SHOP NEW YORK BY MAIL

A PRINT PROJECT BOOK

NOTE ON DATA AND PRICES
Since it takes eight or nine months
for a book to reach consumers after
the text has been completed, you may
encounter some changes in product
lines or prices. Price changes are
more the rule than the exception.
All products and companies listed in
Shop New York by Mail are included
at the discretion of the editors, and
no advertising or promotional fees
are accepted.

SHOP NEW YORK BY MAIL is an original publication of Avon Books.
This work has never before appeared in book form.

AVON BOOKS
A division of
The Hearst Corporation
959 Eighth Avenue
New York, New York 10019

SHOP NEW YORK BY MAIL

Prudence McCullough, Editor
Lowell Miller, Producer

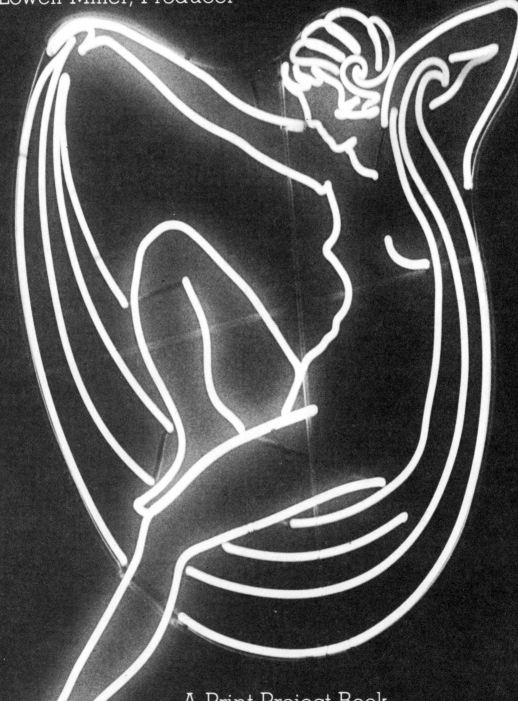

A Print Project Book

 AVON
PUBLISHERS OF BARD, CAMELOT, DISCUS AND FLARE BOOKS

CONTENTS

THE COMPLETE GUIDE TO BUYING BY MAIL

(reprinted courtesy St. Martin's Press, Inc.)

This section is an invaluable tool in ordering by mail. Whether you are a mail-order veteran or a novice about to place your first order, you will find information here that will help you every step of the way. *Read this section* before you order a catalog or write a single letter of inquiry. It will save you time, money, and the miseries of ignorance.

CATALOGS, PRICE QUOTES, AND INFORMATION

Catalogs: Most mail-order firms issue catalogs, which can range in volume and sophistication from mimeographed one-sheet price lists to lavish books with hundreds of color photographs and detailed descriptions. The age of the free catalog is almost over, thanks to higher postage, printing, and handling costs, and most catalogs cost around $2.00. If the catalog's price is listed as "refundable," this means that the company will credit the price of the catalog to your first order, providing you meet the minimum order.

When you write for a catalog, write a complete letter stating which catalog you want (some firms have several), and *always include your return address in the letter.* (You'd be amazed at the number of people who forget to do this, and never receive catalogs.) Mention *Shop New York by Mail,* so firms know the source of the reference. You should also make a point of mentioning any enclosures of coin or checks, so they won't be overlooked. Date the letter and make a carbon or Xerox copy. You'll find that getting into the habit of keeping complete records of all mail-order correspondence will prove helpful later.

If the catalog costs under $1.00, send coins taped securely between thick pieces of cardboard. For catalogs costing $1.00 or more, send a money order, or personal check if you can wait the two weeks while the check clears. *Never* send stamps to any company, unless they request them.

Sometimes the company specifies a "SASE" instead of or in addition to a catalog charge. This is a stamped, self-addressed envelope, and it saves the company the cost of postage and some handling. When you send a SASE, use a long business envelope (No. 10), address it to yourself, *stamp* it, and include it with a letter requesting the catalog.

When firms run out of catalogs, are between printings, or only issue catalogs seasonally, there can be a delay of months before you receive yours. Some firms will notify you by letter or postcard. Most will not. To insure peace of mind, especially if you have to have the catalog by a certain date, take a tip from the pros: Include a stamped, self-addressed postcard with your catalog request and ask the firm to use it to notify you of delayed catalogs, and to give you an idea of when they will be sent. You are most likely to receive a catalog promptly if you order one in October, November, or early December. You are, overall, *least* likely to receive one promptly if you order in January or August and September, when catalog supplies are usually depleted or new catalogs are being printed. As a final note, the best way to assure yourself of the next catalog is to order from the current one.

Price Quotes: Certain firms use price quotes exclusively when selling by mail. They almost always carry name-brand goods, and request that you send them model or style numbers on the products you want so they can make the price quotes. Most of the companies will give quotes over the phone, but a letter is often cheaper, unless the firm has an "800" phone number and *specifies that it can be used for price quotes* (most firms take orders only over these phones). To get the model numbers, style numbers, colors, sizes, etc., you must first find the item in a store or in a catalog. Copy down all the information about the item or items that you can find, and write it all out clearly. Leave space on the letter so the company can enter the price—they often don't have the time to write out another letter. Request prices on only three items at a time—retailers say that they relegate mimeographed sheets requesting twenty price quotes to the wastebasket, since the sender appears to be doing research rather than comparison shopping. *Always* enclose a SASE with a price-quote request.

If you do decide to phone for a price quote, be sure to have all this information in front of you. *Don't* make collect calls. To avoid later problems, make sure you speak to someone in a position of authority, preferably the manager. Take down his name and advise him that you are making a note of all the information he gives you. Treat phone calls as seriously as letters, since the notes you take may be the only tangible records you have.

Requesting Information: There are some firms that are small or do custom work, and to whom you must write with your specific request in order to find out what they have or whether their services are useful to you. Whether you are having linens monogrammed or would like to have an antique doll repaired, you must be very descriptive and include all the information that could possibly help the company serve you. First, read the listing carefully. Send an article for repair or restoration only when the listing so indicates—otherwise, write beforehand, with a description of the article, any damage, the repairs or alterations needed, and send a photo if possible. When sending *any* article, include a cover letter describing the repairs you want done (even if you have already written beforehand—letters are often mislaid), insure the package, and send return postage and insurance by separate cover, in case the firm can't do the work or you decide against it.

HOW TO ORDER

Ordering: Locate the order blank in your catalog and use it. Use any self-sticking address labels as requested. If there is no order blank, use a piece of paper with all pertinent information: code numbers, name of item, number of items ordered, units, prices, tax, shipping, and handling. Observe minimum order requirements. If a catalog is more than six months old, you should write for a new one. Prices do change without warning, and the best any firm can do is guarantee a price as of the order date. You may be billed for the difference between the old price and the new one, especially on imported goods and jewelry.

When the firm advises it, give second choices. If you want them to make substitutions, you must authorize the company to do so on the order form.

Insurance, Packing, Handling, and Sales Tax: The charges for insurance, packing, and handling are usually nominal and are often figured into the transportation costs. Always ask whether insurance is included (if it's not noted on the order form), and request it if it isn't. The small charge is worthwhile, considering what little recourse you have without it if your shipment is damaged or ruined in transit. Add sales tax if you are a New York City or New York State resident and the firm requests it, or if you live in the state where the firm or any of its branches is located and you have a local sales tax—this will be noted on the order form.

Shipping: Virtually all packages are sent by the U.S. Postal Service (parcel post), United Parcel Service (UPS), or by truckers. Some firms, especially those with perishable goods such as food, make use of express services offered through the post office, or private over-night-delivery systems, such as Federal Express. Orders that weigh up to 50 pounds can go by parcel post or UPS, but there are also some restrictions on the size of the package (consult UPS for these).

UPS: The amount of postage you are charged on packages sent by UPS is determined by where you live, where the company that is sending your goods is located, and the dimensions and weight of the package.

UPS has divided the country into sixty-three sections. Each section has a zoning chart that breaks down the rest of the country into seven zones (which run from "Zone 2" to "Zone 8") according to distance, via the first three digits of the Zip Code.

The system works like this: A firm located in Manhattan uses a zone chart that lists Manhattan Zip Codes (prefix 100-) as the No. 2, or closest zone, and California Zip Codes (prefix 900-) as the No. 8, or farthest zone. Almost every firm in this book does business from Manhattan. The exceptions are firms that ship from warehouses in other parts of the country, or distributors who have merchandise "drop shipped" from manufacturers' warehouses.

You can translate these zone numbers into shipping costs by consulting the Common Carrier Rate Chart. This chart lists rates for packages weighing up to 50 pounds, from Zone 2 to Zone 8. Naturally, the lowest charge is on a

shipment of 1 pound to Zone 2, and the highest is on a shipment of 50 pounds to Zone 8.

Some firms will include all the rate charts you need to figure postage, while others will state at the bottom of their order forms, "Add enough for postage and insurance. We will refund over-payment." When a firm leaves it up to you, you should call your local UPS office to find out what zone you are in in relation to the company, and request a rate chart so you can figure the costs exactly. Remember to allow for the weight of packing—the box or crate and padding.

PARCEL POST (PP): The costs for PP are somewhat higher than those for UPS, but there is one distinct advantage: *Only packages sent by parcel post can be delivered to a post office box.* (UPS must have a street address in order to deliver goods.) If you are having a package delivered to a post office box, in order to avoid delays and the possibility that the package will be returned to the company if sent by UPS, write "DELIVERY BY PARCEL POST ONLY; UPS NOT ACCEPTABLE" in bold red letters on the order form, unless there's a box to check to indicate your preference. On the check, write "GOODS TO BE DELIVERED BY PARCEL POST ONLY." When the company endorses or cashes the check, they are implicitly agreeing to this and must send the order by parcel post.

Some companies determine postage on a flat rate, which saves you the trouble of estimating costs. The goods will still be delivered by either UPS or PP, and will be subject to the same limitations.

Consult your local post office for parcel post rates, as these are generally more subject to change than are UPS rates.

TRUCKERS: When the company specifies that the goods must be sent by truck, or if you have a combined order with goods that are both mailable (under 50 pounds, in general) and nonmailable, the entire order will go by truck. Truck charges are always collected upon delivery. Since truck charges are based on weight and distance, the additional expense is a real factor to consider when ordering very heavy items from a firm located far from you. A typical minimum charge for orders up to 100 pounds is $25.00, with an additional charge of $7.00 or more for home delivery. If you can pick up your order at the truck terminal, you will save that much. There is also a fee for delivery notification. For exact fees, you should consult your local carrier.

The term "FOB factory" stands for "free on board," and the location listed after it (for instance, FOB Chicago) is the place from which the goods are shipped, either by mail or truck, depending on which is cheaper.

For very heavy shipments, up to a maximum of 500 pounds, you can contact REA Express instead of a trucker and have the goods delivered by their trucks or by air freight. If you live close to an airport and near the company shipping the goods, REA Express can be cheaper than local carriers, and most goods will take only one to three days to arrive.

When the carrier arrives, you must pay the charges with cash or a certified check—no personal checks.

Payment: Each company lists its preferred methods of payment. A few companies accept only certified checks, but most will take your personal check or money order, and many accept interbank cards (MasterCard, Visa, American Express, etc.). Each method of payment has its own advantages and drawbacks, and can affect how long it takes to receive your goods.

Most firms accept *personal checks,* but often require that you allow ten days to two weeks for the check to clear before they will send out the order. This is the cheapest means of payment for you, and if you can stand to wait two extra weeks for your order, the best.

MONEY ORDERS from banks or the post office are also good forms of payment, and since they are equivalent to cash, don't take any time to clear. A typical *bank* money order costs 75¢ for any amount up to $1,000.00, and, like a check, payment can be stopped on it if you have to cancel the order. *Postal* money orders are comparable in price and also convenient.

STAMPS AND CURRENCY should never be sent through the mails, except in small amounts for catalog costs. Stamps should never be sent unless specifically requested.

COD stands for "cash on delivery." You can pay with cash or certified check. There are always service charges on COD deliveries.

CHARGE CARDS are the ultimate convenience, as most firms accept phone orders with them, and you can order from a hundred firms with a credit card and still receive just one bill at the end of the month. Some firms are now asking phone customers for their addresses, home phone numbers, and bank's numbers before they accept an order. Why? For all they know, you could be reading the card numbers and expiration dates from stolen cards, and give a temporary address as a delivery destination. (It's been done, and the firm has had to absorb the loss.) They'd rather verify the fact that you are the real Jane or John Doe *before* they ship the Trinitron. The only real drawback to plastic money is the finance charge that attacks unpaid balances. Please note that some firms require special minimum-order amounts on charge purchases.

RECEIVING YOUR ORDER

Second Thoughts: If you think better of it, you can cancel your order at any point in the transaction after you send it, unless the firm has already shipped the goods. A refund must be on its way to you within 7 days, or an adjustment made to your charge account within one billing period.

Delayed Orders: Keeping careful records of your orders will come in handy if your order is delayed. Be aware that the company *must* respond to your order within 30 days by either sending it, explaining any delays, or returning your payment. Call or write the company if you haven't heard within 30 days, give them the order number and the items you requested, and ask for an explanation.

When you receive your order, open it carefully. Save all the wrappers and cartons, and report any damages, short shipments, and other problems to the shipper immediately. See the section titled "Refunds, Returns, and Defective Merchandise" for further information.

REFUNDS, RETURNS, AND DEFECTIVE MERCHANDISE

Returns: Return policies vary from company to company. Some give you 30-day trial periods with no-questions-asked refunds. Some require that returns be authorized (which means that you must write a letter detailing the reason for the returns and getting permission from the firm to send the merchandise back). Some firms don't allow any returns at all, especially on personalized or custom-made goods. *Read their policy before ordering, and save the original boxes and wrapping*—some firms accept returns only when packed in the boxes in which they were sent. Anything you send back will be at your own expense, unless the policy states otherwise. Some firms also request a "restocking fee," a charge for the trouble of returning the goods to stock.

Complaints: If you have a complaint about the goods or the firm, the first thing to do is to write that company a letter stating the problem and what you would like done about it. Be clear, concise, and civilized. If you don't get any action, write again, referring to your first letter. If, after the second complaint, you get no response, write a third letter and send copies, along with cover letters, to the Direct Mail/Marketing Association, (DMMA), the Federal Trade Commission (FTC), and the U.S. Postal Service. The U.S. Postal Service investigates *every* complaint and resolves about 85% of the problems, partly because it has the power to withhold mail delivery to a company if it doesn't cooperate. Write to the Chief Postal Inspector, U.S. Postal Service, Washington, DC 20260.

The FTC investigates companies with profiles of bad service and fraud, but probably won't offer immediate action. To lodge a complaint with the FTC, write to the Bureau of Consumer Protection, Federal Trade Commission, Washington, DC 20580.

The Direct Mail/Marketing Association is a trade organization whose members make up about 70% of the major U.S. mail-order businesses. The DMMA will help by referring complaints to appropriate agencies and by putting pressure on the offending firm. Write to them at Mail Order Action Line, DMMA, 6 East 43rd St., New York, NY 10017.

If you are the cautious type, you can check with the branch of the Better Business Bureau nearest the firm you're dealing with to see if it has a "record" *before* you order. You can also register complaints there if you have problems with the firm.

Reordering: If you want to order from a company again, you should request the current catalog if yours is over a year old. You're usually guaranteed a spot on its mailing list as long as you're an active customer.

Guarantees and Warranties: The simplest guarantee, and one offered by many stores, is "satisfaction guaranteed or your money back." This means that if you are not pleased with the product, you can return it for a refund, exchange, or credit. Sometimes the guarantee is conditional or limited to very specific uses or functions of the product, and sometimes it's a no-questions-asked policy. To prepare for the possibility that you might want to return something you have ordered by mail, you should be familiar with the company's rules regarding guarantees and returns. Most returns must be authorized—that is, you must write to the company and receive permission to return the goods. Sometimes you will have to pay a restocking charge, and you will almost always have to pay the return postage and insurance. Remembering to keep all the wrapping and the original carton and invoices will make returns much easier.

Warranties are basically the same as guarantees, but usually cover the life and function of a particular item rather than all the goods a manufacturer produces. Warranty information is included with products that are covered by them, and detail the limits of use of the product, its ideal operating conditions, and conditions that would invalidate the warranty. For instance, immersing many electrical appliances in water will immediately void the guarantee. Warranties usually run from 90 days on goods with a high rate of failure after that point, to 5 and even 10 years for goods that have proven durability records. Products covered by a warranty are usually accompanied by a postcard, which you then fill out and send to the manufacturer or head service station. A warranty is not valid unless the manufacturer has received the completed card.

The most important thing to remember when you are buying a warrantied item is to read the details of the warranty very carefully. You should then try to evaluate the warranty by discerning the real value in terms of time covered, percentage of the item's parts covered, and how difficult it will be to have the warranty honored.

1 | Appliances
Audio
TV/Video

Have you ever found yourself frustrated when, after reading a magazine article about some great new speaker system, or radio, or mini-TV, you find that it's just not available in your town? That never happens in New York. If it plugs in, somebody's selling it in the city. If you can't find the appliance you want from the sources in this chapter, you'd better sign up for a trip on the Space Shuttle.

Aside from variety, New York merchants are known for their fabulously low prices. With so much competition, sellers are forced to accept prices that in many areas of the country would be considered wholesale. But be careful. Many claims of discount "below list price" are actually based on the prices charged by tony department stores. These stores occasionally charge *more* than the manufacturer's suggested list price for appliances. A discount from department store prices is not always meaningful. Needless to say, the smart shopper *never* buys appliances from those department stores—even their sale prices don't represent substantial savings.

Shop around. Find out exactly what you want. Read *Consumer Reports* and specialty magazines to discover the best values and true list prices. Then get in touch with our New York City merchants for availability and big savings. Be prepared to call or write to a few places for prices — their inventories are so large and rapidly changing that few catalogs are available. But before you place a call or write a single letter, do read the Buying Guide in the front of this book, which gives you invaluable information on requesting a price quote.

Problems and Pitfalls: The markets for appliances, TV and video sets, and audio components are enormously competitive. The biggest dealers work on markups of as little as 3% and 4% over cost, and do a huge volume in order to make a profit. There appear to be continual price wars, and mythological "can't be beat" prices. Theoretically, if Loony Larry and Mad Mo both advertise "lowest" prices, you could take price quotes back and forth from store to store and dicker them down to just about nothing. In reality, this doesn't work—Larry or Mo will back

down when they begin to lose money, and in general, there is a price floor below which neither will go. So much for promises. However, you can *get* a good deal if you approach price quotes seriously: Get the name of the person who is giving you the price quote, and proceed to tell him the lowest price quote you've gotten on an item, and ask him if he can beat it. Be prepared to offer the date you got the price quote, the store, and the person who quoted the price. You can also take advertisements of specials that feature prices lower than those quoted by the store you're visiting, and let the salesman know you are serious about buying if he can beat the price. Often, the size of your savings is directly proportional to your persistence. This all applies to mail order: Note all the details when you are getting a price quote by phone, and above all, be sure to ask whether the item is in stock. It is easy for someone to quote a low price on something they no longer have in stock, simply to get your business. Once in the store, or once they've gotten a commitment over the phone and credit-card information, they assume that they will be able to "switch" products and sell you something different, or keep you waiting months for the shipment containing your turntable, TV, or whatever to arrive. *Don't* fall into this trap. When doing business by mail, use credit cards—at least you can refuse to pay later for something you haven't received. Keep good records of phone calls, noting the name of the person you spoke to (get first and *last* names), date, time of day, whether the person said the item was in stock, the price, shipping charges, etc. You can follow the phone call with a letter of confirmation, restating the vital facts of the conversation, if you wish. *Remember your rights.* You must be notified of delays and you have the option of canceling your order in the event of delays of 30 days or more. All the firms in the sections "Machines and Media" and "Cameras, Photographic Equipment, and Services" have been checked with the Better Business Bureau.

Hopefully, "defensive ordering" on your part and decent records on theirs will guarantee that transactions will go smoothly. If they don't, please contact The Print Project (see the "Feedback Page" at the end of this book).

ANNEX OUTLET, LTD.

Dept. NYBM
43 Warren St.
New York, NY 10007
(212) 964-8661
Information: price quote by letter
Minimum Order: none
Accepts: check, MO, certified check

We thought snarky salesclerks were an integral part of buying at a discount until we shopped at Annex Outlet. No barking! No biting! The discounts are friendly, too, at 35% to 40% off list price.

Annex advertises its blank tapes but also sells audio components, TV and video equipment, and car audio parts. Their audio manufacturers are Pioneer, Sansui, Marantz, Teac, Akai, JVC, JBL, Bose Martin, Technics, and Dual. In car audio they sell components by Blaupunkt, Audiovox, Panasonic, Sanyo, Kenwood, Alpine, and Nakamichi. They carry Sony, Panasonic, Hitachi, RCA, and Zenith TVs, video equipment by those manufacturers as well as JVC, Toshiba, and Quasar, and video tapes by Panasonic, RCA, JVC, Fuji, TDK, Maxell, Sony, Ampex, Scotch, and BASF. They have blank cassette tapes by Maxell, Scotch, TDK, Ampex, BASF, Memorex, and Sony.

Annex Outlet is going strong after twenty-five years, and is run by Abe, who says that he got into the business for "the action, the challenge." He gets plenty of both at Annex, which he calls "the store everyone's been looking for."

APNI DOOKAN

42 East Canal St.
New York, NY 10002
(212) 925-5865
Information: price quote—phone or letter
Minimum Order: none
Accepts: check, MO

Apni Dookan means good discounts on audio, TV, video, and car audio components. They've stood up under rigorous comparison shopping and provided New Yorkers with some of the best buys in the city on things like answering machines and calculators. A partial listing of the brands they carry includes Akai, Allison, JVC, Rotel, Sansui, Fisher, Marantz, Sharp, Pioneer, Sony, Mitsubishi, Blaupunkt, Clarion, Technics, and Bose. They have Toshiba portable radios and TV sets, Ortofon stereo cartridges, Koss headphones, and Ego speakers.

Apni specializes in dual-voltage (overseas) appliances, and will give you a price quote over the phone. Be sure to mention *Shop New York by Mail* for the best price!

ARGUS RADIO AND APPLIANCES

507 East 80th St.
New York, NY 10021
(212) 794-1705
Information: price quote
Minimum Order: none
Accepts: check, MO

Argus ships large appliances manufactured by Amana, Caloric, GE, Frigidaire, Hotpoint, Indesit, Litton, Maytag, Magic Chef, Tappan, Welbilt, Westinghouse, and Whirlpool. In the TV and video department, they carry Panasonic, Philco, Quasar, RCA, Sanyo, Sony, Sylvania, and Zenith. Write with complete model information for a price quote.

BARNEY'S

42 West 38th Street
New York, NY 10018
(212) 391-6934
Information: price quote, by letter
Minimum Order: none
Accepts: check, MO, MC

You're guaranteed 30% off list price at Barney's where you can get audio components, TV and video equipment, small and personal-care appliances, calculators, and phone-answering machines.

They sell Panasonic, Sony, and Technics audio components, Sanyo, Panasonic, JVC, and Sony TV and video equipment, and appliances by GE, Moulinex, Oster, Presto, Sunbeam, Hamilton

Beach, Norelco, Clairol, and Gillette. Try them for calculators by Casio, Canon, and Sharp, and phone answering machines by Sony and Panasonic. Barney's has some dual-voltage goods, takes special orders, and has been doing it all well for twenty-five years.

BERNIE'S DISCOUNT CENTER

821 Sixth Ave.
New York, NY 10001
(212) 564-8582
Information: price quote, by letter
Minimum Order: none
Accepts: check, MO

Bernie's sells a little bit of everything, all at substantial savings on list price. Their customers have been spreading the word so effectively since Bernie's set up shop in 1948 that they don't need to advertise, the hallmark of a real discount source.

The core of their stock is in audio components, TV and video equipment, car audio parts, and appliances. Their audio lines are Pioneer, Panasonic, Sony, Zenith, and Hitachi. The TV and video brands they carry include RCA, Zenith, Sony, Panasonic, GE, and Hitachi, and they sell Panasonic, Blaupunkt, Pioneer, Craig, and Audiovox car audio components. Bernie's has Hitachi, Panasonic, and RCA video tapes for VHS systems, and Sony and Zenith for the Beta variety, plus TV games by Atari. They sell large, small, and personal-care appliances. (Large appliances are shipped within New York City and to nearby counties only.) Bernie's has *everything* in other appliances, including air conditioners by GE and Chrysler, and microwave ovens by Norelco, Amana, Litton, and GE.

Bernie's also stocks full lines of Hoover and Eureka vacuum cleaners, fuzzbusters, CBs, calculators by Sharp, Casio, Canon, and Texas Instruments, language translators, phone answering machines by Cod-A-Phone, Record-A-Call, Sanyo, and Phone-Mate, specialty batteries,

power hand tools by Black & Decker, Skil, Rockwell, and McCulloch, and clocks.

Bernie's will special-order and sells dual-voltage and 220-volt appliances. They really live up to their motto, "If it plugs in, we sell it."

BLOOM & KRUP

206 First Ave.
New York, NY 10009
(212) 673-2760
Information: price quote
Minimum Order: $25.00
Accepts: check, MO, MC, Visa

You don't have to visit Bloom & Krup's showroom with its long rows of silent appliances to order from them. You simply have to have the model number of the appliance you want, be it by Amana, Charmglo, Caloric, Arkla, Sub Zero, Country Squire, Frigidaire, GE, Hotpoint, Indesit, Kitchenaid, Litton, Hoover, Eureka, Premier, Norelco, Moulinex, Oster, Waring, Hamilton Beach, Braun, Tappan, Welbilt, or Thermadore. They also carry TVs and video equipment by Admiral, Magnavox, Panasonic, Quasar, RCA, Sony, Sanyo, Toshiba, Sylvania, and Zenith. In another room in the store, there are home products and furniture by manufacturers like Sealy, Simmons, Sa-Z-Boy, Childcraft, Kirsch, Yorktown, El-Kay, Perrego, Bassett, and Lane. Send a model number or description for a price quote. The savings over list price run from 10% to 30%.

BONDY EXPORT CORP.

Dept. NYBM
40 Canal St.
New York, NY 10002
(212) 925-7785
Information: price quote, by letter, with SASE
Minimum Order: none
Accepts: check, MO

Bondy is yet another discount source for typewriters, tape-recorders, TV and video, cameras and movie equipment, small and personal-care appliances, and things like luggage, kitchenware, and watches. They've thrived for twenty-eight years by discounting everything they sell from 30% to 50% and offering a wide variety of appliances in dual voltage.

They carry the top names in everything: S.C.M. and Olivetti typewriters; GE, Sunbeam, Moulinex, Oster, Presto, Norelco, Remington, Gillette, and Clairol appliances; Zenith, Sharp, and Sony TV and video equipment; and cameras by Pentax, Olympus, Minolta, Yashica, Rollei, Chinon, and other firms. They have full lines of discounted Farberware, Corningware, Parker and Cross pens, and Samsonite luggage, and both domestic and imported model Seiko watches (American-made Seiko model numbers are invalid as price-quote references on the latter—*describe* the imported model or send a picture).

Bondy asks that you write for a price quote and include all model or stock numbers and a stamped, self-addressed envelope with the request. Limit yourself to two price quotes per letter. For those who live in New York, Bondy *does* sell large appliances. Since they don't ship anything over 50 pounds out of state, they prefer to sell appliances within the city and invite you to visit their Canal Street store in person for price quotes on these.

BRYCE APPLIANCE & AUDIO-VIDEO CO.
115 West 40th St.
New York, NY 10018
(212) 575-8600
Information: price quote by phone
Minimum Order: none
Accepts: check, MO, MC, Visa

In the back of the mind of every New Yorker is a pile of slogans, jingles, and catchwords that represent the ad detritus of the Big Apple. There's "You've got to eat us to believe us," for Cooky's Steak Pub, "An educated consumer is our best customer," for Syms Clothing Stores, and the unqualified "I Love New York," for

the Big Apple. When it comes to audio and video equipment, you can risk the lunatic promises of Crazy Eddie, whose prices are "insane," or be reasonable and "shop Bryce for price."

Bryce supplies to other stores selling audio and TV equipment, and their retail prices are "very competitive." Even better than the discounts is their selection. Their multimillion-dollar inventory includes audio and video equipment by IMF, ADS, Hafler, Sony, Panasonic, Harmon/Kardon, Pioneer, Rotel, Hitachi, Shure, MXR, Numark, Sennheiser, Mitsubishi (auto audio only), Jensen (home and auto audio), Dual, Craig (auto audio), Koss, KLH, Micron, Clubman (mixers), Aiwa, AKG (microphones), Atari (video games and personal computers), Atlas (audio accessories), Discwasher, GE, Pickering, Sharp (calculators), Smith Victor (video), Toshiba, Stanton, Technics, Allison (speakers), Fanon (intercoms), JBL, Kenwood, Teac, Tascam, R.G. Dynamics, Phone-Mate (answering machines), Recoton (accessories), Sansui, Sonus (cartridges), Soundcraftsman, Akai, Casio (calculators), Mattel (electronics), BSR, and Philips. Zenith products are available by special order only. Bryce also sells the Technics professional series, as well as industrial video by JVC, Pansonic, and Sony. Industrial video is more sophisticated than consumer sets, but falls short of broadcast equipment.

There's hardly anything in the world of audio/video Bryce doesn't carry, and almost nothing they don't know about it. They give price quotes over the phone, and their advice is always free.

DEMBITZER BROTHERS
5 Essex St.
New York, NY 10002
(212) 254-1310
Information: price quote by letter
Minimum Order: none
Accepts: check, MO

The Dembitzers aim to please

everyone with a storeful of goods that include TV and video sets, all sorts of appliances, tape recorders, calculators, phone answering machines, housewares, and gifts, and a sales force that can speak 8 languages fluently.

They have TV and video by Zenith, Sony, GE, and Panasonic, calculators by Casio, Canon, and Sharp, and phone answering machines by Sanyo, Record-A-Call, Code-A-Phone, and Phone-Mate. Their extensive lines of large, small, and personal-care appliances include GE, Westinghouse, Whirlpool, Kitchenaid, Caloric, Tappan, Maytag, Jannair, Sanyo, Phoenix, Waring, Braun, Salton, Hamilton Beach, Sunbeam, Oster, Norelco, Remington, Schick, and Clairol. They also have Parker and Cross pens, Corning and Farberware cookware and dinnerware, and Timex watches.

One of their special items is the Wonder Baker, a contraption that acts as a cake oven but uses a low stovetop flame as heat. This energy saver was developed in Israel and is described in the brochure the Dembitzers will send you (include a SASE with the request). They also have the Magna Wonder Knife ($22.00), a serrated knife with an adjustable "guard" that allows you to slice in exact, even thicknesses of $1/16$ to $1/2$ inch. The blade is stainless steel, the knife needs no sharpening, and comes in models for left-and right-handed people. A brochure is available upon request.

EBA ASSOCIATES
2329 Nostrand Ave.
Brooklyn, NY 11210
(212) 252-3400
Information: price quote by letter
Minimum Order: none
Accepts: check, MO

EBA has been around for twenty-five years and will take special orders on their lines of appliances, TV and video equipment, compact stereos, small audio components, and radios. They do go farther on their price policy: They guarantee

that if you can find a lower price on an item within 30 days of purchase they'll give you the difference plus 10%.

With that in mind, consider EBA if you're looking for a TV or video recorder by Sony, RCA, Zenith, Quasar, Panasonic, GE, Sharp, Toshiba, Magnavox, Philco, or Sylvania. They have compact stereos, audio components, and radios by Sony and Panasonic, and major appliances, shipped FOB Brooklyn, by Admiral, Amana, Caloric, Frigidaire, GE, Hotpoint, Hardwick, Indesit, Jennair, Litton, Kitchenaid, Magic Chef, Maytag, Westinghouse, Whirlpool, Roper, Tappan, Wasteking, and Welbilt. Remember that savings on large appliances or anything over 50 pounds are often consumed by trucking charges, which is the only caveat we could apply to this firm.

FLASH PHOTO ELECTRONIC
1206 Ave. J
Brooklyn, NY 11230
(212) 253-7121
Information: price quote by letter
Minimum Order: none
Accepts: check, MO, MC, Visa

Flash Photo claims to have "the lowest prices available anywhere." Since they also stress the personal service they give store and mail-order sales, they may come close to being all things to all people, at least in the land of electronics.

Flash sells audio components, TV and video goods, all sorts of appliances, and cameras and film. They have all name-brand audio, TV, and video equipment by Admiral, Hitachi, Panasonic, RCA, Sony, Zenith, and GE. Their appliance lines include Amana, Tappan, Magic Chef, Westinghouse, Maytag, Avanti, Caloric, Chambers, Corning, Speed Queen, Frigidaire, Hotpoint, Insinkerator, Kitchenaid, Salton, Sub Zero, Thermadore, and other manufacturers. Try them for cameras by Nikon, Minolta, Canon, Yashica, Mamiya, Leica, Kodak, Polaroid, Hasselblad,

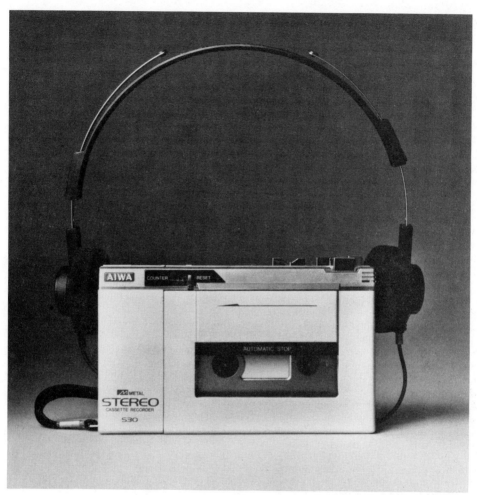

Aiwa Stereo Cassette Recorder,
available from Bryce Audio,
Pam-Lon International, and S.C.A.

Olympus, Eumig, Sigma, Soligar, and Bell & Howell, and brand-name film.

GREATER NEW YORK TRADING CO.

81 Canal St.
New York, NY 10013
(212) 226-2808, 8850
Information: price quote by letter or phone (see text)
Minimum Order: on china, inquire
Accepts: check, MO

Chaos and disorder seem to be the hallmarks of a true discount store, at least on the Lower East Side. The bargain adrenalin hits the blood with one look at the operations at the Greater New York Trading Co., where cartons stacked to the rafters teeter precariously over the rather grubby sales floor. Instincts prove correct: The prices are fabulous.

Mr. Bruce Ochs, the manager, fended off customers long enough to tell us that the Trading Co. sells major and small appliances, TVs, typewriters, vacuum cleaners, china, crystal, stainless, silverplate, sterling, holloware, and gifts. The appliance manufacturers include Amana, GE, Hotpoint, Frigidaire, Magic Chef, Litton, Roper, Whirlpool/Westinghouse, Caloric, Kitchenaid, and Tappan. They have TV and video lines by Sony, Zenith, Panasonic, Hitachi, Toshiba, RCA, Quasar, Sylvania, GE, and MGA. There are Hoover and Eureka vacuum cleaners and typewriters by Olivetti, SCM, Olympia, Adler, and Hermes. The china, crystal, and silver selection is enormous. A sample of the brands they carry includes Lenox, Wedgwood, Royal Doulton, Noritake, Royal Worcester, Minton, Mikasa, Rosenthal, Orrefors, Oneida, International, Reed & Barton, Lunt, Wallace, Gorham, Towle, and Stieff. (They carry some discontinued sterling patterns, too.)

Mr. Ochs proudly says that the store has been in business for fifty-one years with the same owners. He also says that they're usually too busy at the store to spend time on the phone giving price quotes until after 3:00 P.M., and suggests you inquire by mail if you can't get through. One more thing: You can forget your Mastercard and Visa here. "We don't accept credit cards. That's why we're cheap," states Mr. Ochs. Oh.

HARRY'S DISCOUNTS

8701 18th Ave.
Brooklyn, NY 11214
(212) 236-3507
Information: price quote by letter
Minimum Order: none
Accepts: check, MO

Harry's has been making great buys on audio components, TV and video sets, and major appliances for over twenty years and passing the savings on to their customers. They have "almost everything" in the audio department, all the major brands in TV and video equipment, and major appliances from "all companies." They'll ship large appliances and anything over 50 pounds to all five boroughs of New York City, Long Island, and some parts of New Jersey. Harry's also does special orders.

HUNTER AUDIO-PHOTO, LTD.

507 Fifth Ave.
New York, NY 10017
(212) 986-1540
Information: price quote
Video Brochure: SASE
Minimum Order: none
Accepts: check, MO, MC, Visa

Cameras, radios, calculators, pens, and watches can be had here at "the best prices on Fifth Avenue." Hunter Audio sells the major lines of cameras and accessories, radios by Sony, Panasonic, GE, and Sanyo, calculators by Casio, Canon, Hewlett-Packard, and Toshiba, and watches by Casio, Seiko, Texas Instruments, Bulova, and Timex. There are phone answering machines in the name brands, pens by Parker, Cross, and Sheaffer, and both video blanks and movies for the two video formats.

Hunter Audio-Photo does special orders and sells dual-voltage appliances. If knowing you got it on Fifth Avenue at a *discount* gives you a thrill, Hunter Audio-Photo is the place to go.

INTERNATIONAL SOLGO, INC.
77 West 23rd St.
New York, NY 10010
(212) 675-3555
Information: price quote by letter
Minimum Order: $25.00
Accepts: check, MO, MC, Visa

Almost fifty years of discounting experience go behind every sale at International Solgo. They carry audio components, TV and video sets, and large and small appliances. The audio lines include Pioneer, Panasonic, Sankyo, Sanyo, JVC, and Audio-vox, and there is TV and video equipment by Philco, Quasar, GE, Zenith, Sony, RCA, and Hitachi. The appliance manufacturers include Amana, Brown, Eureka, Clairol, Hoover, Charmglo, Garland, Magic Chef, Tappan, Caloric, Admiral, Connair, Hotpoint, Sankyo, Norelco, Mr. Coffee, Maytag, Litton, Rival, Kitchenaid, Proctor-Silex, Bunn, Norge, Sunbeam, Farberware, and more. Solgo also has brand-name watches, cameras by Nikon, Minolta, Canon, Yashica, and Polaroid, luggage, and phone answering machines by Phone-Mate and Sanyo. Write to them with model or stock numbers and descriptions and they will send a price quote.

JEMS SOUNDS, LTD.
785 Lexington Ave.
New York, NY 10021
(212) 838-4716
Information: price quote by letter
Minimum Order: none
Accepts: check, MO, MC, Visa

Jems Sounds is distinguished by their excellent selection of audio components, TV and video sets, cameras, calculators, phone machines, and watches, and their spacious two-floor showroom.
They have TVs by Sony, Panasonic, Sanyo, and Toshiba, audio components in those lines as well as Onkyo, Teac, Akai, Dual,

JBL, Technics, and Marantz, and video by Sony, RCA, Zenith, JVC, and Panasonic. There are video games by Atari and Mattell, calculators by Casio, Sharp, Toshiba, Panasonic, Canon, Texas Instruments, and Hewlett-Packard, and phone answering machines by Phone-Mate, Record-A-Call, Sanyo, and ITT. Try them for watches by Bulova, Citizen, and Seiko, and cameras in all the major lines.
Jems Sounds has been selling at very competitive prices for seven years and credits their success to their policy of treating every customer the way they themselves would like to be treated.

KUNST SALES
45 Canal St.
New York, NY 10002
(212) 966-1909
Information: price quote by letter
Minimum Order: none
Accepts: check, MO, MC, Visa

Kunst makes its sales in audio components, TV and video equipment, all kinds of appliances, and luggage. Many of the appliances are available in dual voltage for overseas use. The audio manufacturers they carry include Sansui, Marantz, Pioneer, Akai, Technics, and Dual. They have TVs and video equipment by Sony, Panasonic, Zenith, RCA, and Hitachi, and appliances by GE, Westinghouse, Whirlpool, Sunbeam, Oster, Farberware, Norelco, and Clairol, to name a few. Their complete lines of Samsonite and American Tourister luggage are popular since, like everything else here, they are discounted up to 50%.

LEWI SUPPLY CO.
15 Essex St.
New York, NY 10002
(212) 777-6910
Information: price quote by letter with SASE
Minimum Order: none
Accepts: check, MO

Lewi's tiny store has some big

discounts on Mikasa china, Brother sewing machines, Olivetti typewriters, Seiko watches, Sony products, and cameras by Yashica, Konica, and Canon—up to 50% off list price. Write to them for a price quote, and include a stamped, self-addressed envelope.

LYLE CARTRIDGES

Box 69, Kensington Station
Brooklyn, NY 11218
(212) 871-3303 (N.Y. orders and inquiries)
(800) 221-0906
Catalog: free
Minimum Order: varies, depending on area of U.S. you live in
Accepts: check, MO

Audio stores are usually state of the art and not much more, which means they seldom stock last year's components or the replacement parts you need to make last year's model run.

Lyle Cartridges carries the cartridges, spindles, drive belts, and diamond styli that will save your stereo from obsolescence. There are parts and accessories for equipment by Garrard, BIC, Thorens, Panasonic/Technics, BSR, Dual, and other manufacturers, made by Shure, Stanton, Audio-Technica, Micro-Acoustics, Satin, Sonus, Acutex, Audio Dynamics, Grado, Pickering, Ortofon, and Empire. They also carry record-care supplies by Discwasher, Watts, Permostat, and Sound Guard.

Lyle is run from a garage-type building in Brooklyn, and what they save in forgoing amenities they pass on to you in phenomenal discounts. For instance, the Shure M95G cartridge, list price $71.50, is $27.75 here; Audio-Technicas AT10, regularly $40.00 is $10.00; the Pickering PATE is $10.50 from $24.50, etc. In addition to what is listed, Lyle carries a full line of ceramic and crystal cartridges and replacement diamond needles available upon request. Everything is covered by a limited warranty that guarantees replacement of defective goods.

PAN-LON INTERNATIONAL, INC.

141 Fifth Ave.
New York, NY 10010
(212) 889-6990
Information: price quote by phone or letter
Minimum Order: none
Accepts: check, MO, MC, Visa, AE, DC

We can't figure out how Pan-Lon does it. Their Fifth Avenue showroom has an open salesfloor the size of a studio apartment, and when commercial space is rented by the square foot, one has to conclude that their overhead isn't low. But their prices are—discounts of 45% on Samsonite luggage, 40% to 50% on Seiko watches, and similar savings on appliances, audio and TV lines, calculators, cameras, and even sunglasses. Their appliance manufacturers include GE, Westinghouse, Moulinex, Oster, Proctor-Silex, Hamilton Beach, and Eureka. In audio components and TV/video sets they carry Sony, Hitachi, Aiwa, Panasonic, Sanyo, JVC, Sansui, Marantz, Pioneer, Grundig, Toshiba, Sharp, National, and Philips (in American Standard, Pal Secam, and Pal/N systems). There are calculators by Casio, TI, Hewlett-Packard, Canon, Toshiba, Sanyo, and Sharp, and a variety of sunglasses, including those by Ray Ban and Porsche Carrera.

Pan-Lon carries dual-voltage goods and is accustomed to shipping all over the world. You can call or write for a price quote.

RCI/RADIO CLINIC DISCOUNT APPLIANCES, INC.

2599 Broadway
New York, NY 10025
(212) 864-6000
Information: price quote by letter
Minimum Order: none
Accepts: check, MO, MC, Visa

Doctor Discount is busy at the RCI Radio Clinic, cutting prices down to size on audio components, TV and video goods, and large, small, and personal-care appliances. A sample of the manufacturers they carry includes Jensen, JBL, Emerson, KLH, Scott, Sony, Zenith, Hitachi, Toshiba, JVC, Casio, Sharp, Melville, Rotel, Intellivision, Atari, Unisonic, GE, Westinghouse, Hankscraft, Edison, Titan, Carrier, Fedders, Airtemp, Frederick, Hoover, Eureka, Panasonic, Presto, Proctor-Silex, Gillette, Toastmaster, and Clairol. You can write or call for a price quote. Discounts can run up to 50% off at sale time. By the way, this really *is* a radio clinic: RCI runs audio clinics for women who don't know the difference between woofers and tweeters, and were too afraid to ask.

S & S SOUND CITY

58 West 45th St.
New York, N.Y. 10036
(212) 575-0210
(NY orders and inquiries)
(800) 223-0360 (rest of U.S.)
Information: price quote by phone or letter
Video Brochure: SASE
Minimum Order on Blank Tapes: 6
Accepts: check, MO, MC, Visa

Electronics bargains on the Lower East Side are *de rigueur*, but decent discounts in midtown Manhattan are hard to find. S & S Sound City has them: They are one of the largest phone machine dealers in the city, and sell full lines of car audio systems, radios, TV and video sets, TV games, blank and recorded video tapes, calculators, and security systems. Discounts here commonly reach 40% and 50% off list price.

The phone machine manufacturers carried here include Phone-Mate, Record-A-Call, Teletender, and ITT. They have car audio by Sanyo, Pioneer, Blaupunkt, and Audiovox, and audio and TV goods by Zenith, Toshiba, Sanyo, RCA, Quasar, Panasonic, Hitachi, JVC, and Emerson. They have the small Pearl-corder tape recorders, Fanon intercom systems, and electronic games by Atari, Mattel, and Intellivision.

S & S is doing all it can to further the state of the art when it comes to video. They've pulled together a great brochure that gives the lowdown on the two video cassette recorder (VCR) formats, BETA and VHS. If you are video-ignorant and planning to buy, this is a must—just send a SASE. VCR owners can purchase blank tapes for either format and choose from hundreds of movie tapes that range in strength from Superman to Blazing Saddles, some of which are listed on the video brochure.

Mel Tillman and Bernard Berman may well have "the nicest company in town." They do special orders. They sell major appliances in all the top brands. Write or call for a price quote.

SAM'S SALE CITI

27 Essex St.
New York, NY 10002
(212) 673-8383
Information: price quote by phone or letter
Minimum Order: $25.00
Accepts: check, MO

Sam's spiffy store is one of the new breed of discount sources. Clean, carpeted, and civilized, it even sells crystal along with the standard lines of plug-in goods, and all at savings of 10% to 40% off list price.

Sam carries compact stereos and some audio components by Panasonic and Sony, TV and video sets by those manufacturers and Sharp and Zenith, and *anything* in small and personal-care appliances. He has phone machines by Sanyo, Phone-Mate, Code-A-Phone, and ITT, and even sells the ITT phones themselves. There are Atari video games here, Samsonite attaché cases, watches by Seiko, Pulsar, Bulova, and Timex, and cameras by Pentax, Yashica, Olympus, Nikon, and all the other major brands. Remember that the minimum order here is $25.00.

Mail Order Tip: Most returns must be authorized: that is, you must write to the company and receive permission to return the goods.

STEREO CORP. OF AMERICA

1629 Flatbush Ave.
Brooklyn, NY 11210
(212) 253-8888 (NY orders and all inquiries)
(800) 221-0974 (U.S. orders)
Catalog: free; also price quote by phone or letter
Minimum Order: none
Accepts: check, MO, MC, Visa

SCA, a.k.a. Stereo Warehouse, bills itself as "the low price safe sound place." The implication is that one often takes risks with discount audio outlets. Reassured, we're faced with the task of choosing components from SCA's 60 manufacturers, among them Technics, Dual, BIC, Teac, Bose, Onkyo, Shure, Akai, Marantz, Phase Linear, Aiwa, Pioneer, Kenwood, Sony, ADC, Harman/ Kardon, Sansui, TDK, JBL, and many others. The savings are a risk-free 30% to 70% off list price (higher discounts reflect prices on closeouts and specials). Price quotes are given over the phone and by mail.

UNCLE STEVE

343 Canal St.
New York, NY 10013
(212) 266-4010
Information: price quote by phone or letter
Minimum Order: none
Accepts: check, MO, MC, Visa

Uncle Steve, a.k.a. Steve Schwartz, sells appliances, audio components, TV and video equipment, and cameras at great discounts from his madhouse on Canal Street. He sells "every major brand" and is more than happy to give price quotes over the phone, as well as by mail.

WISAN TV AND APPLIANCES

4085 Hylan Blvd.
Staten Island, NY 10308
(212) 356-7700
Information: price quote by letter with SASE
Minimum Order: $100.00
Accepts: check, MO, MC, Visa

Wisan has been selling appliances, audio components, and TV and video equipment for over forty years at savings of 10% to 40% on list price. They carry the major manufacturers of audio goods, and TV and video sets by Zenith, Quasar, GE, RCA, Sony, and Panasonic. Their appliance lines include Frigidaire, Whirlpool, Caloric, Maytag, Magic Chef, Gibson, Westinghouse, Tappan, Speed Queen, Sub Zero, Amana, Chambers, Wasteking, Kitchenaid, and Jennair. They make regular deliveries within New York, New Jersey, and Connecticut, but can have goods shipped anywhere. Send a stamped, self-addressed envelope with your request for a price quote and shipping charges.

SEE ALSO: Cameras, Photographic Equipment, Services
Home
Office Supplies

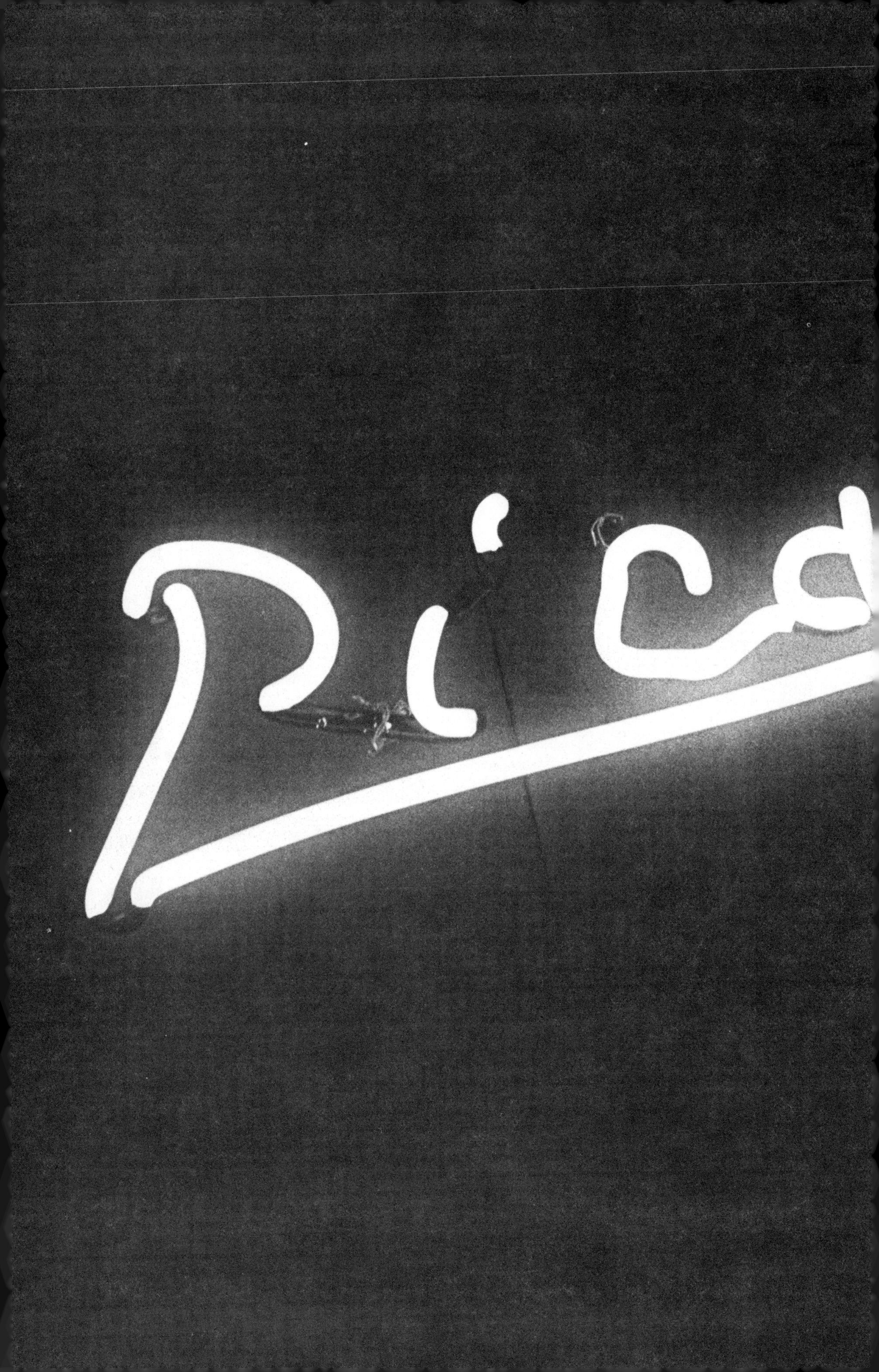

2 | Art
Antiques
Restoration Services

The density of art galleries and antique shops per square mile is probably greater in New York than anywhere else in the world. New Yorkers can often be seen on a windy fall day trooping from exhibition to exhibition, "gallery guide" in hand, working across 57th Street, up Madison Avenue, or hopping in a cab to the recycled-for-art factory district of Soho. Most of the important museums in this country are located in the city. So are the major auction houses. While there are museums and galleries elsewhere, New York is the only city in this country where art is a really *significant* part of the urban experience.

Since most art and antiques—except for prints—are one of a kind, they don't lend themselves particularly well to mail-order catalogs or purchasing. We've emphasized in this chapter, for that reason, services such as fine art restoration and antique repair. These services *are* available by mail and exist at a level of breadth and professionalism that would otherwise be unavailable to non-New Yorkers. The city is full of talented craftspeople who serve the art world, but you needn't live here, or be a museum curator, to take advantage of their skills.

ALL-ART RESTORERS
140 West 57th St.
New York, NY 10019
(212) 489-6937
Information: letter with photo and SASE
Minimum Order: none
Accepts: check, MO

Patricia Hammel handles all kinds of art objects at All-Art, including those made of porcelain, pottery, jade, enamel, glass, cloisonné, and tortoise shell. Although she works primarily with dealers, she does do work for individuals and smaller museums that don't have their own conservators.

Ms. Hammel does business by mail on the following terms: Write a letter stating in explicit detail the object and the nature of the damage and repair desired, and include a stamped, self-addressed envelope and a clear photo of the piece taken at close range, OR send the piece directly with a cover letter and include a stamped, self-addressed envelope for her estimate *and* a check or money order for return shipping and insurance, in case All-Art can't do the piece or you think better of it. (Just duplicate the amount that it costs to ship the insured package to All-Art and send the check or money order with a separate letter, explaining what it's for.)

ANTIQUE FURNITURE WORKROOM
225 East 24th St.
New York, NY 10010
(212) 683-0551, 0552
Information: write including SASE
Minimum Order: none
Accepts: check, MO

Your precious American and European antiques are safe at the Workroom, where refinishing *doesn't* mean a dip in the strip tank followed by a glossy coat of polyurethane. It *does* mean careful refinishing by hand and French polishing with techniques that will leave your furniture with the deep gleam of age and its market value, in most cases, unimpaired.

In addition to polishing and refinishing furniture, the Workroom repairs fine chairs, restores Chinese lacquer screens, and even does woodwork restorations. For the latter and for large antiques, the Workroom will come to your home (provided you live in New York City).

Those doing business by mail must write to the Workroom with a complete description of the item to be refinished or repaired, including dimensions, and a photo if possible. They'll tell you if the job is within their capabilities. Please note that the services listed are the only services the Workroom offers. They stress that they don't make furniture, bind books, repair silver, or mend quilts.

ASSOCIATED AMERICAN ARTISTS, INC.
663 Fifth Ave.
New York, NY 10022
(212) 755-4211
Catalog: $1.00
Minimum Order: none
Accepts: check, MO

Associated American Artists has been selling prints and lithographs of famous and unknown American artists since 1934, when it was established. Its aim is to make the less expensive prints available to a large number of people.

Originally, "less expensive" meant $5.00 for a Thomas Hart Benton. Today, his lithographs are $1,200 to $1,750 here. Prices range from $90.00 for a still life by John Taylor Arms to $6,000.00 for a litho called "Sarah Wearing Her Bonnet and Coat" by Mary Cassatt. There are works here by Ivan Albright, Milton Avery, Will Barnet, George Bellows, John Steuart Curry, Jim Dine, Stuart Davis, Lyonel Feininger, Childe Hassam, Edward Hopper, John Marin, Reginald Marsh, Robert Motherwell, Raphael Soyer, James McNeill Whistler, and Grant Wood.

Every work is matted, and framing can be arranged at an added cost. Each print is sent with a Certificate of Authenticity, and shipped insured. All works mentioned are subject to prior sale, and the artists listed may not always have work available through AAA. The current stock can be viewed at the AAA gallery.

CENTER ART STUDIO
149 West 57th St.
New York, NY 10019
(212) 247-3550
Information: write, including SASE
Minimum Order: none
Accepts: check, MO

Across the street from the Russian Tea

Room and Carnegie Hall is another New York City institution, but you'll never find it on a tourist map. Tucked away on the second floor, the Center Art Studio has been doing museum-grade repairs and restorations on ceramics, metalwork, glass objects, stone, tortoise shell, lacquer, and other precious things since 1919. "Precious" is the key word here. Center Art handles only the best art and objects. Mr. Fritz Pohl, who manages the Studio, says that they repair Tiffany and glass objects of that quality, but they don't grind the chips off rims of drinking glasses unless they are very valuable. (Waterford is laughed at here, so you have an idea of what is meant.) Referring to glasses that are less than the best, Mr. Pohl wearily declares, "I don't want to see them." He doesn't want to see your antique coverlets or old family portraits either, as Center Art doesn't restore or repair oil paintings or textiles.

If you have the best but it's in need of help, write to Center Art with an explicit description of the object and the repair needed. Include a stamped, self-addressed envelope.

CLIFF SILVER CO.
159 East 55th St.
New York, NY 10022
(212) 753-8348
Information: inquire with description of work, photo, and SASE
Minimum Order: none
Accepts: check, MO

What to do when the garbage disposal turns Grandmother's heirloom gravy ladle into a free-form sterling sculpture? The dishwasher has dulled your flatware? Constant use has worn the finish on plated utensils down to the base metal?

Rush them off to Cliff Silver. Mr. Ziegler of Cliff Silver has seen victims of every sort of use and abuse known to the metal. Garbage disposals, dishwashers, acidic foods, and normal use are the biggest banes. Cliff Silver can correct the damage by straightening, recoating, replating, and otherwise repairing the sterling or silver-plated objects. They also handle articles made of pewter, do copper retinning, and can put new bristles in old silver-backed brushes.

Write to Cliff with a complete description of the repair needed, a photo of the object (if possible), and a SASE. They'll tell you whether they can do the work and may even give you an estimate then. They've been in the business for seventy-five years and their work is excellent.

MICHAEL J. DOTZEL AND SON
402 East 63rd St.
New York, NY 10021
(212) 838-2890
Information: inquire; include photo and SASE
Minimum Order: none
Accepts: check, MO

A repair service that has the business of the City of New York, the prestigious antiques firm of Stair and Co., and interior designers like James Robinson, Elisabeth Draper, and Mark Hampton has to be doing something right. In this case, it's repairing and refinishing metal objects.

Michael Dotzel has been in business since 1935, and his son, Michael, Jr., joined him twenty years ago. They refinish and rewire articles made of silver, brass, copper, and tin. They wire solid brass chandeliers originally made for candles, cast silver bobeches, and clean and repair pewter. They also make metal lampshades and will reproduce metal articles.

The emphasis at Dotzel is on fine work, just as the specialty at International Retinning and Refinishing is retinning. In fact, when International gets work it can't handle, it sends it to Dotzel, and Dotzel farms out big retinning jobs to International. "One hand washes the other, at least in this business," observes Michael, Jr.

Write to Dotzel with a photo or picture and a complete description of the work you need done, and include a stamped, self-addressed envelope, and they'll tell you whether to send the piece. You'll receive an estimate on the work once they've actually seen the article.

MARGO FEIDEN GALLERIES
51 East 10th Street
New York, NY 10003
(212) 677-5330
Information: inquire, including SASE
Minimum Order: none
Accepts: check, MO

Margo Feiden may be best known to art-conscious New Yorkers as a frame artist.

Every frame she makes is created to suit each individual work of art, and often the frame and mat make use of novel finishing techniques and materials like lace and brocade. Graphics and posters are sometimes pressed between a sheet of clear Plexiglas and a back sheet of colored plexi, which forms a tinted border.

Regardless how immortal and enduring the art, the materials of which it is made are subject to the ravages of age. The acids in common wood pulp paper and mat eventually spot and darken prints, and most tapes and glues also have destructive effects. Margo uses acid-free 100% rag board for backing and matting, and noncorrosive products in all the mounting and framing procedures. She also restores prints. People send paintings, art objects, and documents to her to take advantage of the preservative techniques she employs, and the original frames. Write to Ms. Feiden with a complete description of the work you need done (framing, restoring, matting, etc.) and include a stamped, self-addressed envelope.

FOSSNER TIMEPIECES CLOCK SHOP

826 Lexington Ave.
New York, NY 10021
(212) 249-2600
Information: inquire
Minimum Order: none
Accepts: certified check, MO

If your grandfather clock stops short, never to go again, and you live in the metropolitan area, you can call Fossner and have them pay a house call. Mr. Fossner, his wife, and his son run this business with the expertise gained from half a century in a clock repair business in Europe. Their specialty is repair and restoration of old works in clocks and watches, and they offer their experience on these to all by mail (sorry, no grandfather clocks). You can mail the timepiece, insured, to Fossner with a description of the damage, and they'll send you an estimate. Those who can stop in at the shop should—the ticking of scores of old, beautiful clocks is mesmerizing. When you think that in twenty years the imperceptible whir and slap of digital numbers flipping over will signify the passing of time, you're bound to enjoy the antediluvian "tick-tock" even more.

FULTON GALLERY

799 Lexington Ave.
New York, NY 10021
(212) 832-8854
Information: write, including photo
Minimum Order: none
Accepts: check, MO

Once upon a time, before real-estate developers had torn down many of the eighteenth-and nineteenth-century buildings, artists lived on Fulton Street. They were attracted by the picturesque surroundings and the rents of $25.00 and $30.00 for lofts. Stanley Crantson ran his Fulton Gallery there, and above him resided Jasper Johns and Robert Rauschenberg. His own gallery had been the skylit studio of the great Duncan Phyfe. The area predated Soho as a genuine Left-Bank-type of community where artists, musicians, and writers enjoyed the low cost of living and the beauty of the waterfront. Urban renewal changed that, and the buildings that remain are now preserved as landmarks. A whole block of buildings has become the South Street Seaport Museum and related shops.

As the developers rushed in, Mr. Crantson rushed uptown to his present locus on Lexington Avenue. His gallery retains the charm of earlier days, with its comfortable chairs, greenery, and the exhibitions of choice, primarily Expressionist paintings. But the Fulton Gallery not only exhibits, it also restores. Mr. Crantson applies his expertise to oil paintings and works of art on paper. He can repair cracked, burned, torn, and flaking paintings, and mend, flatten, and bleach paper. Most of his work is done on a referral basis, primarily for museums and important collectors. He's worked on paintings by Joshua Reynolds, Gainesborough, Rembrandt, and other masters, and recently completed restorations on two Toulouse-Lautrec graphics. Mr. Crantson's twenty-six years in the art business serve him well; he has a respect for the patina that a painting gains with age, and among other good points he avoids the tendency to overpaint common to many restorers.

If your work of art merits the museum-grade restorations and repairs done here, Mr. Crantson invites you to write, fully describing the damage or condition, and include a photograph. He'll be able to give you a rough estimate then, and a firm estimate when he receives the art, which should be packed well and insured. Appraisals are also done here; inquire.

also done through The Greenland Studio. Include a stamped, self-addressed envelope with all inquiries.

GEM MONOGRAM & CUT GLASS CORP.
623 Broadway
New York, NY 10012
(212) 674-8960
Information: inquire, including SASE
Minimum Order: none
Accepts: check, MO

Glassware is a far cry from crystal in price, but sometimes almost indistinguishable in appearance. Put a $6.00 glass "bubble" next to the $48.00 crystal version, and few can tell them apart (without a flick of the fingernail against the rims).

Glass has another advantage over crystal: Glass can be monogrammed, whereas crystal is usually too delicate. Gem does glass monogramming. They also do glass repair, restoration, and sell glass liners. Write to Gem with complete details concerning what you need done, whether it's monogramming or repair, and send a photo if you have one.

THE GREENLAND STUDIO
147 West 22nd St.
New York, NY 10011
(212) 255-2551
Information: inquire, including SASE
Minimum Order: none
Accepts: check, MO

Stained-glass repairs are the specialty at The Greenland Studio. Mel Greenland, the owner, has thirty years of experience in restoring windows, lampshades, and other articles made of stained glass to their original conditions. Mr. Greenland does small repairs as well as complete restorations, and has been employed by the Metropolitan Museum of Art and the Los Angeles County Museum of Art. If you have a broken stained-glass window or lampshade that merits his services, send him a photograph of the object and a description of the damage and what you'd like done. He'll tell you whether to send it or not. Yes, windows *can* be sent: Remove and pack them very, very carefully. If you live in New York City, Mel Greenland can have someone come to your home and remove and replace the windows themselves. Appraisals are

HESS REPAIRS
200 Park Ave. South
New York, NY 10003
(212) 260-2255
Information: see text
Minimum Order: none
Accepts: check, MO

Bernice Hirsch runs Hess Repairs, where it's easier to mention what they *don't* fix—furniture, electrical appliances, and mechanical devices—than to list what they do. They've repaired or restored china, textiles, glass, ivory, bone, jade, mirror, jewelry, and all kinds of art objects and bibelots, as well as odd things like fishing rods.

They seem bent on returning everything to useful service. Chips in the rims of goblets can be ground down. Hess is prized as a source for blue glass liners for silver saltcellars, pepper dishes, and sugar bowls. Mrs. Hirsch also has collections of crystal chandelier prisms and faceted crystal bottle stoppers. Whether you have an object that needs repair, a bottle without a stopper, a chandelier drop to match, or sterling cellars that need new liners, you should send the item to be fixed, stoppered, matched, or lined to Mrs. Hirsch *insured,* with any necessary explanations or specifications. She'll send you an estimate for the work. This is another service used by museums and antiques dealers, who insist on the best.

HIRAM H. HOELZER
1411 Third Ave.
New York, NY 10028
(212) 288-3211
Information: inquire
Minimum Order: none
Accepts: check, MO

You can find Mr. Hoelzer in his studio, peering through a microscope in order to do minute conservation work on a painting. You can also find him suspended forty feet above a museum floor, doing detail work on murals. He does cleaning and restoration of paintings of oil, *gouache,* and tempera, works on frescoes, and specializes in murals. He's done some watercolor

Nineteenth century Redware Crock,
one of many types of objects
restored by All Art Restorers

restoration but emphasizes that he doesn't do prints or other art on paper.

Mr. Hoelzer has an added feature: He travels to jobs if they're immovable or too large to be sent. He'd just come back from Des Moines when we spoke to him, and was heading off for Virginia the next week. If your painting can't be sent to be cleaned or restored, you can probably schedule a visit with Mr. Hoelzer if you're willing to wait until he shows up in your part of the country. If you're able to send the work, write first anyway with a complete description of the painting and the repair needed, and he'll tell you whether to forward the art.

In addition to repairs and restorations, Mr. Hoelzer makes appraisals of damages for insurance purposes and gives free estimates on jobs, something few professionals of his caliber will do. His references include the University of Pennsylvania, the City of New York, and the U.S. Government—he's the man who keeps the WPA murals in shape.

KAREKIN BESHIR, LTD.
1125 Madison Ave.
New York, NY 10028
(212) 838-3763
Information: price quote by letter; send photo if possible
Minimum Order: none
Accepts: check, MO

Fine antique rugs and tapestries are repaired and restored at Karekin Beshir. They are retained by museums and have a corresponding level of workmanship. Write, describing your rug or tapestry and the damage, and send a photograph if possible. They will tell you whether to forward the article and may be able to give you a price quote then.

LA CHAMBRE PERSE
347 Bleecker St.
New York, NY 10014
(212) 243-4287
Information: $1.00, SASE, and description for Polaroids
Minimum Order: none
Accepts: check, MO

If you could cross an American Indian rug with a dhurrie, you'd probably come up with a kilim. These rugs are woven tapestry-style by the nomadic tribes-

people of the Mideast, and are often used to cover the floors of their tents. When Fred Parvin discovered them while traveling in Iran seven years ago, he was taken both by their artistry and the uniqueness of the weave, and was amazed that no one else was seriously exporting them to the United States. He came back and opened La Chambre Perse, a large, airy store on Bleecker Street. There, the flat-weave kilims and embellished variations called Soumacks that he sells hang from the walls and lie folded in piles on the floor. Mr. Parvin can usually be seen sitting at a desk in the back of the store, dwarfed by the carpet hanging behind him, ready to answer all questions on kilims and advise in their purchase.

Mr. Parvin feels that because kilims are usually made from start to finish by one person, they are closer to "art" than Orientals, which are usually collective efforts. Each rug is truly individual, and prices average anywhere from $650.00 to $1,200.00, though some rugs are cheaper and some rare ones are dearer. La Chambre Perse also sells pillows made from scraps of kilims, which cost $8.00 to $10.00 for a hand-sized one to about $65.00 for the large throw-pillow size.

You can write to Mr. Parvin describing the sort of rug you're looking for, including: dimensions (kilims are oblong); hue (soft and pastel or loud and brilliant, the predominant color desired, and the optimum color combination); age and/or rarity (Mr. Parvin sells only antique and semi-antique rugs, which appreciate with time); and the tribe, if you can be that specific. Mr. Parvin will send you Polaroids of the rugs he has that best match your description— enclose $1.00 and a SASE. His current stock includes over 1,000 carpets, and you know that if he can locate the perfect rug for William Kunstler, Ali MacGraw, and Dan Ackroyd, he can probably do the same for you.

LET THERE BE NEON
451 West Broadway
New York, NY 10012
(212) 473-8630
Catalog: inquire
Minimum Order: none
Accepts: check, MO

Let There Be Neon has been promulgating the creative possibilities of neon since 1972. Its driving force is artist Rudi Stern, whose biography traces roots in the fine arts, video, television and kinetic projections. His gallery is the focus of almost every new interpretation and manipulation of the tubes of colored light we know as neon.

Mr. Stern's clients include Atlantic Records, Henri Bendel, the Jefferson Starship, Saturday Night Live, Ken Howard, Uri Geller, and Salem Cigarettes, to name a few. His studio has produced work for every conceivable place and purpose, including neon architecture, logos, displays, stage designs, residential interiors, book covers, and even furniture, among others. Much of the work done at Let There Be Neon is made to order, but there are some delightful stock pieces that can be seen in illustrations throughout this book (see Acknowledgments). Mr. Stern has published a book, also titled *Let There Be Neon,* detailing the history, technology, and craft of neon. The book and sculptures are available through his catalog—please inquire. Custom neon can also be ordered by mail.

JULIUS LOWY FRAME AND RESTORING CO., INC. AND SHAR-SISTO, INC.
511 East 72nd St.
New York, NY 10021
(212) 535-5250
Information: price quote
Minimum Order: none
Accepts: check, MO

Framing is an art unto itself, and at the eighty-year-old firm of Julius Lowy/Shar-Sisto, it reaches its zenith. The company spreads its frame-making and restoring operations over two floors, but even so, the only space not absorbed by frames is occupied by craftsmen, working away. Their skills include frame restoration, reproduction of antique frames, modern frames made to order, and alterations on frames to fit them to different works of art.

Julius Lowy/Shar-Sisto also works with the art itself. They clean, reline, repair, and restore oil paintings, and do cleaning, mounting, deacidification, and laminations of works of art on paper. Their work is museum level; indeed, most of their clients are museums, galleries, and collectors, and they are members of the International Institute of Conservation. In their years of restoring they've handled works by Picasso, Monet, Rembrandt, Renoir, El Greco, and scores of other greats, and have encountered that rarity collectors dream of: a valuable painting, in this case by Fujita, concealed beneath one that's expendable. Much of the art business is devoted to appraisals and conditions analyses, which are done by visual examination, photography, X-rays, and infrared photography.

Julius Lowy/Shar-Sisto accepts all kinds of restoration jobs, appraisals, and conditions analyses via mail. Write first, describing your artwork or frame and the service you need, and they will tell you whether to send it. Estimates are usually given upon examination of the work.

MALCOLM & HAYES, INC.
694 Third Ave.
New York, NY 10017
(212) 682-1316
Brochure: SASE
Minimum Order: none
Accepts: check, MO

Malcolm & Hayes is a diversified graphic arts emporium that was established in 1894 and now occupies five full floors, each with a different function. The framing shop, where Portuguese craftsmen oversee the framing of all types of art large and small, and also do needlepoint mounting, is on the main floor. Printing and thermography are done on the second, and the third is where the "art"—hand lettering, manuscript, ornamental borders, and scrolls— is done. Engraving and plaques occupy the fourth, and "heavy medals" and awards the fifth. They even have a letterpress for the old-timers there who know how to set each individual font to get certain printing effects.

Malcolm & Hayes offers the services of the "art" floor by mail: calligraphy, hand-lettered certificates done in the manuscript style, borders and scrolls, engraving, etching, etc. Send a stamped, self-addressed envelope for the brochure, which lists the services and the current prices. If you are able to stop in, they'll be glad to show you around.

Mail Order Tip: Truck charges are always collected upon delivery.

NOVAL'S ANTIQUES SERVICING

378 Third Ave.
New York, NY 10016
(212) 684-8293
Information: see text
Minimum Order: none
Accepts: check, MO

Mr. Noval has been "servicing" antiques for almost twenty years, and is one of the best in the field. He's expert at repairing and restoring furniture and oil paintings, and does a brisk business in the refurbishing of antique light fixtures. He can rewire and repair chandeliers and candelabras, and restore electrified lights to their original condition. His huge inventory of old parts, combined with his experience, almost guarantee that he'll be able to handle any job you give him. Mr. Noval prefers that you send the article that needs servicing, insured, rather than writing to him, and he'll give you an estimate upon receipt.

ORIGINAL PRINT COLLECTORS GROUP, LTD.

215 Lexington Ave., Dept. SNY1
New York, NY 10016
(212) 685-9400
Catalog: free
Minimum Order: none
Accepts: check, MO, MC, Visa, AE

Ask any New Yorker about the art at the Metropolitan or the Whitney, and you'll probably hear a discussion of aesthetics and the importance of artists from the Old Masters to minimalists. Ask him about the art on his own walls, and you'll hear about appraisal values, rates of appreciation, and tax shelters. As art becomes invaded by corporations and as record prices are set at auctions almost daily, emphasis shifts from the picture to the price tag. The Original Print Collectors Group thinks this is a shame. They are a small organization of art enthusiasts who have joined forces to purchase original art—limited editions of prints—by known and unknown artists. The prints are chosen by experts for their aesthetic appeal and potential price appreciation.

A recent color catalog shows prints by Joan Miro, Marc Chagall, Hector Saunier, Jean-Pierre Cassigneul, Ronald Christensen, Claude Weibusch, and many others. Prices for the signed,

numbered, and framed works run from $98.00 for "American Oriental" by David Olson to $9,500.00 for "La Grande Corniche" by Marc Chagall. A brochure with a short biography of each artist and information on the genesis of every work accompanies the catalog. The actual printing procedure is detailed in the discussion of Thom De Jong's work. Each print is certified as original and authentic.

The Original Print Collectors Group sells only to members. Membership, which includes a year of catalogs and newsletters and a $25.00 credit voucher good toward any purchase made within a year, costs $25.00. Since you can gain membership with all the benefits by ordering from the catalog, it appears to be a mere formality. You can return anything you buy within 30 days for a full cash refund, or a credit or exchange at any time as long as you are a member.

SAXON & CLEMENS, INC.

979 Third Ave., Room 1411
New York, NY 10022
(212) 759-5791
Information: inquire
Minimum Order: none
Accepts: check, MO

Saxon & Clemens creates "treasure boxes" for collections of small Oriental *objets d'art,* yours or theirs. They fashion an Oriental-style frame and fit it with small niches that showcase your collection of jade, onyx, gold, wood, ivory, or porcelain objects beautifully. The boxes are made to look like miniature library walls, but the concept can be modified to suit your taste. Once, a wedding ring manufacturer provided them with the materials and they built a box that began with a lump of gold, showed the successive stages of refining, beating, and working the metal, and ended with the completed ring. The boxes average 16" by 20", although they have created some as large as 3' by 4'. Max Saxon told us that surgeons and dentists respond most strongly to them, a phenomenon that remains unexplained. Mr. Saxon and Lou Marrero, who does much of the actual work, also design boxes using their own collections of objects, such as netsukes, antique silver whatnots, and tiny eighteenth-century wood carvings. One box they made featured tiny clay figures seated at a mother-of-pearl table.

Needless to say, treasure boxes are as precious as the objects they house and should be considered only if you have a collection of value. Saxon & Clemens sell their own boxes and Oriental artifacts from the shop only. They will accept Oriental objects for restoration—scrolls, screens, prints, woodcarvings—but write before you send anything, and include a photograph of the piece. They've been in business since 1940 and have had orders for their boxes from as far away as South America, Australia, and Italy. Their work is excellent, and if your collection is worth the expense, the boxes should be considered as an interesting form of display.

SAY IT IN NEON
444 Hudson St.
New York, NY 10014
(212) 691-7977
Catalog: $3.00, refundable
Minimum Order: none
Accepts: check, MO, MC, Visa

Light to order: Custom-made neon is the stock in trade at Say It In Neon. Designer Pacifico Palumbo, more easily known as Tony, will create "anything from your sketches, ideas, whims, phobias, or fantasies, for home or commercial use." Anything in neon, that is.

Say It In Neon handles the medium with taste and ambition. We have yet to ask them to capture agoraphobia in a mode suitable for office use, but they are well equipped to handle less abstract assignments with refreshing design concepts.

One of the more recent innovations at Say It In Neon is the neon lamp sculpture, which requires no special outlets or wiring, and adds pizzazz to the most tired decor, as well as illumination. Mr. Palumbo tells us that the sculptures use less energy than conventional lamps, and "give a glowing aura you'll find you can't afford to live without." Hmmm.

The catalog illustrates previous work done for other clients by Say It In Neon. Some pieces are featured in the chapter openings in this book (see Acknowledgments). Inventive and whimsical, they prove Mr. Palumbo's point that "we're light-years ahead of our time." Neon art is becoming quite collectable and may well prove a good investment.

SPANISH REFUGEE AID
80 East 11th St., Room 412
New York, NY 10003
(212) 674-7451
Brochures: free
Minimum Order: none
Accepts: check, MO

Spanish Refugee Aid is an organization that supports the survivors of the people who fought fascism—and lost to Franco—in the Spanish Civil War that ended in 1939. The fate of these people is an atrocity itself: They fled to France after Spain fell, were held in detention camps there during World War II, and were sent to die in the concentration camps of Buchenwald, Dachau, and Mauthausen. Despite the fact that Spain is no longer ruled by the Fascists, there are still members of Franco's administration in power, and most of the thirty thousand survivors of the war live in France, many on small French pensions of a few dollars a day. Spanish Refugee Aid exists to help seven hundred of these people, who live in desperate conditions.

SRA claims Bruno Bettelheim, Noam Chomsky, Mary McCarthy, Alfred Kazin, Stephen Spender, Lewis Mumford, and other luminaries as its sponsors. They work with direct donations to the refugees, "adoptions," and scholarships for the children of the exiles. They also sell original art, primarily limited editions of prints. Artists contribute their work to SRA, which sells the prints to the public at prices that run from $40.00 to $1,000.00. Previous contributors include Alexander Calder, Joan Miro, James Brooks, Saul Steinberg, Robert Motherwell, Constantino Nivola, and Esteban Vicente. The graphics are all bold, modernistic, and colorful, and the prices are usually less than those typically charged in galleries. *Every cent* of the proceeds goes to help the refugees. The cause needn't be personally compelling to justify buying and enjoying the prints, but it *is* nice to know that it's eminently worthy. The literature and prints brochures are free upon request.

Mail Order Tip: When you receive your order, open it carefully. Save all the wrappers and cartons, and report any damages, short shipments, and other problems to the shipper immediately.

SPRING AGAIN, INC.

107 Spring St.
New York, NY 10012
(212) 226-3710
Information: price quote by phone
or letter
Minimum Order: none
Accepts: check, MO

Gustav Stickley designed the electric chair, which secures him a position, if strange, in American jurisprudence. He also designed the ordinary chairs, rockers, recliners, settees, tables, cupboards, and other furniture known as Mission. A few years ago, Mission was recognized as an important part of the arts and crafts movement of the early twentieth century, prices skyrocketed, and Mission dealers opened shops all over town. Today, a few remain, including Spring Again.

Michael Carey, the owner, carries all kinds of signed and unsigned furniture by Gustav Stickley, L. & J. G. Stickley, and Limbert, as well as Roycroft copperware, Fulper pottery, and the Navajo rugs that complement the plain Mission style so well. Prices, he says, range from $10.00 to $6,000.00.

Fortunately, the Stickleys kept catalogs of their work, and Dover Books (see listing under "Books") has published a facsimile of the general catalog. Mr. Carey invites you to write or call concerning any piece listed in the catalog, and if he doesn't have it in stock he can retain your want list. Condition, presence of signature, and other particulars are all described in accurate detail by Mr. Carey.

STAIR & CO., INC.

59 East 57th St.
New York, NY 10022
(212) 355-7620
Catalog: free
Minimum Order: none
Accepts: check, MO

We venture into Stair & Co. every year or so, gaze longingly about at the seventeenth- and eighteenth-century English furniture, paintings, and porcelains, and then buy a can of furniture polish. Like the store, the polish, Stawax, is superlative. It is recommended for all kinds of wood, is white, pleasant-smelling, comes packed in a red 1-pound tin, and costs $10.00. Consistent use of Stawax and thorough polishing eventually yield a finish closer to satin than the effects produced by the heavier waxes sold in hardware stores. Stawax is *the* proper polish for valuable antique pieces.

Those with the money for valuable antiques shouldn't miss the Stair collection. Recent highlights include a handsome English oak dresser the color of cherry with open plate racks above and cupboards below, circa 1740, an English Charles II black lacquer side table circa 1660; a wonderful Chinese export porcelain of a boy carrying a fish, and a pair of English William and Mary blue-glass-bordered mirrors, circa 1695. A small color catalog of representative pieces is available, and prices are given upon request.

Across the street from Stair & Co. is their subsidiary, The Incurable Collector, which specializes in eighteenth- and nineteenth-century paintings and Oriental furniture and lacquered pieces.

Another subsidiary, operated through Stair itself, is Oxford Antique Restorers, Ltd., which will repair and restore antiques, paintings, and lacquer. Inquiries are invited regarding Stawax, the Stair catalog, the antiques in stock, and the restoration services.

Mail Order Tip: The Postal Service resolves about 85% of mail order problems: it has the power to withhold mail delivery if a company doesn't cooperate. Write to the Chief Postal Inspector, U.S. Postal Service, Washington, D.C. 20260.

SEE ALSO: Books, Records, Tapes, Stationery, Films, Educational Supplies
Home
Unusual, Rare

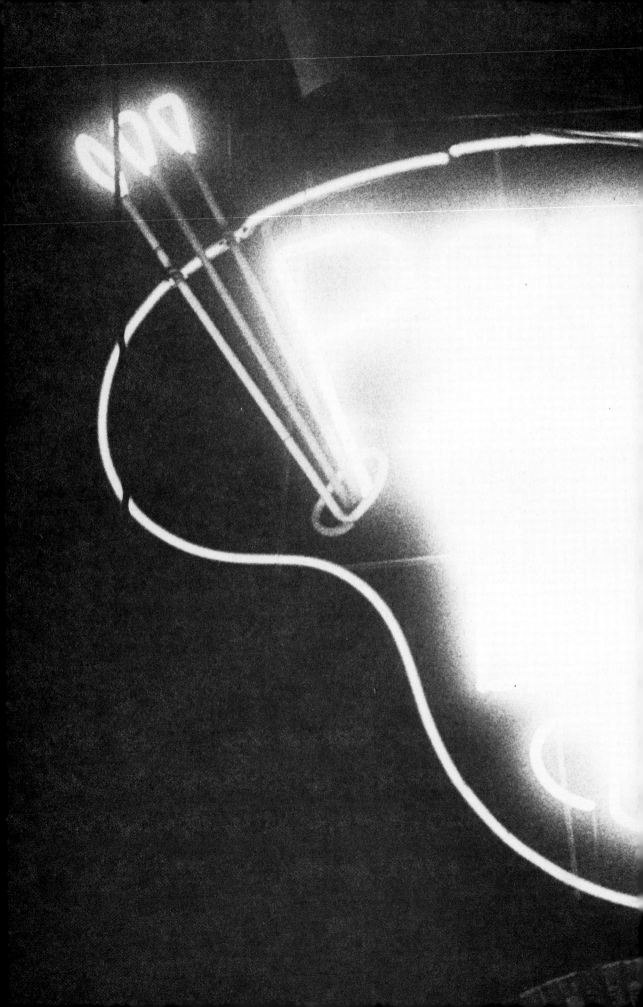

3 | Art Supplies
Craft Supplies

Because New York City has so many people crammed into a very small geographic area, and because so many of those people are artists or would be (estimates run as high as twenty would-be's for each real artist, higher yet in Soho and the East Village), the city is the nation's capital for art supplies. Even if you have access to art materials where you live, it would be silly not to buy them by mail from New York stores instead. Why? Across the country, art materials are made for consumers, or at best, student grade—poor in quality and high in price. New York suppliers would quickly go out of business, on the other hand, if they sold anything less than the very best-quality professional materials at the lowest possible prices.

Many suppliers offer their own specialties, you'll find, in addition to a range of goods pictured in something called "the general catalog." The general catalog is a compendium of basic art materials from a variety of top-name manufacturers that forms a core list of necessary products. Individual stores add or subtract pages from the general catalog, and offer discounts, sometimes, from the standard list prices. In most cases, a supplier distinguishes himself by extensive offerings in an area of concentration (such as Art Brown's pen catalog), in addition to the general catalog. Some merely offer good service and prices on general catalog items only. In all cases, the range of goods available is stupendous.

ADVENTURES IN CRAFTS

218 East 81st St.
New York, NY 10028
(212) 628-8081
Catalog: $2.00
Minimum Order: $12.00
Accepts: check, MO, MC, Visa

Découpage, the art of "cutting out," is the main enterprise at Adventures in Crafts. This tiny store is run by Dee Davis, a dynamo who seems to know everything there is to know about *découpage.*

Her store boasts one of the most extensive collections of basswood containers used for *découpage,* available anywhere. There are hinged boxes of all types, purses, planters, shadow boxes, decoys, footstools, wastebaskets, and the like, plus others of tin, bisque, and glass that can also be découpaged. She has a complete selection of gessoes, paints, fillers, glazes, metallic waxes, crackling mediums, solvents, and varnishes. The tools you'll need, such as brayers, burnishers, brushes, X-Acto knives, rulers, abrasives, and scissors are here, as well as materials like gold carbon, embossed gold paper trim, braid and cartouches from Germany, prints, tea papers, lapis and malachite papers, rice papers, and bronzing powders. Should *repoussé,* eggeury, or papier-mâché be more to your liking, supplies for those crafts are here too.

New Yorkers can take courses in découpage, repoussé, papier-mâché, and three-dimensional découpage at Adventures in Crafts from Dee, who has also written one of the best books around on the craft, *Step-by-Step Découpage.* Advice is freely given at this friendly store.

ALJO MANUFACTURING

116 Prince St.
New York, NY 10012
(212) 226-2878
Catalog: free
Minimum Order: none
Accepts: check, MO

Aljo Manufacturing has been selling fabric dyes to craftspeople, schools, and institutions for many years. Their dyes are used extensively in batik, tie-dyeing, and fabric painting, as well as in screen and block printing, photo and map coloring, costume making, and for other purposes.

Aljo sells tepid water dyes for batiking cotton and rayon, permanent machine-washable hot-water dyes for cotton and rayon; cold-process dyes for batiking that can be thickened with urea and gum, forming a solution suitable for fabric painting, brilliant alcohol-water dyes for silk painting, and acetate/nylon dyes. Commercial dyes incorporate different dye formulas for cotton, rayon, acetate, and other fabrics within each package. Since cotton dye doesn't "take" properly on acetate and vice versa, some dye is inevitably wasted, and colors usually differ from fabric to fabric. Aljo dyes are formulated for individual fiber types, creating deeper, truer colors overall. Each type of dye is available in 24 to 30 colors that range from palest yellow and pearl gray to black, starting at about $1.00 for a ½-ounce package. Aljo carries pound cakes of beeswax ($6.50), tjanting tools ($4.50 each) in small, medium, and large sizes, gum thickener, and hydrosulphite. Their booklet on Aljo aniline dyes gives hints and procedures for successful dyeing.

Once you've mastered the art of fabric dyeing, you might want to try coloring lacquer and shellac, leather, wood, and fresh and dried flowers—Aljo has dyes for all of them. Write for information.

AMERICA'S HOBBY CENTER, INC.

146 West 22nd St.
New York, NY 10011
(212) 675-8922
Model Kit Catalog (mainly wood models),
Model Car Catalog (radio-controlled),
Ship Catalog, all $1.50 each, published every 24 to 36 months
Subscriptions to 12 issues of Sales Catalogs for HO-and N-Gauge trains, and planes, boats, and vehicles are $2.50 each, published 3 to 4 times a year

---

Marshall Winston can tell you everything you ever wanted to know about vehicular hobbies, and then some. He runs America's Hobby Center, which was founded by his father in 1931. "Vehicular hobbies" include model cars, ships, airplanes, trains, and radio-controlled equipment. The Hobby Center offers separate catalogs of cars, ships, and a general catalog of models and tools, and subscriptions to 12 issues of sales catalogs of HO-and N-gauge trains, planes, boats, and vehicles. The Center claims, "If you can't get it from ... it's just not available." They get orders from places like Rio and Iron Curtain countries, and Japanese tourists buy models and materials imported from their own country at the Center, where they're cheaper, and take them home.

BELL YARN CO.
75 Essex St.
New York, NY 10002
(212) 674-1030
Mail Order:
10 Box St.
Brooklyn, NY 11222
(212) 389-1904
Price List: free
Yarn Cards: $2.00
Minimum Order: none
Accepts: check, MO

This yarn and needle-arts source is famous for the great freebie they throw in with every purchase: free instructions given right there in the store by qualified teachers. These are even available by mail (upon request), as well as all the yarns and accessories. Bell carries domestic and imported materials for needlepoint, crewel, embroidery, and rug hooking by Columbia Minerva, Coronation, Fox, Wonoco, Bucilla, DMC, Dimension, Penquoin, Paragon, Margot, Sunset Designs, and other major brands. Everything is discounted, and prices drop even lower during the eagerly awaited sales, announced via flyer to all those on the mailing list.

B & M YARN CO.
151 Essex St.
New York, NY 10002
(212) 475-6380
Color Card and Prices: $1.50
Minimum Order: none
Accepts: check, MO

B & M's huge selection of materials and supplies for knitting, embroidery, needle-point, bargello, and rug hooking is available by mail at discount prices. They carry all the brand names in addition to their own private-label yarns. Advice is free here and the salespeople are very helpful.

Mail Order Tip: Only packages sent by parcel post can be delivered to a Post Office box.

ARTHUR BROWN & BRO., INC.
2 West 46th St.
New York, NY 10036
(212) 575-5555
The International Pen Shop at
Arthur Brown
same address as above
(212) 575-5544
General Art Catalog: $2.00 refundable
Minimum Order: $50.00
Accepts: check, MO
Catalog: free
Minimum Order: $15.00
Accepts: check, MO, MC, Visa, AE, DC

Arthur Brown & Bro. claims to be America's largest supplier of artists' materials. Having visited the store, we leave that assertion unchallenged. Art Brown excels in many departments, and has an amiable, informed staff on duty to answer all your questions. Regrettably, the mail order is limited to what is contained in the "general catalog." Art Brown *does* have a separate catalog for its pen department, called The International Pen Shop, which illuminates what we mean by excelling. Even this 40-page brochure is too small to illustrate a fraction of the stock of the 43 manufacturers they carry. We are treated to photos of gold-plated and sterling models by Cartier, the unparalleled Mont Blanc pens in gold (including the Diplomat in 18K solid gold for $4,500.00) and others in rhodium, Parker pens in many styles and finishes, platinum pens, sleek designs by Lamy of Germany, elegant French instruments by Dupont and Waterman De Paris, and others by Pilot, Christian Dior, Sheaffer, Cross, Caran D'Ache, Fisher, Pentel, Garland, Anson, and Aurora. There is also a first-class selection of calligraphic supplies, including books, pens, paper, and accessories. When the pens and automatic pencils run out, Art Brown is there with the refills, ink cartridges, leads, and inks to keep them going, plus an on-premises repair shop.

None of these pens cost 19¢. Then again, no one ever throws them away. In fact, they're usually passed down through the family. Have you ever heard of an heirloom BiC?

Mail Order Tip: If the catalog's price is listed as "refundable," this means that the company will credit the price of the catalog to your first order, providing you meet the minimum order.

CHARRETTE

212 East 54th St.
New York, NY 10022
(212) 593-1633
Mail-order Address:
31 Olympia Ave.
Woburn, MA 01888
(617) 935-6000
Catalog: $2.00
Minimum Order: none
Accepts: check, MO, MC, Visa, AE

Every architect and draftsman in New York knows about Charrette and their famous cash card. For $6.00, anyone can buy a "cash privilege card" that entitles one to a 20% discount for a year on all purchases made *in the stores* on cash-and-carry basis. (Alas, no such card or discount for mail-order customers, but regular prices are competitive).

The current catalog begins with illustration board and ends with a list of customer services available through Charrette. In the 250 pages between are thousands of tools and supplies for architects, artists, and students. There are all sorts of boards for illustration, matting, and mounting, acetate films, drafting film, tracing paper, all kinds of papers for layout, sketching, watercolors, printing, and calligraphy, plus photographic background paper. Brands include Charrette, Strathmore, Bainbridge, Winsor & Newton, Fabriano, Three Candlesticks, Arches, and Rives. Charrette sells projectors, viewers, visualizers, Diazo machines, supplies, and film, all kinds of drafting and engineering tools, architectural specialties that include basswood for modelmaking, tools, parts bins, tweezers, scissors, calipers, paper cutters, tapes and adhesives, dry-mount machines, office supplies, artists' supplies, pens, pencils, and markers, templates, and books. Charrette has an enormous selection of modern office furniture, including chairs by Wilde and Spieth in a rainbow of colors, the Krueger Vertebra chairs that respond automatically to changes in position, Royalmetal chairs and stools, Luxo lamps, Vemcolites, taborets, flat files in oak, gray metal, and white and gray enamel, desk pedestals and tops, and standard office files (suspension, lateral-file, and vertical-plan storage). There are drawing tables, drafting tables, easels, and shelving systems.

Charrette's reproduction division, Stone Reprographics, offers Diazo printing, offset, Xerographic reproduction, binding, photographic reproduction and mounting and finishing, and an array of other custom services. Charrette themselves make registration stamps for architects for $12.00, but will render the service free to new architects from Massachusetts and New York.

Much of Charrette's stock can be used in the home or office—their handsome black "pickled" stainless-steel scissors for $8.95, tapes and dispensers, calendars, index files, portfolios, binders, and cases, frames, dust brushes, magnifying glasses, etc. When Christmas rolls around, don't forget their "cash privilege card" for your student, artist, or architect friends who live in Massachusetts or New York City.

ALBERT CONSTANTINE & SON

2050 Eastchester Rd.
Bronx, NY 10461
(212) 792-1600 (inquiries)
(212) 792-1602 (N.Y. orders)
(800) 223-8087 (U.S. orders)
Catalog: $1.00
Minimum Order: $5.00; $10.00 on charges
Accepts: check, MO, MC, Visa

Constantine's was founded in 1812 by Thomas Constantine, whose mahogany desks and chairs are still being used in the U.S. Senate. Today it is run by Dorothy Docherty, a Constantine descendant. Although their main lines are tools and supplies for woodworking and marquetry, so many items they sell have other applications that the catalog is a favorite of people who can't tell a dowel from a dado.

Even they, however, can succeed at veneering since the development of contact cement several years ago. Constantine's Veneer Glue, $2.75 a pint, saves you hours of setting veneer with clamps, cauls, and presses. They sell 101 veneers, from ash to zebrawood, at 20¢ to $1.50 a square foot. For projects with long surfaces, you can apply Monarch veneers, which run 7 feet and longer. These are sold in exotic woods like limba, bubinga, Brazilian rosewood, and figured avodire. Constantine sells many veneer packs and assortments at special prices, a "complete course" with veneers and tools, and for the novice, a box of 50 4"-by-9" samples of cabinet veneers. The tools—rollers, edge trimmers, veneer punches, routers, planes, trimming chisels, veneer pins, veneer tape, and saws—are all here. Once you've become proficient at handling veneers, you can attempt marquetry. Constantine sells inlays and overlays in designs that range from two strawberries on a panel, to the Shriners' emblem. Marquetry pictures are even more rewarding, and there are kits here depicting animals, landscape scenes, and even Da Vinci's *Last Supper.*

The craftsman who works in solid wood needn't settle for lowly pine when he can get kiln-dried cherry, mahogany, maple, oak, poplar, walnut, and even exotic c woods like ebony, teakwood, and padouk. There are also plywood panels in walnut, maple, oak, and mahogany stripe. Constantine has professional Marple carving tools, chisels, turning sets, gouges, carving and whittling knives, and much more. They sell specialty tools we haven't seen elsewhere, such as the inshave used for hollowing out the seats of Windsor chairs ($18.95), screw and wire gauges, a graining tool for imprinting grains on glaze coats, and French curve scrapers. In addition to all this, Constantine sells decorative cut nails and workshop project ideas, clock kits, movements, and parts, basswood boxes for *découpage* and crafts, briar blocks and stems for pipe making, a full line of guitar making materials, casters and furniture legs, wood-finishing products, wood moldings, handles and hinges and all sorts of furniture hardware, woodworking plans and patterns, upholstery tools and materials, chair seat reweaving materials, picture frame moldings, lamp parts, and dollhouse and birdhouse kits.

Ignorance is no excuse at Constantine, where there are scores of books on framemaking, antique reproductions, cabinetmaking, musical instrument making, and upholstery, as well as classic core reference texts on marquetry, woodworking, and carving.

CROWN ART PRODUCTS
75 East 13th St.
New York, NY 10003
(212) 673-0150
Catalog: $1.00
Frame Sheet: SASE
Minimum Order: none
Accepts: check, MO, MC, Visa, AE (add 5% for charges on frames)

Raymond Topple is known by

craftspeople across the country as "the silk-screen doctor." He's a chemist who has developed his own line of silk-screening inks and invented many silk-screening devices. He's a teacher at the Learning Annex, where he gives courses on silk-screen technique. He's also a president—of Crown Art Products.

Crown sells the inks Mr. Topple developed, as well as a complete line of silk-screening supplies and equipment. The inks are water-base and emulsion textile inks, and there are fluorescent colors, adhering liquids, film removers, screen washes, thinners, and other related solutions for silk-screen use. You can get screens, fabrics, hinge clamps, screen cable by the running foot, and other supplies here. Specifications are given on the inks and fabrics so you are sure of buying the right thing.

Crown also sells their own unprimed, primed, and stretched canvas at great prices—the stretched canvases are currently 40% off list price. They also sell stretcher bars and sectional frames, which they'll cut to fractions. Stretchers available from the catalog run to 60", frames to 40", but there is a much wider size range at the store—from 5" to 10' on frames. (Mail order is limited to sizes within UPS dimension regulations.) The store also offers cutting services on glass, Plexiglas, boards, and mats.

Future attractions at Crown that will be appearing in the catalog are silk-screen poster ink, glitters, bronzing powders and vehicles, and glass stain. Send a stamped, self-addressed envelope for the latest items to be offered by mail and/or the price list for sectional frames (specify what you want in your request). The catalog lists the other products and is $1.00 by mail, free if you pick it up at the store.

A. FEIBUSCH—ZIPPERS
109 Hester St.
New York, NY 10002
(212) 226-3964
Information: price quote by phone or letter (include SASE)
Minimum Order: none
Accepts: check, MO

Eddie Feibusch *is* zippers. He has the largest collection we've ever seen, running from minuscule doll clothing zips to heavy, industrial-weight closures. "If I don't have it, you can't get it," is how

Fine Sable Brushes from
Fine Art Materials, Inc.

he sums it up. You'll find metal, plastic, nylon, separating, and every other sort of zipper imaginable in over 200 colors in his little shop. He doesn't publish a catalog, but will give you a price quote if you send a swatch of the color you need matched, and tell him the length, material, and type of zipper you're looking for. Include a stamped, self-addressed envelope.

FINE ART MATERIALS, INC.

539 LaGuardia Place
New York, NY 10012
(212) 982-7100
Information: inquire with SASE or call
Minimum Order: none
Accepts: check, MO

Fine Art Materials is located in Greenwich Village, south of Washington Square Park in the New York University complex. Fine Art Materials is run by David Davis, who is known nationally and internationally as a manufacturer and importer of the finest quality materials in the art supply field. Goods are imported from and exported to all parts of the United States and the world daily. Fine Art Materials is known to guarantee (to the best of their ability, they note) the quality of the merchandise they sell. Since Mr. Davis is the manufacturer and direct importer of so many goods, the prices are sometimes as low as half the cost normally paid for supplies and tools of the same caliber. Specialties of the house include stretcher strips, oil colors, papers, pastels, lead-primed linen, easels, and various related products. Mr. Davis has the stretcher strips and his architects' cabinets made for him from imported woods. He is the largest distributor of LeFranc in the United States, carries 600-piece lines of pastels from Sennelier, LeFranc, and Rowney of England, Blocs oils, handmade colors from Holland, Andrews Nelson Whitehead supplies, all kinds of oak easels from France, a huge selection of brushes from Raphael, Rowney, and the Orient, and imports fine papers from England and the Orient. Many of the goods he carries are designed by Mr. Davis and made especially for him. Fine Art Materials also produces its own lines of artists' mediums, oil colors, sketching inks, and does custom work. Send a stamped, self-addressed envelope with your inquiry,

and they will forward information and current prices.

SAM FLAX

111 8th Ave.
New York, NY 10011
(212) 620-3000
Commercial Products Catalog: inquire
Flax Madison Avenue Catalog: inquire
Minimum Order: $25.00
Accepts: check, MO, MC, Visa, AE

Like many commercial art supply stores, Sam Flax has enjoyed enormous success in New York City. They sell supplies, equipment, and furniture to artists, designers, architects, draftsmen, printers, photographers, and institutions in the visual arts, as well as to the ordinary person who wants a fine pen or a picture framed. The catalog reflects stock prices, but David and Leonard Flax, sons of the original Sam, are constantly running specials in the stores. The stores also sell things not shown in the catalog, such as art books and handmade papers, and offer on-premises services like framing and glass cutting.

The Sam Flax catalog is not the "general catalog" put out by most firms. The stress is on commercial and fine arts products including pigments by Grumbacher, Winsor & Newton, and Liquitex, canvas, inks, watercolors, brushes, and paper in the store as well as the catalog. The commercially oriented goods run from Academia stools to zippy paper cutters. There are all kinds of paper and board for drawing, drafting, and presentation, background paper for photography, beautiful drawing tables and art furniture by Bieffe, Stabilus, Opus, and others, taborets for storage, Luxo lamps, files and storage units of every description, pencils, pens, erasers, sharpeners, adhesives, drafting tools, markers, templates, airbrush equipment, presentation cases and portfolios, slide projectors, and much more. The brands are the best—Vidalon, Strathmore, Arches, Eagle, Carb-Othello, Stabilo, Caran D'Ache, Pentel, Kohinoor, Castell, Rapidograph, Speedball, Platignum, Gaebel, Kiskar, Letraset, Chartpak, Eberhard Faber, etc. Many of the goods, like the artists' smocks, rototrays, bulletin boards, unprinted labels, X-Acto knives, and scratch pads, come in handy around the house as well as in the studio.

Sam Flax has branched into gift items like Fante papers, tabletop picture frames, desk sets, and a fine selection of fountain pens in gold, chrome, and sterling. Write and ask for the free "Flax Madison Avenue" catalog if you're interested.

GRAND CENTRAL ARTISTS' MATERIALS, INC.

18 East 40th St.
New York, NY 10016
(212) 679-0023
Catalog: $2.00
Minimum Order: $25.00
Accepts: check, MO, MC, Visa, AE

Grand Central puts out the standard "general catalog" of materials and drawing and drafting supplies. They also have a large framing shop on the premises, which does custom frames in metal, wood, and Plexiglas. Framing is available in the store only.

GURIAN FABRICS, INC.

276 Fifth Ave.
New York, NY 10001
(212) 689-9696
Brochure: $1.00
Minimum Order: 1 yard
Accepts: check, MO, MC, Visa

Interior designers and decorators have patronized Gurian's for over thirty years for its fine selection of decorator fabrics, all at good prices. Stephen and Eli Gurian have made their line of crewel embroidered fabric available to all through mail order. The crewel sold here is embroidered by hand in Kashmir using colored or white wool yarn on handloomed, all-cotton background cloth called dsuti. Crewel embroidery dates back to the fifth century, but the curling, twisting patterns of vines and flowers have a fresh look that make them well suited for home decorating. Nine patterns are currently available, some in a variety of colors that include brown tones, gold tones, blues, greens, reds, multicolors, and white on white. The material is 50" wide, and prices are $14.00 to $24.00 a yard, depending upon the complexity of the embroidery. Unembroidered dsuti is $4.50 a yard.

Gurian's also offers ready-made bedspreads ($80.00 to $120.00), tablecloths, throw-pillow covers, seat covers, and a tote bag with wood handles. The catalog is in color, but if you are matching the fabric to other colors you can buy swatches for 50¢ or $1.00 depending on the size. Crewel is sturdy, can be dry-cleaned or hand-laundered, and is not easily overused—the Gurian catalog illustrates a room done entirely in crewel that succeeds beautifully. You can return anything you buy within 15 days for a complete refund, providing the material hasn't been cut.

GUTCHEON PATCHWORKS

611 Broadway, 2nd Floor
New York, NY 10012
(212) 673-0990
Brochure and Swatches: 50¢ and SASE
Minimum Order: 1 yard
Accepts: check, MO

It is absolute irony that some of the finest craftspeople around today live and work in the city of steel and glass. Beth and Jeffrey Gutcheon are well known among patchwork artists everywhere, and they've been designing quilts, teaching classes, and selling materials out of their Broadway loft for years. They are authors of the classic books *The Perfect Patchwork Primer* and *The Quilt Design Workbook,* which have helped many quilters solve their problems in design and execution, and have even been the inspirations behind prize-winning quilts.

The Gutcheons offer instruction, accept commissions and orders for custom quilts, and lecture and teach all over the world. They also serve as a source for quality fabrics, batting, interfacing, thread, hoops, and books.

The patchwork quilt has undergone an evolution from the ultimate in recycled bedding to an art form exhibited in galleries and museums. Cloth is the patchwork artist's color and canvas, so it's no surprise that the Gutcheons are experts on every kind of quilt textile on the market today. They sell broadcloth, printcloth, and sheeting, all of which are cotton. The current *Fabric Newsletter* they publish contains specifications on the weave, weight, and finish of the fabrics they sell, and other information germane to patchwork quilting. Stapled to the newsletter is a bag of samples of the current fabric stock. Our packet ran from white to black and included bright sapphire, punk pinks, hospital-gown greens, and passionate purples in addition to more muted browns, sky blues, sun yellows, beiges, grays, heathers, and greens. There were also unusual prints included in the samples. The Gutcheons are selling all the fabric at $3.50 a yard, based on a 45" width. If the fabric you choose is 36" wide, you'll receive 1¼ yards, or a light type of sheeting; you'll get 1⅛ yards for every yard ordered. Jeffrey suggests that you tape up your samples and move the swatches around to find the color combinations that appeal to you. Then order promptly (within 6 weeks), as the stock has a rapid turnover.

If your aspirations outdistance your information, you can turn to the Gutcheon bookshelf for help. Their own volumes head the list, followed by books like *The Quiltmaker's Handbook* by Michael James, *Patchwork Patterns* by Jinny Beyer, *The Sampler* by Diana Leone, *The Log Cabin* by Leman/Martin, and more. You get 10% off the list price of all books if you order more than one title at a time, and the Gutcheons pay shipping.

Jeffrey Gutcheon has yet to add interfacing, batting, hoops, and thread to the catalog, but says that eventually everything the store carries will be available by mail. You can also look forward to their forthcoming books *Diamond Patchwork* and *Precision Patchwork,* on "intense works of a lesser dimension." This sounds great for the craftsperson in cramped spaces— apartment patchwork!

HOLE IN THE WALL

229 East 14th St.
New York, NY 10003
(212) 533-1350
Information: inquire for a price quote
Minimum Order: dozen, gross
Accepts: check, MO

Jewelrymaking is a beautiful art, but expensive. Here at Hole In The Wall you can save a bundle by buying in quantity. They sell findings, jewelry tools, chains, Art Nouveau-style filigree and Art Deco findings. They also have gold-filled and sterling findings, wire, and chain. Most of the items sold here are subject to minimum orders of a dozen or a gross, but you can take this up with the owner, Harry, when you call or write to him for a price quote.

LEATHERCRAFTERS SUPPLY CO.

25 Great Jones St.
New York, NY 10012
(212) 673-5460
Catalog: $2.00
Minimum Order: $25.00
Accepts: check, MO, MC, Visa

Every former hippie in New York remembers Leathercrafters Supply as the store that beat Tandy Crafts hands down when it came to stamps, tools, and leathers. Leathercrafters still carries stock that recalls those days, like the stamps of marijuana plants, and the signs of the zodiac, but the bulk of the catalog is devoted to hard-core, no-nonsense tools, leathers, hardware, and equipment, dyes and finishes, buckles, and lacing kits.

There are Osborne tools, Maun punches, Craftool hardware and knives, scissors, stamps of every description, needles, awls, leather goods, hardware, brushes and cements, leather preparations, precut kits, books, and a huge selection of leather skins and scraps. They've got Arkansas sharpening stones, all kinds of edgers, punches, modelers, bone folders, mallets, thread, laces, lace cutters, rivets, riveters, and many more tools, books, and supplies necessary to leatherworking.

Leathercrafters has been serving individuals and institutions since 1919 and will be here in 2019, providing the cows survive. The prices are excellent and the people are friendly.

LEE'S ART SHOP, INC.

220 West 57th St.
New York, NY 10019
(212) 247-0110
Catalog: $2.00
Minimum Order: none
Accepts: check, MO, MC, Visa

Lee's is a huge art supply source with an emphasis on the newest materials, especially imports from Italy and France. They send out the "general catalog," which just begins to tap the wealth of materials and equipment for fine and commercial art, drafting, advertising, and architecture.

What you don't see listed is the complete line of Mecanorma transfer lettering, which is the most popular brand in Europe. It doesn't dry out (has no shelf life), retains sharp edges, holds in a blowup, and you get 50% more letters on

Mecanorma sheets than typical brands for the same price or less. Lee's also carries Letraset (complete catalog, $1.00), and Formatt graphic art aids. The small office can use the Kroy lettering machine, also sold here. There are all sorts of drafting machines and instruments by Mutoh, storage units for architects, artists, and engineers by Martin, Bankers Box corrugated fiberboard files for rolled and flat document storage, Akro plastic bins and drawer sets, and the top-notch storage and studio furniture by Foster. There are all kinds of plastic furniture systems and tabourets by Beylerian, Eberhard Faber, and Martin.

Lee's Art also has a huge selection of lights, including the modernistic lines by Basic Concept, Ltd.; the entire collection of George Kovacs, which includes designs by Robert Sonneman, Ingo Maurer, John Mascheroni, and Isamu Noguchi, Halo Power-Trac lights, and the Verd-A-Ray fluorescent lights that reproduce daylight. Lee's even sells clocks by Howard Miller. You must write to Lee's with model numbers for any of these items not listed in the general catalog.

Across the street from the art store is, appropriately, a gallery of posters and graphics by Steinberg, Munch, Oldenburg, Kertesz, Chagall, and other greats. Prices for these run from $5.00 to $70.00 and the catalog is available upon request.

JOSEPH MAYER CO., INC.
22 West 8th St.
New York, NY 10001
(212) 674-8100
Catalog: free
Minimum Order: none
Accepts: check, MO

Joseph Mayer Co. has been in business since 1914. They put out the "general catalog" that most art firms carry, but unlike others, they levy no charge for it. Nor do they have a minimum order. Enough said.

ALICE MAYNARD
133 East 65th St.
New York, NY 10021
(212) 535-6107
Information: inquire
Minimum Order: none
Accepts: check, MO

Charles Quaintance, the grandson of one of the original owners of Alice Maynard, informs us that needlepoint has been supplanted by knitting as the hottest needleart in New York City. It seems that every woman who remembers how to purl has taken a look at the price tags on this season's handknit sweaters and dusted off her needles. At Alice Maynard, she can choose from a beautiful selection of yarns in wool, cotton, silk, and mohair. They specialize in natural fibers and fashion yarns, in a wide range of colors and gauges (one cotton "yarn" runs from thread-fine to one-stitch-to-the-inch, rope thick). Inquiries about specific brands, colors, and weights are invited, but there is no catalog.

Alice Maynard really excels in the service department. You can get your needlepoint or knitted articles blocked and finished here. Needlepoint can be mounted on pillows, piano benches, stools—everything but framed. They will also complete your half-finished projects, and execute your needlepoint or knitting designs from scratch. Sweater collectors who are handy with knitting needles take note: If you send Alice Maynard your measurements plus a photo of any knitted garment, they'll send you instructions on making it. This service, currently $10.00 (for customers buying Maynard's yarns), makes those beautiful sweaters seen in magazines like *Vogue* available to anyone who can knit, at a quarter to a third of the cost. If you are lazy and well-heeled, you can have the experts at Maynard copy a photo or another garment themselves. This is not cheap, but nothing made to order ever is. Write for prices of the services you need, and send a stamped, self-addressed envelope for information on taking measurements if you're having knitting instructions made.

FRANK MITTERMEIER, INC.
3577 E. Tremont Ave.
Bronx, NY 10465
(212) 828-3843
Catalog: free
Minimum Order: none
Accepts: check, MO

Frank Mittermeier sells tools to chiselers and gougers, but not the shady sort. His customers are woodcarvers, sculptors, ceramicists, and potters. The tools he carries are made by David Strasmann & Co., a firm that has been making fine chisels, gouges, chip knives, and other cutting and carving tools since 1835. In addition to general professional tools, there are special instruments for inletting gunstocks, wood inlaying, and violin making. They also have clamps, buffers, sanding and polishing kits, planes, calipers, steel scrapers, rubber mixing bowls, palette and fettling knives, glass engravers, wax carvers, anvils, and oilstones. Prices are subject to "the world monetary situation, the wildly fluctuating prices of imported wool, bristle, steel, wood, and other commodities," which almost guarantee that the current prices of less than $5.00 to over $50.00 per tool will be obsolete as you read this.

Mr. Mittermeier has collected a number of books on related arts and crafts that bear mentioning: *Ben Hunt's Big Book of Whittling, Carving Animal Caricatures* by Elma Waltner, *Direct Carving in Stone* by Mark Batten, books on *repoussage*, monographs and ciphers, glass etching and engraving, turnings, wax carving, and more. Between the books and the tools, Mittermeier gives you the edge on all kinds of carving and sculpting crafts.

MODERN NEEDLEPOINT MOUNTING

11 West 32nd St.
New York, NY 10001
(212) 279-3263
Catalog: $2.00
Minimum Order: none
Accepts: check, MO

Modern Needlepoint is run by the same Mr. Paul who oversees the Modern Leather Goods Repair Shop, but neither place suffers for the diversification. The needlepoint side of the business offers blocking and mounting services. They will mount needlepoint on handbags, as wall hangings, in frames, as bell pulls and eyeglass cases—in any way you'd like it except on clothing or shoes. The shop maintains high standards by employing European craftspeople, despite the fact that it has about 600 needlepoint accounts and is the biggest needlepoint mounting business around. Modern has forty-five years of experience dealing with all kinds of mounting jobs, and according to Mr. Paul, "we're rarely ever stymied." So bring your problem to Modern.

NEW YORK CENTRAL SUPPLY CO.

62 Third Ave.
New York, NY 10003
(212) 473-7705
Art Materials Catalog: $3.00
Fine Paper Catalog: $2.00
Printmaking Catalog: $2.00
Artists' Colors, Canvas, and Easels Catalog: $2.00
Calligraphy Catalog: $2.00
Catalog price refundable with order
Minimum Order: $10.00 to $35.00
Accepts: check, MO, MC, Visa, AE

The New York Central Supply Co. would be just another busy art supply store were it not for the presence of Steve Steinberg. Mr. Steinberg, grandson of the founder of this sixty-five-year-old firm, has a thing for paper. Between his enthusiasm and his access to superb sources around the world, he's assembled a collection that's the best in New York City, and possibly anywhere. The Fine Paper Catalog lists art and decorative papers from England, Holland, Ireland, France, Italy, Japan, Nepal, Germany, Egypt, and the U.S.A. The papers include those for fine artwork, calligraphy, printing, etching, silk-screening, sumi, woodcuts, rubbings, and books. The weight, texture, color, finish, content, watermarking, edging, manufacture method, function, origin, and pH level (when available) of each kind of paper are listed. Some of the extraordinary finds here are silk tissue from Japan, 140-pound unbleached linen paper of John and Cathy Koller, real papyrus from Egypt, calfskin parchment, a limited supply of the paper of the J. Whatman mill (closed for twenty years), and handmade lace paper. Although these papers are designed primarily for art use, New York Central does have a stationery department with smaller writing sheets of comparable quality, including sets from Arches, the Kollers, India, Richard de Bas, the Wookey Hole Mill Co. of England, and Swedish Lessebo stationery. There are also one-of-a-kind handmade blank books of Arches 100% rag paper with marbled covers and leather bindings, and similar blank books covered in Belgian linen. Prices run from $11.50 to $40.00, depending on size.

The Calligraphy Catalog is as exhaustive as the one on fine paper, listing inks by Pelikan, Higgins, Stephens, Winsor and

Newton, and Artone, pens and nibs by Gillott, Hunt, Speedball, William Mitchell, Pelikan, Osmiroid, and Montblanc, for drawing, calligraphy, mapping, cartooning, lithography, and music notation, plus a collection of papers suited for calligraphy.

The Printmaking Catalog includes tools and supplies for marbling, etching, lithography, block printing, silk-screening, rubbings, and batiking. They even have supplies for silverpoint, an old art form that involves drawing with a stylus of sterling on a prepared surface and allowing the silver to tarnish, giving the picture its shadings.

Last but not least, there is the catalog of Artists' Colors, Canvas, and Easels. Pigments, solvents, and finishes by Block, Grumbacher, Markal, Permanent Pigments, Rembrandt, Rowney, Shiva, Sennelier, Winsor and Newton, Bocour, Hyplar, Liquitex, Dr. P.H., and Luma are all available. There are stretcher bars, stretchers in round, triangular, oval, and half-oval shapes, stretched canvases, primed and unprimed canvases of cotton and linen by several firms, and pages of easels. Their comprehensive Art Materials Catalog is bound to have whatever you can't find in the other four, and the price of each is refundable with your first purchase.

New York Central has been serving the art world since 1905, and claim no less than Andy Warhol, Robert Motherwell, Lowell Nesbitt, Jasper Johns, Frank Stella, and Larry Rivers as customers. If for nothing else, New York Central must be noted for the definitive collection of paper.

PEARL PAINT
308 Canal St.
New York, NY 10013
(212) 431-7932
Catalog: $2.50
Minimum Order: $50.00
Accepts: certified check, MO, MC, Visa

Pearl Paint began forty-five years ago as a store selling house paint and related supplies. Some of their customers complained that there were no art supply sources in the area, so Pearl introduced artists' paints. Today, all that's left of the house paint business is 2 pages of paint and varnishes in their 350-page catalog and a narrow shop on the ground level of their five-floor store, although they still mix paint to order and carry a good assortment of sealers, varnishes, strippers, and personal-protection products.

New Yorkers, especially artists and craftspeople, know Pearl for what lurks above the paint store. There are four floors of art and crafts supplies stocked to the rafters, discounts of up to 50%, jocular salesclerks, and the utter mayhem of what seems like a million artists searching for the perfect paint or paper simultaneously.

You can get an inkling of how this chaos comes about with the Pearl Paint catalog. There are 225 pages of art materials and equipment that cover everything from Academy watercolors to zinc plates for etching. They have all the standard supplies—paint, paper, brushes, canvas, templates, pens, adhesives—and equipment like drawing boards, drafting tables, lamps, chairs, easels, and artbins that are listed in any "general catalog." They also carry French marbled papers, hake brushes, scented instant water-colors, curving rulers, and supplies for calligraphy, silk-screening, lithography, and sumi.

In the crafts section there's a little bit of everything. If your hobby is sculpting, woodcarving, enameling, candlemaking, textile weaving, quilting, knitting, rugmaking, macrame, jewelry, metalworking, *découpage*, or seat reweaving, your supplies and tools are here. There are many hard-to-find items for all kinds of crafts, like gold leaf, textile paints, braid-aids, ceramic frog eyes, and miniature music boxes, as well as all kinds of crafts books. The minimum order is a little steep, but get your friends together and you'll have no trouble meeting it.

THE TRAIN SHOP, LTD.
23 West 45th St.
New York, NY 10036
(212) 730-0409
Information: price quote by phone, or by letter with SASE
Minimum Order: $5.00 on charges
Accepts: check, MO, MC, Visa

The Train Shop is housed in the former quarters of the now-defunct Model Railroad Equipment Company. They are carrying on in the same tradition, offering over 200 different lines of equipment, including all the major and minor brands, handmade imported brass models, and N-, HO-, and O-scale trains. They also carry the German Marklin models in HO- and Z-gauge. Manager Paul Schulhaus says a catalog would be impossible, and will give you a price quote over the phone as well as via letter. You can check the store's ads in *Model Railroader Magazine* for the monthly specials.

UTRECHT LINENS CO.

33 35th St.
Brooklyn, NY 11232
(212) 768-2525
Catalog: free
Minimum Order: $40.00
Accepts: check, MO

Utrecht began selling art material in 1949, and has since ventured into drafting supplies and related miscellany. They manufacture their own paints, canvases, brushes, and stretchers, which are ranked as some of the best by New York artists.

The Utrecht catalog devotes entire pages to describing the quality and amounts of pigments and vehicles used to make their paints, and includes a chart of the pigment composition of the oils and acrylics. Prices on these run from 95¢ to $6.18 per studio tube of oil, and $2.00 to $10.85 per pint for acrylics, which are also sold in tubes. Utrecht carries tempera, primer, gesso, linseed oil, Damar crystals, and rabbit-skin glue, and even includes some how-to information on making Damar varnish and sizing and priming canvas. They also carry ten kinds of linen canvas in different weaves, widths, weights, and threads-per-square-inch, and four types of cotton duck. Prices run from $11.40 to $160.00 per 3-yard roll in linen, and $30.20 to $41.50 per 10-yard roll for duck. Utrecht paints and Utrecht canvas deserve the best tools, which are the Utrecht brushes. They make their own of Kolinksy red marten, pig's bristle, nylon, squirrel hair, or other fibers that are bound and clamped in nickel ferrules, and then mounted on hardwood handles. There are brushes for oil acrylic and water-colors, all competitively priced.

Utrecht also carries art products by other manufacturers. There are Strathmore papers, Bienfang pads, printmaking paper by Arches, Rives, Copperplate, and Tovil, the exquisite handmade Fabriano papers, Eberhard Faber and Castell pencils, Conte charcoal, Winsor & Newton brushes, Luxo lamps, and much more.

The prices at Utrecht are good to begin with, get better with quantity purchases, and all Utrecht products are subject to staggered discounts of 5% to 20% when they total over $75.00 to $450.00. The minimum mail order is $40.00, but this doesn't apply to purchases made in person at their store.

THE WHOLE KIT & KABOODLE CO., INC.

8 West 19th St.
New York, NY 10011
(212) 675-8892, 0245
Catalog: $1.00, plus SASE
Minimum Order: none
Accepts: check, MO

Jim Fobel and Jim Boleach once ran The Picture Pie Co., which featured pies hand-painted with any picture a customer desired. They were selling their pies and other decorated foods through a Manhattan department store bakery, and found that they couldn't keep up with their orders for hand-painted food. Then one of them hit upon the notion of stenciling the food instead. The idea worked beautifully, and they began to diversify. Their "status breads" shaped like handbags and stenciled with the logos of the designers (or parodies thereof) were a hot item until one of the designers sued for a million dollars. The case was later dismissed, The Picture Pie Co. disbanded, and The Whole Kit & Kaboodle Co., a firm devoted exclusively to stenciling, was formed.

The Whole Kit & Kaboodle sells stencil kits under the name Stencil Magic. These are often featured in the crafts sections of magazines like *House & Garden* and *Family Circle*. These kits include precut plastic stencils that are soft enough to go around corners, and some also contain paint, brushes, and materials for different projects such as stenciling a butcher's apron, placemats, labels, notes, and greeting cards.

Serious stencil artists prefer designing their own projects to buying them in kit form. They can buy stencils in a variety of classic and contemporary patterns that include flowers, vines and borders, patchwork patterns, letters, American motifs, and buildings. There is also a line of stencil patterns (from which you cut the stencils) that include designs for holiday themes, borders, Americana, storybook characters, natural themes, animals, tile patterns, Egyptian motifs, and a quartet of "jumbo" patterns, two feet by three feet, that illustrate a stylized cow and sheep grazing, Egyptian motifs, flowers and insects, and authentic early Americana. The stencil paper, knives, and brushes you will need are also here (no paint). Depending upon the medium you use, you can stencil on fabric, ceramic, leather, wood, walls, and floors—instructions are included with each package of Stencil Magic stencils.

The Whole Kit & Kaboodle does not stop at stencils. They also market a line of bargello card kits, pillow kits in primitive American painting prints, and picture frame kits that are assemblages of German paper prints. They plan to diversify further, but, as authors of *The Stencil Book,* Boleach and Fobel assure us that they'll continue to produce "stencil magic."

SEE ALSO: Books, Records, Tapes, Stationery, Films, Educational Supplies

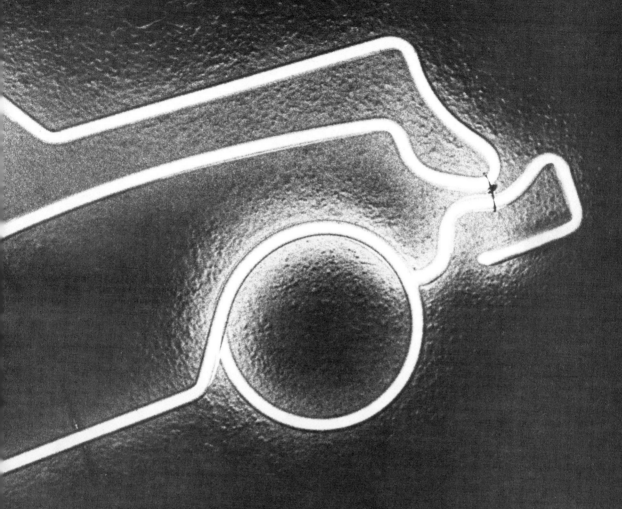

4 | Auto
Marine

The automobile is not nearly so important in New York as it is in other cities. This may result from the fact that cars seem to spend most of their time standing in traffic jams. And, after all, on our dense island of Manhattan you can go almost anywhere by subway or bus or taxicab (rent-a-jam). Car owners pay nearly as much monthly for parking space as out-of-towners do on their mortgages.

Surrounded by water, Manhattan was once an extremely boat-oriented town (back when it was still a town!). The big cruise ships still dock here, and over at 79th Street on the Hudson River there's a marina where several score of nautical city-dwellers live full time on houseboats. (Much cheaper than an apartment. Cold in winter.) In their leisure time, some New Yorkers take to the waters of Long Island Sound for sailing and power-boating. So the city retains fascinating old-line sources for marine items, sources that make your local sporting goods store or marina shop look like bare bones operations. Even if you get seasick just lying on a beach you'll find much here of interest for your wardrobe, and nice things for home decor.

COMMODORE NAUTICAL SUPPLIES

396 Broadway
New York, NY 10013
(212) 226-1880
Catalog: $1.00
Minimum Order: none
Accepts: check, MO, MC, Visa, AE

Yacht owners dock their crafts at marinas on City Island, but buy their uniforms and gear at Commodore, in the middle of the fabric district.

Anyone willing to spend tens of thousands of dollars on a boat, yacht club dues, marina fees, and maintenance costs owes it to himself to get a full-dress uniform and proclaim himself captain, from cap to shoes. Commodore sells tropical worsteds for year-round use for $175.00, polyester uniforms for $125.00, and club blazers for $110.00. Suits made to order are 25% extra. Commodore sells embroidered silk and gold-bullion insignia for sleeves and caps denoting rank, as well as discs and lapel pins. There are caps for everyone from the gob to the commodore himself, sandals and topsiders, foul-weather suits and boots, life vests for children and adults, oiled wool sweaters, and tote bags. Commodore has things like floating sunglasses, foam-insulated waterproof vinyl gloves, and space blankets that can be used for outdoor sports and other activities.

There are all kinds of yacht appointments and gear to make life at sea more comfortable, like glassware and dishes emblazoned with burgees and boating motifs, split sheets for boat bunks, galleyware, soap that lathers in salt water, teak and Lucite racks and accessories, as well as yacht logs, signal launchers, first-aid kits, navigational instruments, maintenance products, nautical jewelry, and insignias, flags, signals, and burgees. There are enough things that could serve equally well on land as at sea to make this a catalog worth looking at, even if you're a confirmed landlubber!

Mail Order Tip: Charge cards are the ultimate convenience, as most firms accept phone orders with them, and you can order from a hundred firms with a credit card and still receive just one bill at the end of the month.

GOLDBERG'S MARINE

Store Only:
12 West 46th St.
New York, NY 10036
(212) 840-8280
Mail Order and Store:
202 Market St.
Philadelphia, PA 19106
(800) 523-4506 (orders only)
(215) 627-3700 (inquiries and orders from Pa.)
Catalog: free
Minimum Order: $25.00 by phone
Accepts: check, MO, MC, Visa, AE

Only a New Yorker can understand why Goldberg's Marine seems so out of place in Manhattan, which is, after all, an island. The closest most residents come to sailing a pleasure craft is taking the three-hour sightseeing cruise on the Circle Line. For the few with some sort of vessel or the many who appreciate practical clothing and hardware, Goldberg's provides a complete selection of goods at their stores and in their comprehensive catalog. Here you can get the famous boat-neck French pullover in striped cotton for $17.79 (on sale), flashy yellow foul-weather gear for everyone in the family, deck moccasins and sailing shoes, yachting caps, and duffel bags.

There are all sorts of fishing and anchor lines that can be used for a variety of other purposes, a selection of anchors and tackle, maintenance products, navigation and communications instruments, galley equipment and utensils, and an assortment of gift and novelty items. Goldberg's even sells inflatable life boats and dinghies, which means you don't need a space at the marina to sail. Their top model, the K88 Runabout, holds three people and sells here for $666.66, compared to others like it retailing at $1,295.00. There are things here that landlubber and boat owner alike will find useful: an assortment of wall-mounted fire extinguishers by Kidde and Fireboy on sale from about $10.00 to $219.00, teak and brass fixtures and hardware for kitchen and bath, binoculars, mildew killers, flares, CB equipment, and much more. Goldberg's runs a great catalog sale every summer that features savings of up to 50% over list prices, and has a staff of well-informed salespeople on duty year-round at the stores in New York City and Philadelphia, who can advise on all boating matters. Mail order is handled only through the store in Philadelphia.

HANS KLEPPER CORP.

35 Union Square West
New York, NY 10003
(212) 243-3428
Catalog: free
Minimum Order: none
Accepts: check, MO

The Hans Klepper Corp. is as misplaced as the bulb specialists on Wall Street or the saddlery shops situated miles from the nearest stable. Klepper, home of the folding kayak, is located across from Union Square Park, whose largest body of water is an occasional puddle.

Johann Klepper, an ingenious tailor from Rosenheim, Germany, invented the folding kayak in response to the needs of local Germans who needed inexpensive, easily transported vessels that could navigate still and fast water. The idea, an adaptation of the skin-covered Inuit kayak, was improved over the years, but even early Kleppers proved eminently seaworthy. C.E. Layton crossed the English Channel in one in 1909, just two years after the first was designed. Admiral Byrd used Kleppers on his 1928 South Pole expedition, the same year that Captain Romer made the first Klepper crossing of the Atlantic. In more recent years they've been navigated on the Nile, through the Grand Canyon, up the Yukon, down the Amazon, around Cape Horn, and on other bodies of water.

The Klepper derives its versatility from its design. It is wider than a traditional kayak, more stable, and because of built-in air sponsons, it's virtually unsinkable. The collapsible hull is made of mountain ash and Finnish birch, and the covering is rubberized canvas. Assembly time is about 30 minutes for a beginner working alone, and as little as 15 minutes for an experienced owner. The disassembled boat fits into two canvas bags that can be stored—and toted—anywhere. The two-seater Aerius II is 17' long and weighs 70 pounds, and one-seater Aerius I is 15' long and weighs 50 pounds. Both boats come completely outfitted for paddling at under $1,400.00 each. The "Sail-equipment" package converts either into a sailing vessel at under $500.00. The folding Klepper can handle calm water, white water, rapids, and open seas—the rougher the water, the more experience advisable, of course. Mr. Stiller, the manager at the New York City store, says that a program of instruction in use, care, service, and handling of the boat is available by mail if you're not located near a Klepper dealer. Who shouldn't buy a Klepper? "A slob of a person who doesn't take care of his things, an overly generous person who lends all his things out, and the person who wants to shoot the rapids the first day," says Stiller.

Slobs and others can be more negligent with Klepper's handmade rigid fiberglas kayaks that seat from one to three and cost from $500.00 to under $800.00. There are all sorts of paddles and spray covers for both kinds of kayaks, rudder assemblies for rough water, life jackets, white-water helmets, boat carts, seat cushions, car carriers, maintenance products, replacement parts, and books. The only thing missing is *Popeil's Pocket Fisherman,* the perfect complement to a boat you fold up and put in your closet.

MANHATTAN MARINE AND ELECTRIC CO.

116 Chambers St.
New York, NY 10007
(212) 267-8756
Annual Catalog: $2.00
Minimum Order: $25.00
Accepts: check, MO, MC, Visa, AE

Once upon a time, long before Battery Park was created on landfill at the southern tip of Manhattan, ships docked along the lower end of the island, and Chambers Street served as the marine supply center, with four or five chandlers.

Today, Manhattan Marine is the only one left. Established in 1924, it publishes "the world's most complete catalog for naval architects, shipyards, marine stores, and boat owners" that is, this year, 432 pages long. Manager Tom Wrenn calls his supply house the Tiffany's of the marine trade. If their 21 floors of inventory don't make them special, then their know-ledgeable staff of seasoned seamen who back up every sale with years of experience do.

The majority of the goods at Manhattan Marine are geared for boats 23' to 80' long, although many items apply to general marine use. Their catalog lists all

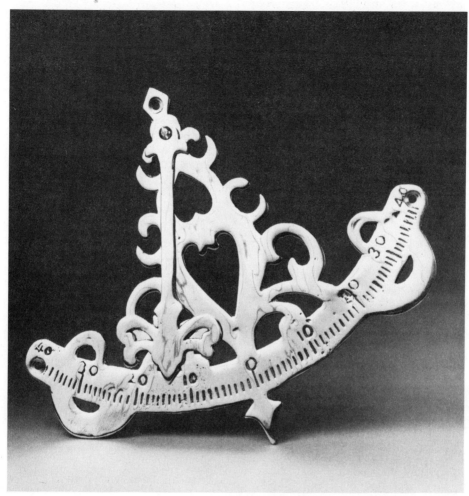

Brass Inclinometer
from Goldberg's Marine

the teak racks and cabinets, solid brass porthole mirrors, handsome copper ship lamps, galleyware, life jackets, boatwear, foul-weater gear, life rafts and sportboats, chairs and ladders, flags, signals, and first-aid kits found in other marine catalogs. They also have a comprehensive selection of maintenance products, Nautolex vinyl decking, flooring, and planking, hardware, chain, portholes, vents, fans, lighting, plumbing supplies, wiring, horns, navigation instruments, gas-fume detectors, bilge pumps, optics, depth finders, sounders, radar, receivers, line, and *three* kitchen sinks.

Mr. Wrenn estimates that about two thirds of his customers own powered vessels, average length 48', and the rest sailing crafts, the average 35' long. They prefer to forgo the discounts offered at other marine supply stores for the comprehensive selection and invaluable assistance of the staff at Manhattan Marine, who can help determine the best part or article to suit the individual purpose, and will repair or replace defective goods promptly.

NEW YORK NAUTICAL INSTRUMENT AND SERVICE CORP.

140 West Broadway
New York, NY 10013
(212) 962-4522
Information: phone or letter with SASE
Minimum Order: $10.00
Accepts: certified check, MO, or COD

We all know what to do with a drunken sailor, but a broken navigational instrument is another matter. Sober sailors bring theirs to New York Nautical.

This firm can handle repairs on barometers, compasses, clocks, chronometers, sextants, binoculars, and telescopes. They handle mechanical navigational equipment only, no electronics, and although they can repair antique instruments they don't ordinarily become involved in restoration projects—just the the repair. You can call Mr. Spina at New York Nautical and describe your instrument and he'll tell you whether he can repair it. You can also send him the instrument directly. He prefers to do business COD, but if you ship him the instrument, ask him for the repair bill plus shipping and insurance charges, and you can prepay and avoid the COD charges.

TIME MACHINES, INC.

Dept. S.C.
13 Neptune Ave.
Brooklyn, NY 11235
(212) 743-8874
Catalog: $1.00
Minimum Order: $15.00 on charge cards
Accepts: check, MO, MC, Visa

Manhattan probably harbors fewer auto enthusiasts per capita than any other place in the country, owing mainly to the expense of garage rental and maintenance, the skill of metropolitan car thieves, and the accessibility (if not reliability) of the public transportation system.

New York City redeems itself with Brooklyn, where cars are the main mode of transportation, and the American passion for automobiles thrives. It is here that Time Machines was founded about five years ago, evolving from a basement hobby into a top source for off-market parts and accessories.

Time Machines is for the person who *loves* his car. Eric Levy, manager, says that one of his customers owns a 1964 Plymouth Duster, which he has "nurtured and cared for" since he bought it new. Eric says he would hate to see the man have to choose between the car and his wife. This kind of devotion is expressed by refitting every possible standard part with one of much better design and performance, and adding special features for street racing, safety, security, and energy conservation. Time Machines carries the Electra-Fan, which replaces the less efficient belt fan, high performance coils by Mallory and Accel, Sonic Sentry theft alarms, Waxoyl antirust compound, NGK spark plugs, Cibie headlights and searchlights, quartz halogen head and auxiliary lamps by Hella and Marchal, spoilers, stabilizers, and antisway bars.

Time Machines is not just for the car nut. For instance, the "Cyberlite Deceleration Warning Light System" appeals to any driver who wants to lessen the chances of rear-end collision. It's an amber brake light that pulses on stopping—the shorter the stop, the faster and brighter it flashes. On the other hand, only those familiar with car and road parlance would understand this description of the advantages of "understeer": "It keeps you from pulling a brodie off into the tall timber if you foul up, and if you're really hurrying, it allows you to leave a turn under power in a neutral mode rather than hanging the tail out."

Those who do more than maneuver stop-and-go traffic will appreciate the performance shock absorbers, racing-style steering wheels, V.D.O. automotive instruments (tachometers, temperature and pressure gauges, etc.), Scheel and Recaro car seats, tools, and stopwatches for the performance driver. Eric Levy says they "carry only the very best." Time Machines backs up every purchase with a 30-day guarantee, and all parts have warranties—some lifetime— that Time Machines honors.

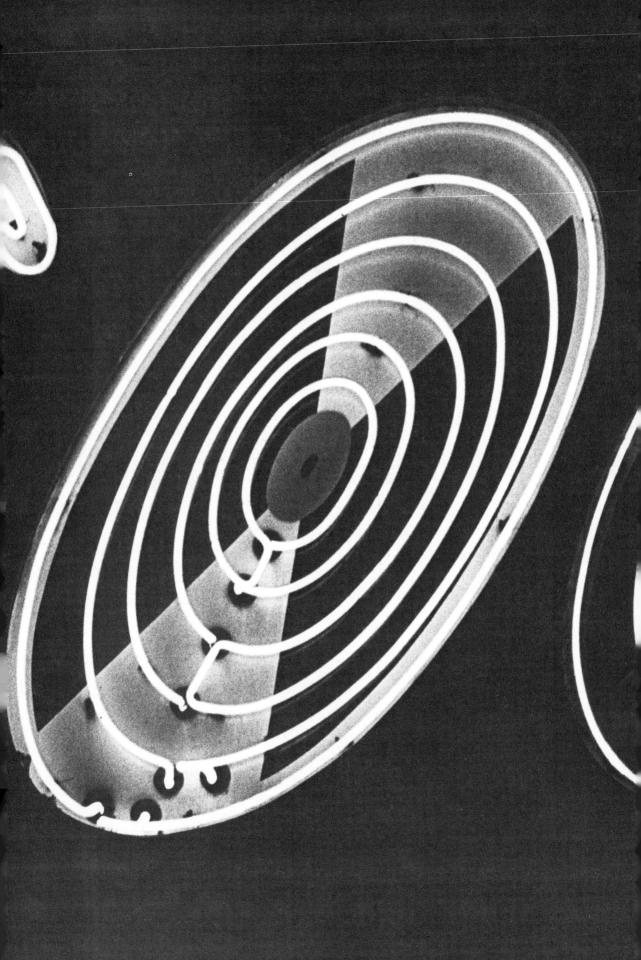

5 | Books
Records
Tapes
Stationery
Films
Educational Supplies

The typical New Yorker, on a typical day, processes more sensory input and information than is produced by the entire state of Wyoming in a year. Well, maybe.

While that statement may be bogus, it's true that New York has more bookstores than any other city, and more newspapers, and more magazine stands, and more TV stations, and more radio stations, and more orchestras, and more students, and more intellectuals. We don't have the exact figures, but information and communication is probably New York's major product area, exceeding even designer jeans. (Well, perhaps real estate and finance involve more real dollars.) Certainly New York's intelligentsia—its artists, musicians, writers, editors, teachers, publishers, academics—exert its most powerful influence on the nation at large.

Books and music are a way of life. Lacking the beauties of nature in their environment, New Yorkers turn to the life of the mind (or take up roller skating). Take a ride on a bus or subway and you'll see most of the commuters reading something—a newspaper, a book, typewritten reports, a computer printout. Words pour out of New Yorkers, over them, under them, and through them. In every language known to man. In print or out of print, you can possibly find every book, magazine, folio, diary, daybook, whatever—in our sources. The same goes for records and tapes. America may be a cultural wasteland, but New York City is its oasis.

ACADEMIC PRESS

111 Fifth Ave.
New York, NY 10003
(212) 741-6800
Catalogs: free; see listing
Minimum Order: none
Accepts: check, MO

Academic Press publishes about 650 titles a year for the professional in the behavioral sciences, medicine, and higher mathematics. The only title we could fathom was Schachter's *Everyday Mother Talk to Toddlers,* a study of the styles of speech a mother uses with her child in different situations (and even that description is a gross simplification). We wouldn't like to have to say *"submillimeter spectroscopy"* quickly five times, much less read it. Minds so attuned will find a real wealth of reference texts from this firm, which publishes three separate catalogs of books on the behavioral sciences, mathematics, and medicine. Academic, which is a subsidiary of Harcourt Brace Jovanovich, also publishes scholarly journals in the same fields, with titles such as *Ultrasonic Imaging* and *Theoretical Population Biology,* which are offered through Academic Press.

AMES & ROLLINSON, INC.

215 Park Ave. South
New York, NY 10003
(212) 473-7000
Brochure: $1.00
Minimum Order: none
Accepts: check, MO

The people at Ames & Rollinson probably recognize more academic excellence and render more citations on a single day than most people do in a year. Ames & Rollinson produces hand-lettered scrolls and certificates marking achievements of all kinds—retirements, special services, and other acts of distinction.

Certificates are either composed to suit each occasion, or reproduced from blank copies of originals that are filled in with appropriate names, dates, and titles. This involves many hours of precise calligraphy, and artwork when the scroll is bordered or illuminated. Since Ames & Rollinson has been in business since 1869, there's a good chance they produced one of the diplomas or certificates in your life, either drafting the original or filling your copy.

The Ames & Rollinson brochure illustrates some examples of certificates they have designed or filled in. Among them is one bestowing the title of "Ambassador of Good Humor" upon an ice-cream salesman, a certificate of appreciation from the American Institute of CPA's, membership certificates for dozens of businesses and organizations, diplomas and scholastic awards, testimonials, memorials, commemoratives, charters, professional oaths, coats of arms, books of remembrance, and guest registers. Ames & Rollinson can design your certificate or scroll, help you with the wording, execute the original on sheepskin, vellum, or parchment in styles that range from medieval to modern, make any necessary reproductions, fill in names and dates, embellish certificates with 24-karat-gold illumination, and copy existing scrolls and certificates. They can frame or plaque-mount the certificate or bind it in a leather-covered folio with a silk-lined slip case. Other Ames & Rollinson services include the reproduction or design and execution of book plates, family trees, poems and mottos, wedding invitations, statements of principles, and the like. Prices for the scrolls and certificates begin at just under $100.00 and go up to several hundred dollars, but reproductions of originals are as low as $1.00 each when bought in quantity. Ames & Rollinson has introduced a new miniature scroll suitable for desk display that comes mounted on a 3"-by-5" block of Lucite and starts at $50.00 for originals and $12.00 for copies in quantity.

There's no reason to limit the uses of the scrolls to red-letter occasions. If you've got the money, you can tell someone exactly what you think of him or her (either way). This Christmas, try giving the doorman, superintendent, newsboy, and housekeeper miniscrolls citing their years of unstinting service. They'll be awed to their shoes and if you buy enough scrolls it won't cost you half of what the bonuses would.

APPELFELD GALLERY

1372 York Ave.
New York, NY 10021
(212) 988-7835
Catalog: free
Minimum Order: none
Accepts: check, MO

If knowledge has an odor it is surely the

smell that prevails at Appelfeld—a fine blend of old paper, aging bindings, leather preservative, and glue. Mr. Appelfeld has been handling old and rare books, English and American literature, standard sets, and fine bindings for many years. He also appraises books, manuscripts, and literary property.

There are 350 books in the current catalog, all listed with specifics on condition, age, rarity, and any distinguishing details. Included are *Historical Essays* by Henry Adams in a first edition dated 1891, the complete works of George Eliot circa 1880, a folio of the works of Machiavelli, James Fenimore Cooper's *The Deerslayer* with color plates by Wyeth, and many other sets and volumes by Mark Twain, Henry James, Robert Burns, Boswell, Dickens, Dos Passos, and other authors great and obscure.

Prices are reasonable, beginning at $15.00. Mr. Appelfeld retains want lists, and is always looking for interesting collections of antiquarian books.

BARNES & NOBLE BOOKSTORE

Mail Order Dept.
126 Fifth Ave.
New York, NY 10011
(212) 620-7430 (information)
(212) 620-7435 (customer service)
Catalog: free
Minimum Order: $5.00; $15.00 on charges
Accepts: check, MO, MC, Visa, AE

Barnes & Noble is not just for college students and cheapskates, despite the fact that they have the most comprehensive textbook department in the city, and more recently published books at better prices than anyone else. Everyone goes there to pick up books on *The New York Times* best-seller list (at 35% off), the *New Columbia Encyclopedia* ($29.50 from $79.50), and all kinds of new and used books in cloth and paper that are reviewers' copies, remainders and over-stocks, hurt books, misprints, remaindered reprints, small-press specials, backlisted books, special purchases, and odd lots from post office auctions. The main store at 18th Street sells (and buys back) college textbooks for every course given *anywhere* (or so it appears), educational outlines, study guides, medical texts,

engineering texts and technical books, crafts and repair how-to books, law texts, reference tools, juvenilia, literature, and books on business.

The Sales Annex, across the street from the main store, is where one goes for hard-core savings on "regular" books. The bargains are so seductive, the selection so overwhelming that shopping carts are provided. Purists argue that books shouldn't be purchased like lamb chops and canned peas, but even the most resistant usually gives in and loads up. A sample of the sorts of books in the Sales Annex includes: reference tools, religion, Americana, world history, art and the arts, literature, puzzles, self-improvement, mysteries, food and wine, politics, economics, business, sports, language, travel, poetry, philosophy, autobiography and biography, antiques and collecting, film and drama, New York, Judaica, social sciences, and nature. The Barnes & Noble catalog, published several times a year, lists books from all these categories, in addition to textbooks and reference material on genetics, medicine, the social sciences, technical sciences, math and computers, business and economics, languages, writing, and literature. The catalog is available free of charge. If you don't see what you want there, Barnes & Noble runs a special-order service that can obtain any book published in the U.S.A. Send them the title, author, and publisher and they'll send you a deposit request, then notify you by postcard when the book is ready. They offer a money-back guarantee on all books, accept returns within two weeks, and give you full credit or a cash refund.

The bright, colorful B & N Annexes with their charcoal carpeting and bold wall graphics can be seen all over town. One, on 8th Street, took over the location of the ill-fated Marboro books. Many carry, in addition to a reduced range of the books sold in the 18th Street Sale Annex, discounted records, tapes, and games.

It is said that at Barnes & Noble you can fill a Christmas shopping list in less than an afternoon without killing your checkbook. It's even easier when done by mail.

Mail Order Tip: The best way to assure yourself of the next catalog is order from the current one.

BENNETT BOOK STUDIO

920 Broadway, Room 1703
New York, NY 10010
(212) 674-8520
Information: inquire; send SASE
Minimum Order: none
Accepts: check, MO

Great books deserve beautiful bindings, which are the stock in trade at Bennett Book Studio. Mr. Sal Fria runs the Studio, which has been in business for over a century doing bindings in cloth and leather, tooling and lettering in 23-karat gold, and making slipcases for fragile or rare volumes that need protection.

Bookbinding is a complex art that can combine the skills of printer, weaver, leatherworker, and goldsmith, which means prices aren't low. Write to Mr. Fria at Bennett with a description of what you need done and he'll tell you whether he can handle it, and may be able to give you an estimate then.

BLACK SUN BOOKS

667 Madison Ave.
New York, NY 10021
(212) 688-6622
Catalog: 1 year, $2.00
Minimum Order: none
Accepts: check, MO

Bibliophiles whose tastes turn to French, English, and American first editions from the eighteenth through the twentieth centuries, fine bindings, and rare and privately printed books can expand their libraries at Black Sun Books.

Linda and Harvey Tucker run Black Sun, which was founded when their collection of books outgrew their apartment. The current catalog lists gems like a limited facsimile edition of William Blake's *Illustrations of the Book of Job* ($1,500.00), a three-volume first edition of George Eliot's *The Mill on the Floss* ($400.00), *The Intelligent Woman's Guide to Socialism and Capitalism* by George Bernard Shaw ($15.00), a first edition of *Madame Bovary* ($1,500.00), and *A Picture Book Without Pictures,* by Hans Christian Andersen. The Tuckers are members of the Antiquarian Booksellers' Association of America, guarantee satisfaction, and will help you build your library. Each book is described fully and accurately.

The Tuckers' newest venture in

publications is a collection of original motion picture scripts, made available to film buffs in a catalog that is probably the only one of its kind in existence. The current issue lists 853 different scripts, beginning with *Accidents Will Happen* (starring Ronald Reagan and Gloria Blondell, among others) and ending with *Zulu.* You're as likely to find atrocities like *Willard* and *Rollerball* here as the classics of every film genre: *Bananas, West Side Story, Bikini Beach, Forbidden Planet,* etc.. Prices range from $25.00 for *Dr. Goldfoot and the Bikini Machine* to $250.00 for *Johnny Got His Gun.* Satisfaction is guaranteed on every purchase, and that includes *I Married a Monster From Outer Space.*

BRENTANO'S, INC.

586 Fifth Ave.
New York, NY 10036
(212) 757-8600
Mail-Order Address:
Dept. 1021
Tinton Falls, NJ 07724
(800) 228-2028 ext. 130 (orders)
Christmas Catalog: free
Minimum Order: none
Accepts: check, MO, MC, Visa, AE

Brentano's is the bookstore that sells chess sets, Miss Piggy dolls, sterling bead chokers, gumball machines, and hobby horses. Their wonderful gift department is a store unto itself, carrying sculpture, jewelry of gold and semiprecious stones, silver candlesticks, lacquered roses, embroidered silk pillows, jewelry boxes, toys, games, desk accessories, and Christmas decorations (in season). They also sell a full line of calendars, playing cards, posters, and stationery.

The bookstore proper carries books from all major publishers on subjects that range from architecture to zoology, with an emphasis on new hardcover releases. They also carry books of university presses, small presses, have an extensive selection of reference and business books, and a huge paperback department. Brentano's is also a member of the Antiquarian Booksellers Association of America, and has a rare books department that sells limited editions, rare books, facsimiles of rare books, eighteenth- and nineteenth-century literature, and fine bindings. Among their current offerings are the complete works of Jane Austen, bound in three-quarter morocco leather, the boxed set $850.00, and a facsimile edition of the Dead Sea scrolls printed on sheepskin, which comes in its own earthenware jar and costs $7,900.00.

In short, you can find just about everything at Brentano's except a discount price until sales time.

CHESTERFIELD MUSIC SHOPS, INC.

12 Warren St.
New York, NY 10007
(212) 964-3380
Catalog: free; published 4 to 6 times a year
Minimum Order: $10.00 on charges
Accepts: check, MO, MC, Visa

Chesterfield Music runs the country's largest mail-order record business, selling all sorts of records and tapes by all publishers at savings of up to 80% on suggested retail prices. Their specialties are classics, jazz, shows, and collectors' items. From 500 to 1,000 records and tapes are listed in every catalog, and they take special orders for items not included in the catalog that are in stock.

If you've looked in vain for *Songs and Chants of Ghana, Music of the Alps,* or *The Flutes of the Andes,* your search ends here. These and other recordings of the music of Argentina, Arabia, Bali, Greece, Portugal, Romania, old Russia, and a plethora of other times and places are here for $3.99 each or 4 for $15.49. You can get records of classics by Bartok, Stravinsky, Dvorak, Brahms, and the like performed by the Austrian "Rundfunk" Symphony Orchestra for $4.99 each. The "real" budget collection of classics are $1.99 each, or $9.25 for 5, which is about as cheap as any good thing gets. Our favorites are the jazz greats by masters like Louis Armstrong, Cab Calloway, Artie Shaw, Fats Waller, and Duke Ellington, at $3.98 each, or 4 for $11.94. Previous catalogs have listed movie soundtracks, folk music, and children's records, so write with requests for items you want that aren't shown in the current catalog.

Mail Order Tip: If a catalog is more than six months old, you should write for a new one (before ordering).

CHINA BOOKS & PERIODICALS, INC.

125 Fifth Ave.
New York, NY 10003
(212) 677-2650
Mail-order Address:
2929 24th St.
San Francisco, CA 94110
(415) 282-2994
Catalog: $1.00
Minimum Order: $10.00
Accepts: check, MO

Since the United States normalized relations with China, it seems that every department store in town is opening a Chinese boutique or emporium. A huge exhibition of Chinese antiques, industrial products, crafts, and general goods is now touring the United States. China Books couldn't be happier.

The surge in interest in the land, people, arts, and politics of China has created a new demand for their books, which run the gamut from children's picture books to studies of Chinese medicine, literature, and history. The children's books are brightly illustrated morality tales in which the proletariat rabbits, monkeys, birds, and elephants work toward good ends. In one, four animals "cooperate to build a bridge despite intimidation and harassment from an enemy fox." *The Stuck-up Kitty* who thinks too much of its looks has its comeuppance, and in *Looking After Myself* a little girl makes her own breakfast, takes care of her toys, and works in the garden. Move over, Maurice Sendak and Dr. Seuss! The books run from 75¢ to $3.95. The literature and poetry selections for adults share similar concerns. There are the poems of Mao Tse-tung; Tsa Yu's *Thunderstorm,* which portrays the conflict between parents from old China and their children; *Rickshaw,* a classic tale of social corruption in modern China; and *A Dream of Red Mansions,* which chronicles generations of an eighteenth-century noble family whose lives of luxury and pleasure conceal "symptoms of decline and self-destruction." This story, which sounds like China's answer to *Rich Man, Poor Man,* is sold in three silk-bound volumes at $14.95 each.

China's politics are covered in books by Mao, and there are volumes by and about Marx, Engels, Lenin, Stalin, and Mao. Chinese history, from the earliest dynasties through the aftermath of the Cultural Revolution, is cataloged in a collection of books by John Fairbank, Jean Chesneaux, Han Suyin, and others. Contemporary Chinese subjects are also covered in books like *Favorite Dim Sum* ($4.50), *Chinese Meatless Cooking, The Good Food of Szechuan* ($7.95), *A Barefoot Doctor's Manual* (which is the translation of the official Chinese paramedics' guide), *Chinese Medicinal Herbs,* acupuncture books and charts, fundamentals of T'ai Chi Ch'uan, and Chinese archaeology and arts, including *Modern Chinese Woodcuts, China Folk Toys and Ornaments, The Wonder of Chinese Bronzes,* and books on the ancient Chinese painters.

You can keep abreast of current events, science and medicine, technology, political issues, and the arts of China as seen through the eyes of the Chinese by subscribing to English-language periodicals, or you can go to China and see it all for yourself. Now that the People's Republic is no longer red hot, travel to China is booming. All the maps, guides, souvenir books, dictionaries, and phrase books you could want are here in a selection comprehensive enough to take you from Tibet to Peking.

The books in the catalog are in English, but the stores carry a wide variety of books in Chinese, in addition to beautiful papercuts, bookmarks, brocade-covered diaries, art prints, and sandalwood soap. There's one book in the current catalog that gives us a clue to some of the motives behind the new relations: *How to Sell to the People's Republic of China,* a businessman's guide to penetrating the world's largest market, by Sal Massimino. We can see it now: T'ai Chi abandoned for disco, golden arches atop the Great Wall . . . .

DAYTON'S
824 Broadway
New York, NY 10003
(212) 254-5084
Information: inquire
Minimum Order: $20.00
Accepts: MO only

Dayton's stocks current and out-of-print albums in every category—classical, jazz, blues, rock, pop, show tunes, etc. Their mail-order department handles *only* mint-condition LPs, with a minimum value of $20.00 each. Records of lesser value are probably available in the store, but won't be sent via mail. Write to Dayton's with the name of the album, the artist, the label, and the catalog number (if possible) of the record you want, and state that you know it's worth at least $20.00 (this way, they know that you're serious and prepared to meet the minimum-order requirement). If you don't know the market value of the LP you're trying to find, it makes sense to consult other search services and rare-records departments before writing to Dayton's.

DJUNA BOOKS
154 West 10th St.
New York, NY 10014
(212) 242-3642
Catalog: 35¢
Minimum Order: none
Accepts: check, MO

Djuna Books is a tiny bookshop in Greenwich Village that carries books by, for, and about women. Along with backlisted classics they have the latest information on women's health and political issues. Owners Sue Perlgut and Shirley Walton-Fischler can help in locating all kinds of material, and if their store doesn't have what you need they probably know where to find it.

The current Djuna Books catalog includes *The Pure and the Impure,* by Colette; *Tell Me a Riddle,* by Tillie Olsen; *The Little Disturbances of Man,* by Grace Paley: *To the Lighthouse,* by Virginia Woolf, and many other works of fiction. Under the heading "Lost and Found Women" are Kate Chopin's *The Awakening; The Yellow Wallpaper,* by Charlotte Perkins Gilman; and *The Haunted Pool,* by George Sand. There are two pages of "Lesbian/Gay" books by Adrienne Rich, Andrea Dworkin, Rita Mae Brown, Kate Millet, and others, anthologies and essays on the condition of women, biographies of well-known women, Marxist/socialist books, women's journals and diaries, books on women and religion, and bibliographies. There are books on the women's movement, women's health, violence against women, sports, childbirth/ parenting, sexuality, the behavioral sciences, art, drama, and humor. They even have women-oriented science fiction. There are symbols to designate the small or women's press books,

Lesbian-oriented works, and books for children and teenagers. You don't have to be a feminist to drop in at the store, which is open seven days a week.

DOVER PUBLICATIONS,INC.

180 Varick St.
New York, NY 10014
(212) 255-3755
Catalog: free
Minimum Order: none
Accepts: check, MO

Dover, the publishing house that brings you Tom Tierney's John Wayne and Marilyn Monroe paper dolls and books of surrealistic postcards, also give you Albert Einstein's *Investigations on the Theory of Brownian Movement,* and Trollope's *Rachel Ray,* a reproduction of the 1863 edition. Dover specializes in reprints of rare or out-of-print books, arts and crafts handbooks, technical books on science and math, and reproductions of pictures from the archives of copyright-free art, although their entire range encompasses everything from the fine arts to gardening and cooking. Dover's distinction among publishing houses is not their books list so much as their methods of production. They use low-acid, high-opacity paper that won't yellow and crumble with age. The pages are sewn together in signatures rather than glued to the spine, so they don't fall out and the spine won't break when the book is opened flat. Unlike the common paperback, Dover soft covers are designed to last forever.

Dover books are also cheap. Most are $1.00 to $5.00 and very few are over $10.00. Fifty drawings of Bellini from the rare Goloubew edition are here for just $2.50. The complete score of Mozart's *Don Giovanni,* from Leipzig editions that cost $200.00 to $300.00, is $10.00. There are books on Tibetan art, posters from World War I, *Frank Lloyd Wright's Fallingwater* by Donald Hoffman, *Coptic Textile Designs,* books on antiques, dolls, photography, music, dance, literature, magic, the behavioral sciences, history, cooking, the sciences, and math, all very reasonably priced. The children's books include reprints of Andrew Lang's fairy tales, Beatrix Potter books, *The Wonderful Wizard of Oz* and other books by Frank Baum, and many more classics. Dover's collection of copyright-free art has inspired coloring books of common weeds, mythical beasts, prismatic designs, tropical fish, Civil War uniforms, and other unusual subjects, at just $1.50 each.

Creative souls know Dover for their large selection of books of art instruction and technique and their crafts handbooks. Here is *Animal Sketching* by Alexander Calder ($1.50), *A Manual of Veneering,* a book of templates for 12 quilt designs, cut-and-use stencil books of Art Deco, Victorian, Christmas, Egyptian, and Early American designs, *Creative Lithography and How to Do It,* and many other practical and informative source books.

Dover is celebrated by no less than *The New York Times* for making reprints of books on mathematics, physics, chemistry, engineering, astronomy, geology, biology, and other sciences available at low prices. These and all other Dover books are covered by an unconditional money-back guarantee on books returned within 10 days. There's a book here for everyone, and the catalog is a must-see for Christmas shopping.

M. M EINHORN MAXWELL, BOOKS

80 East 11th St.
New York, NY 10003
(212) 228-6767, 2129
Book Lists: free, include a SASE
Minimum Order: none
Accepts: check, MO

Marilyn M. Einhorn is interested in books on food and drink. Lawrence R. Maxwell, her husband, is interested in the performing arts. It comes as no surprise, therefore, that when they launched their book business they decided to specialize in those two areas.

Thanks to frequent buying trips here and abroad, they have accumulated a tremendous stock of hard-to-find books. Their Xeroxed lists, which appear several times a year, are highly specialized and appeal to sophisticated clients who know exactly what they want. For example, a recent list on "Baking and Confectionery" brought an order from a former White House pastry chef now with the CIA (Culinary Institute of America) at Hyde Park, and a list of books on "American Wines" was purchased *in toto* by a client in Scotland. Among other goodies, they boast a collection of books on dance from all over the world, and the most extensive collection of books on puppetry in the United States.

Since their stock changes daily, their catalogs never reflect their entire inventory and they invite you to list your *desiderata* with them without charge. New York City bibliophiles take note: This is primarily a mail-order source. Visitors are welcome, but only with an appointment.

FOUR CONTINENT BOOK CORP.

149 Fifth Ave.
New York NY 10010
(212) 533-0250
Catalogs: free; see text
Minimum Order: as noted in each catalog
Accepts: check, MO, MC, Visa

The Four Continent Book Corp. is probably the only store in the city that carries books, periodicals, posters, and records from Soviet Russia, Poland, and Czechoslovakia.

Four Continent does a large mail-order business and issues many separate catalogs for books, records, and subscriptions. *Art, Social Sciences, Russian Science and Technology, Literature, Literary Criticism & Children's Books* and *Music from Russia on Records* are published in English. *Subscriptions to Periodicals & Scientific Journals, Dictionaries & Encyclopaedias,* and *Folk and Popular Music on Records* are in Russian and English. The catalogs *Art, Linguistics, Literary Criticism, For the Classroom* (teaching aids for Russian- and English-speaking students), *Magazines, Journals and Newspapers on Microfilm,* and *Slides and Film Strips* are all in Russian. Not cataloged but quite wonderful and worth a trip to the store are the Russian arts and crafts that can be seen there, as well as all sorts of posters and cards

When requesting any of the catalogs, spell out the full title and specify whether you need it in Russian or English, as they may issue some of the catalogs in both languages.

Mail Order Tip: You are most likely to receive a catalog promptly if you order one in Oct., Nov., or early December.

THE FRENCH AND SPANISH BOOK CORP.

115 Fifth Ave.
New York, NY 10003
(212) 673-7400
French Books Catalog: $2.95
Spanish Books Catalog: $2.95
Dictionary Catalog: $4.95
Minimum Order : $10.00
Accepts: checks, MO

Emanuel Molho presides over what is probably the most extensive collection of books in French and Spanish in North America today. Between La Librairie de France on the promenade at Rockefeller Center and La Libreria Hispanica at the corporate headquarters on Fifth Avenue, the firm stocks roughly a million books in French, Spanish, and other languages. Both stores carry reference books, textbooks, bilingual books, French and Spanish translations of books in English, literature, criticism, juvenilia, texts on business, pure and applied sciences, math, domestic arts, history, philosophy, the fine arts, hobbies, Americana, and every other possible topic. They also have a special "Third World" section featuring books on and from Haiti and French-speaking African nations.

The newest department at the French and Spanish Book Corp. is The Dictionary Store. Mr. Molho aspires to offer every dictionary on any subject in any language currently available, and after perusing 175 pages of titles in *The Dictionary Catalog,* we think he may have succeeded. There are books here for every possible occupation from accounting to zoology, in monolingual, bilingual, and multilingual editions. *The Dictionary of Rubber?* A Serbo-Croatian dictionary of cattle-rearing terms? A *Glossary of Micrographics?* They're all here, as well as thousands of others.

Within both the Spanish-oriented store at 115 Fifth Avenue and the French-oriented store at Rockefeller Center there are French and Spanish daily papers and periodicals, calendars, records, tapes, games, maps, posters, paintings, graphics, and *objects d'art,* as well as books. Catalogs are sent free to schools and libraries requesting them on letterhead, and teachers are given in-store discounts.

Mail Order Tip: The age of the free catalog is almost over.

THE GOLDEN DISC

239 Bleecker St.
New York, NY 10014
(212) 255-7899
Oldies Catalog: $2.00
Minimum Order: none
Accepts: check, MO, MC, Visa
(U.S. funds only)

The Golden Disc specialty is 45s, specifically rock 'n' roll and rhythm 'n' blues singles. Their list begins in the day of Bo Diddley and the Platters, and runs into the 1960s. This is where you'll find Frankie Lymon and the Teenagers on Gee, Johnny Ace on Duke, the Orioles on Jubilee, and the Flamingoes on the Chance label. In addition to hard-to-find 45s they carry "mainstream" rock of the 1960s and 1970s, the albums by the Beatles, the Who, the Jefferson Airplane, and others of that ilk that are still in demand but not stocked in large record stores.

When the New Wave washed across the Atlantic from Britain, it made a big splash in the United States—names like the Clash, Sex Pistols, the B-52s, Devo, Elvis Costello, and Patti Smith became household words in homes where, as one Golden Disc employee put it, "punk is thunk." The Golden Disc sells New Wave imports and specials as well as the big labels, and is presently compiling a New Wave catalog.

In the world of LPs, the Golden Disc carries current releases on major labels like United Artists, Epic, MCA, Asylum, Columbia, and Warner/Elektra/Atlantic. The specialty labels go from Apple to Ze, and include imports. They also carry reggae, salsa, and calypso.

Records aren't the only draw at The Golden Disc. Kids of all ages come here for the fine collection of picture buttons, used to communicate rock 'n' roll affiliations to the rest of the world. A father and son were seen making a selection from over 360 then available (not by mail). The boy settled on a Pink Floyd and the Stones. His father passed on the buttons but asked if the store carried direct discs (they don't). But what they *do* have in the record department is enough to win them customers like Johnny Cash and keep other collectors coming back.

It's too bad you can't "listen-by-mail," but if you know what you want Golden Disc likely has it.

HACKER ART BOOKS, INC.

54 West 57th St.
New York, NY 10019
(212) 757-1450
Catalog: free
Minimum Order: none
Accepts: check, MO

New Yorkers believe that art books are better read than just plopped on the coffee table and left to gather dust from Christmas to Christmas. When they want a good art "read," they can stop in Soho at Jaap Reitman, on Madison Avenue at Wittenborn, or down the street from Henri Bendel's, at Hacker Art Books.

Hacker has been selling new and out-of-print art books on the fine and applied arts for over fifty years. They claim the title of the largest art book store in the country, and put out catalogs listing 500 books at a time, most of which are unobtainable elsewhere.

The books are described with style—to wit, "A good wine needs no bush, and a book by Kenneth Clark needs no fanfare" introduces the writeup of *Animals and Men* by the same author (published at $19.95, sold here for $12.95). You can get volumes on a diversity of topics, such as *300 Years of American Seating Furniture* ($16.95), *Plastics for Kinetic Art*, and a monolithic collection of *The Drawings of Paul Cezanne*, which contains 1,223 plates and costs $99.95 (from a published price of $140.00).

Primitive Erotic Art features not only pictures but also fresh insights drawn from psychoanalysis and anthropology. There are all sorts of books on the art and architecture of southern Arabia, Spain, the Dark Ages, Greece, Japan, India, Red Grooms, Peru, Eskimos, the Shakers, and many more. The selection is large enough to include those odd books that few would think of writing, and fewer reading, but that are often fascinating. The history of wallpaper, a three-century overview of collars, stocks, and cravats, and a handbook of penny banks must surely fill some void. Whether your art library is thin or your coffee table is bare, you'll find something to fill the empty spaces at Hacker Art Books, and at up to 50% off list price.

Mail Order Tip: When firms run out of catalogs, are between printings, or only issue catalogs seasonally, there can be a delay of months before you receive yours.

HOUSE OF OLDIES

267 Bleecker St.
New York, NY 10014
(212) 243-0500
Catalog: $2.00
Minimum Order: none
Accepts: check, MO

Everything about the House of Oldies is vintage, including their catalog, circa 1968. They have hundreds of thousands of rock 'n' roll and rhythm 'n' blues 45s that date from 1949 to the present. The catalog lists records released before 1968, but want lists for records from the 1970s, as well as oldies not listed in the catalog, are all welcome.

You don't realize how far music has come in a generation until you look at the titles here. Remember "Blame It on the Bossa Nova" by Eydie Gorme, "Bewitched" by Doris Day, and "Onward, Christian Soldiers" as sung by Perry Como? Remakes (or duplicative titles) were common even when R&R and R&B were young. Both the Spaniels and the Shirelles did "Baby It's You," and the Cadillacs, Chariots, Five Thrills, and the Passions all took a stab at "Gloria." You'll find all your old favorites here, even those you'd probably never own up to liking. Our list includes "I Love My Baby" by Neil Sedaka and the Tokens, Hank Williams's "Jambalaya," both the Bobby Darin and Louis Armstrong versions of "Mack the Knife," "On Top of Spaghetti" by Tom Glazer, "Stormy Weather," and "Sixty-Minute Man" by the Dominoes.

House of Oldies also has a selection of rare R&R and R&B albums, and some of the assorted group collections like *Alan Freed's Golden Pics* and *Murray the K's Blasts* that are priceless to any oldies fan.

The last few pages of the catalog consist of reproductions of several Cash Box Top 100 charts from November 30, 1963 to January 13, 1968 that will really take you back. Even if you never order a record, you'll have a good time looking at the charts and the rest of the catalog. Until we saw it here, we wouldn't have believed that Anita Bryant had recorded "Till There Was You." No prices are given on any of the records, so you have to write House of Oldies with a list of titles (include artists) and they will send it back with current prices.

Check out some of your dusty old platters here. Market values have been soaring.

J & R MUSIC WORLD

23 Park Row
New York, NY 10038
(212) 732-8600 (N.Y. orders and all inquiries)
(800) 221-8180 (U.S. orders)
Information: price quote
Minimum Order: 4 albums or tapes
Accepts: check, MO, MC, Visa

J & R is really a world unto itself, with an inventory of millions of record albums, sheet music, and some audio components. They sell their records at prices that have withstood professional comparison shopping, and make the savings available by mail to all. Just about any current release of a classical, operatic, pop, rock, jazz, easy-listening, show-music, country 'n' western, or soundtrack recording can be found here, at savings of up to 30%, sometimes more. Call J & R with the names and labels of the albums you're looking for and they'll give you a price quote.

LITERARY MART

1261 Broadway
New York, NY 10001
(212) 684-0588
Price List: SASE
Minimum Order: none
Accepts: check, MO

Owning an encyclopedia may not solve all of life's problems, but it will answer many of its questions. Literary Mart not only sells all the major encyclopedias and a plethora of other reference tools, but also sells them at up to 30% off list price.

The most recent editions of encyclopedias by Britannica, Americana, and Collier's are here, plus the one-volume compendiums by Columbia and Random House. For the children, there are sets by World Book, *Britannica Junior*, Compton's, Funk & Wagnalls, and the *New Book of Knowledge*.

In the dictionary department, there are all sorts of editions by Merriam-Webster, Random House, Webster's, Funk & Wagnalls, World Book, Grolier, Thorndike-Barnhart, and American Heritage. The authoritative *Oxford Dictionary,* in 13 volumes with two supplements, is also available in its current printing.

Literary Mart has pages of listings of "special reference" tools, including esoterica like *1,200 Years of Italian Sculpture*, the Funk & Wagnalls *Jewish Encyclopedia*, *Great Disasters of the 20th Century*, and *Pro Football A to Z*. They also carry the staples of inquiry: atlases, volumes of quotations, foreign-language volumes, thesauruses, the Bible, and the Great Books series on literature.

Last but not least, there is the *Scholar's Britannica*, the famous Eleventh Edition of 1910, which was edited at Cambridge University and includes essays by Gladstone and Macaulay. It may not have much on nuclear physics, but it does showcase some of the best scholarly writing by the finest minds of the day. If they were alive today, they'd probably buy all their tomes from Literary Mart.

LUSTRUM PRESS, INC.
Box 450, Canal St. Station
New York, NY 10013
Book List: SASE
Minimum Order: none
Accepts: check, MO, MC, Visa

Some photographers simply document a split second of time, while others explore the possibilities of the limited image. The latter is the métier of the darkroom artist, and the focus of Lustrum Press.

Lustrum takes its direction from the photographers who run it: Ralph Gibson, the editor; John Flattau, the producer; and Arne Lewis, the creative director. Their focus is best illustrated by their *Theory* series, which examines the process involved in different aspects of photography. Prominent photographers describe their trade secrets and the techniques used to achieve a particular "style." Lustrum's *Darkroom* books provide access to the darkroom methods of photographers such as Larry Clark, George Tice, and Duane Michaels. The *Theory* series begins with *Nude: Theory*, an elegant insight into the problems and aesthetics of photographing the nude. Articles and photographs by Duane Michaels, Manuel Alvarez Bravo, and Helmut Newton are included. *Landscape: Theory* confronts the technical concerns of this particular genre, illustrated by the work of Harry Callahan, George Tice, Brett Weston, Robert Adams, and several others. The process of selecting a print from the contact sheet is delineated in *Contact:*

Theory, which includes contact sheets, essays, and final prints from over 40 well-known photographers. The latest in the series is *Fashion: Theory*, which has less to do with clothing than with the absence of it. This book, not lightly called erotic, contains work by Horst, David Bailey, Chris Von Wangenheim, Erica Lennard, and others. (Only Lustrum could do a book on fashion photography and get away with omitting Helmut Newton and Irving Penn.)

Lustrum's focus is on the newer photographers who are forging new aesthetics and developing the techniques that are changing photography. Lustrum's underground classic, *SX-70 Art*, showcases single photographs in experimental modes by a plethora of current artists. *SX-70 Art* is introduced by Isaac Asimov and Max Kosloff, and costs $20.00. Lustrum books range from $6.95 for *Darklight* by Michael Martone to $35.00 for books in the *Theory* series.

Photography is now considered an art, as well as one of the most individual meetings of man and mechanical device. Lustrum books address the concerns of both the art and the craft of photography, and enhance a general appreciation of photography while providing technical tools invaluable to the photographer himself.

JAMES MAC DONALD CO.
43 West 61st St.
New York, NY 10023
(203) 853-6076
Information: inquire
Minimum Order: none
Accepts: check, MO

For over a century the James MacDonald Co. has been restoring old, rare books to their former glory and making slipcases for those that just need protection. They can take an antique volume that's falling to pieces, dismember it, repair and rebuild it, and leave it looking like an old book but with the strength of a new one. They do fine quarter and half bindings, in calf, French morocco, and cloth, some full-cloth bindings, and make slipcases of equally fine materials.

Restorations are tedious, time-consuming, and the materials are often expensive, so the cost is not low. The James MacDonald Co. works mainly for the rare-books departments of univer-sities and institutions, among them

Whittier's Poetical Works,
from Strand Book Store

Harvard and Yale. Your book has to be quite valuable to warrant spending what you will here to have it restored, but if you think it is, write with a full description of the book and the damage or condition. They'll tell you whether to send it. Just for the record: They've actually restored a Gutenberg bible.

NATIONAL BOOK STORE

15 Astor Place
New York, NY 10003
New (212) 475-4946
Information: price quote by phone
or letter
Minimum Order: $5.00
Accepts: check, MO

Sun-bleached math and physics books fill the window of the National Book Store at Astor Place. Inside, it's library quiet, and every book is in its place. Students and faculty from nearby Cooper Union and NYU know National for its comprehensive math section, the variety of university presses it carries, and the philosophy collection, which some customers claim is the best in the country. Literature, poetry, and general interests are also represented.

National sells the Riverside series, the Loeb Classical Library, the Everyman Library, Greek and Latin texts, and the Dover math and science series. They also have fine selection of student outlines and study helps, the Arco Civil Service series, and chess and puzzle books. They will retain want lists for books that are in print but hard to find. Their store at 725 Broadway, just below 8th St., is all paperback but also academically oriented.

NATIONAL EDITION AND LIBRARY BINDERY

244 West 49th St.
New York, NY 10019
(212) 246-4392
Information: inquire
Minimum Order: none
Accepts: check, MO

National is the closest thing to a no-frills bindery this side of staples and rubber bands. They specialize in library bindings, which are good, protective, and utilitarian, but because the bindings are oversewn rather than bound in signatures, they are somewhat stiff and tight and don't allow the book to lie flat. If you don't mind grappling with your reading material or if you need a little-used volume rebound, this service is for you. National does a brisk business in theses, reports, magazine collections, dictionaries, and Bibles. Bindings are done in cloth, buckram, and leather, buckram being the top choice as it outlasts leather and is half the cost.

Library bindings have the advantage of being cheap: Currently it costs $10.00 to have a year of *National Geographic* bound. Write to National with the type of magazine and the number of issues you need bound, the binding material you prefer, and they'll give you a price quote. Send books, theses, and other material directly, insured, and they'll send you the bill.

THE PHOENIX BOOKSHOP

22 Jones St.
New York, NY 10014
(212) 675-2795
Catalog: free
Minimum Order: $3.00
Accepts: check, MO
Note: all articles mentioned are subject to prior sale

Robert Wilson used to drop in at The Phoenix Bookshop every Friday after he was paid. One afternoon it occurred to him that he hadn't bought a book there in three weeks. "Sell me a book, Larry," he challenged the proprietor. "You can buy them all," was the reply. "How much?" Robert shot back, and after three years of negotiations they agreed on a price and Robert bought The Phoenix.

That was over twenty years ago. Since then, Mr. Wilson has changed the specialty of religion to poetry and first editions. Phoenix was one of the first bookstores east of San Francisco to carry the beatniks (Ginsberg et al). They carried W. S. Merwin before he became well known, bought the poetry collections of Marianne Moore and W. H. Auden, and served as Anaïs Nin's agents before she had achieved fame and glory.

They still buy virtually every piece of poetry published, no mean feat considering the volume produced and the realtive obsurity of many small presses.

Most of the books listed in the catalog are by known poets and authors. William Burroughs's *Naked Lunch, The Ticket that Exploded, Nova Express,* and a scarce title, *Roosevelt After Inauguration,* are here, as well as volumes by Ginsberg, Creely, Delmore Schwartz, and John Giorno. You can find *Dharma Bums* by Jack Kerouac, *Sea and Sardinia* by D. H. Lawrence, and a translation of Baudelaire's *Flowers of Evil* by Edna St. Vincent Millay and George Dillon, books by Lawrence Ferlinghetti, E. M. Forster, James Joyce, and Archibald MacLeish, collages by Ray Johnson, little magazines and periodicals, anthologies, collections, and odd items like the card by Louis Zukofsky called *Finally a Valentine,* one of 500 numbered copies. Prices on the books run from under $2.00 to hundreds of dollars, depending upon the condition and rarity.

The irony of this store is that it reflects a deep appreciation of the poetic form, but Mr. Wilson is, by his own admission, a failed poet. This doesn't seem to bother him at all.

PILOT BOOKS

347 Fifth Ave.
New York, NY 10016
(212) 685-0736
Catalog: SASE
Minimum Order: none
Accepts: check, MO

Pilot is "America's leading publisher of impartial, authoritative franchising books." In plain English, they specialize in books on business and moneymaking ideas. Their current book list includes *Starting A Business After 50, Franchise Investigation and Contract Negotiation, Protecting and Profiting From Your Business Ideas,* and other similar titles. They also publish travel guides that are aimed at the vacationer on a budget— *National Directory of Free Tourist Attractions,* a directory of fast-food restaurants on the East Coast, *Travel Guide to Canada,* etc.—and "personal" guides, which range from *150 Ways to Save Energy and Money* to *The Modern Woman's Zodiac to Love and Fullfillment.* The books, all paperback, run from $1.50 to $15.00 each, and there are at least 25 new titles published every year. Maybe Pilot could be franchised?

THE RECORD HUNTER

507 Fifth Ave.
New York, NY 10017
(212) 697-8970
Catalog: free
Minimum Order: $25.00
Accepts: check, MO, MC, Visa, AE, CB, DC

The Record Hunter stalks albums and tapes of every description, but bags only bargains. They've been sending records all over the world for over thirty-five years, and tell us that they offer the same great prices—up to 50% off suggested list—to those who buy by mail as well as in the store.

The Record Hunter carries jazz, country, blues, rock, classical, opera, folk, disco, juvenile, soundtrack, and show-tune recordings, cassettes, and tapes. The catalog, published four times a year, lists limited-time specials and the Record Hunter discount rate on records not on special. You'll never pay list price here.

RIZZOLI INTERNATIONAL BOOKSTORES, INC.

712 Fifth Ave.
New York, NY 10019
(212) 397-3706
Catalog: $1.00
Minimum Order: none
Accepts: check, MO, MC, Visa

Rizzoli gives the impression of being an elegant private library that just happens to sell its books. The walls are polished mahogany, the floors marble, and the air is pervaded by the hush common to churches and museums. The business of selling books is conducted discreetly, in undertones, by the solicitous staff.

Ah, the books. Rizzoli carries books by all major publishers, but showcases Rizzoli Publications, which are usually serious, comprehensive, and beautiful books on the fine and decorative arts, architecture, and art history. The store also carries a wide variety of fiction, non-fiction, reference works, literature, travel guides and maps, and periodicals from France, Germany, Italy, Spain, and England.

The Rizzoli Publications catalog lists current publications and backlisted titles (other books are available through special orders). Some of the highlights in the current season are *Feminine Beauty* by Kenneth Clark, a liberally illustrated portrait of the feminine ideal through time; *Mariano Fortuny: His Life and Work,* the history of the man who gave us those incredible pleated "Delphus" dresses; *Chinese Art,* an examination of Chinese *objets d'art* made of gold, silver, bronze, cloisonné, enamel, lacquer, and wood; *Mackintosh Architecture,* the buildings of Charles Rennie, better known for his wonderfully constructed chairs; *Impressionists and Impressionism,* the classic compendium of the movement. One of our favorite Rizzoli series are the *Every Painting* books, which catalog and illustrate an artist's life work chronologically. So far, books on Rembrandt, Gauguin, Brueghel, Bosch, Botticelli, Durer, El Greco, Holbein, Michelangelo, and Velasquez have been compiled. Prices at Rizzoli range from reasonable—$5.95 for each paperback volume of the *Every Painting* series, to dear—$150.00 for elegant, limited, numbered editions on Erte, Isadora Duncan, Lewis Carroll, Arcimboldo, and others, which are made on Fabriano paper with hand-tipped four-color illustrations, gold stamping, silk binding, and fine slipcasings.

When, at Rizzoli, you tire of browsing through the exquisite volumes, a visit to the balcony is in order. The classical-records department is there, and a small art gallery as well. Art! Books! Music! We feel cultured already.

THE SCRIBNER BOOK STORE
597 Fifth Ave.
New York, NY 10017
(212) 486-4070
Christmas Catalog: free
Minimum Order: none
Accepts: check, MO, MC, Visa, AE

Legend has it that the Scribner Book Store actually predates Charles Scribner's Sons, the publishing house, which was founded in 1846. Not so, says Mr. Scribner himself, although he isn't sure exactly *when* the store came into being. At any rate, the book store, with its sedate blue and white striped awnings and genteel salespeople, carries on in the grand old tradition of book stores where the printed word commands respect, if not downright reverence. The book store carries the 300-odd titles that Charles Scribner's Sons, located above the store, publish each year, in addition

to books from every other major press. All in all, there are about 50,000 titles on everything from acting to woodworking, in addition to classics in fine bindings, travel books, small-press books, a selection of art and high-fashion magazines, and calendars. The book store publishes a mail-order catalog for the Christmas season, and also runs a search service for out-of-print books. If it's been published, Scribner can probably find it. Write with the title, author, date of publication, and publishing house of the book you're looking for and include a stamped, self-addressed envelope. It's a service like this that endears Scribner to book lovers and places it above other book stores.

STRAND BOOK STORE
828 Broadway
New York, NY 10003
(212) 473-1452
Catalogs: free, see text
Minimum Order: none
Accepts: check, MO

The Strand is to book stores what Zabar's is to delis: the place you can get almost anything you're looking for. While Zabar's doesn't have eight miles of cheese or pastrami, the Strand *does* have eight miles of books on every conceivable subject.

Their catalogs reflect the diversity and volume of the stock: There are separate booklets for art book specials, literature, reviewers' copies, and book specials, which list only a fraction of the volumes available. Many people go to Strand just for the reviewers' copies, which are brand-new, recently published books (mainly hardcover) that are sold at half price. Others go for books on history, architecture, crafts, food, Americana, the fine arts, literature, poetry, antiques, drama, health, photography, sports, and innumerable other topics.

The Strand also has a rare-books department that will hold the true bibliophile in thrall. Mail orders for rare books are handled through want lists, as there is no catalog. They are always interested in acquiring rare or fine books, art volumes, or scholarly tomes, but will also buy "just books." You can call or write to see if they're interested in yours.

The Strand Book Store itself is a dingy, cavernous affair with a rather disorganized shelving system (or so it appears) that appeals to the person who doesn't mind perusing entire stacks before locating that book. The staff can be divinely helpful or thoroughly insouciant, depending, it seems, on the weather or the type of Danish they had that morning. One caveat for the prospective mail-order customer: Strand often seems to be out of catalogs at the moment you need them, owing to the fact that they are free and everyone writes for them. Be prepared to wait while they print new ones and/or make several requests. The good news: Once you get the catalogs, you'll see that the selection and great prices—up to 75% off publishers' list—make Strand worth the wait.

U.S. COMMITTEE FOR UNICEF

P.O. Box 5050, Grand Central Station
New York, NY 10161
(212) 686-5522: inquiries and NY orders
(800) 331-1000: U.S. orders
(918) 664-8300: OK orders
Christmas Catalog: free
Minimum Order: $5.00
Accepts: check, MO, MC, Visa

You can make a few people richer by buying Christmas cards from your stationery store. You can help purchase food, shelter, medical attention, and care for many unfortunate children and refugees around the world by buying cards from UNICEF.

UNICEF cards are known for their fine contemporary designs, often contributed by established artists, and the classic traditional motifs. Most of the cards are printed with non-denominational messages, such as "Season's Greetings" or "Happy Holidays," sometimes in several official United Nations languages, although there are a few blank cards. Many are available with your personal imprint (at an extra cost). UNICEF also sells all-purpose card and note assortments, stationery, desk and wall calendars, paper dolls, books and games for children. The catalog is published in the fall.

Mail Order Tip: Read "The Complete Guide" (p. 8) before you order a catalog or write a single letter of inquiry. It will save you time, money, and the miseries of ignorance.

VIDEO TO-GO

169 West 57th St.
New York, NY 10019
(212) 757-7616
Information: price quote, inquire by letter
Minimum Order: none
Accepts: check, MO, MC, Visa

After shelling out $1,000 for a video cassette recorder, do you find youself using it to record little more than Jacques Cousteau specials and the episodes of *General Hospital* you miss while at work? Make your VCR cost-effective with movies. Video To-Go, a brand-new store in mid-Manhattan, sells everything that's been released for the home video market. This includes all the motion pictures on cassette by United Artists, Paramount, Allied Artists, 20th Century-Fox, Columbia, and other studios. Video To-Go offers not only recent releases but also classics, concerts, documentaries, foreign features, humor, science fiction, children's programs, adult films, and more. They have 60 minutes of Merrie Melodies and Looney Tunes by Warner Brothers, Alfred Hitchcock greats like *Sabotage and The Man Who Knew Too Much,* Buster Keaton classics, *The Third Man* with Orson Welles, *Diabolique,* Bergman's *Persona,* and the hilarious college favorite, *Reefer Madness.*

TV is represented with an *Avengers* episode and a selection from *Star Trek,* to name just two. Cultists will enjoy George Romero's great *Night of the Living Dead,* the Bruce Lee flicks, the original Sherlock Holmes series with Basil Rathbone and Nigel Bruce, and the collection of "B" Westerns with the likes of John Wayne, Roy Rogers, and John Ritter's father, Tex. If it's music you want, the selection here runs from Satchmo and Benny Goodman to Cream's farewell concert and the Rolling Stones. Those who simply want a copy of a movie favorite can choose from *The Story of O, Papillon, Grease, Blazing Saddles, Patton, Superman,* and *The Exorcist,* as well as thousands of others. Video To-Go has a 30-pound resource book at their store that lists everything in print, and will answer mail-order inquiries about specific films. Prices generally begin at $59.95, which means that you should be able to make the movies pay for themselves by inviting all the neighbors over, providing soft chairs, cold drinks, and hot buttered popcorn, and passing the hat at the end of the show.

SAMUEL WEISER, INC.

740 Broadway
New York, NY 10003
(212) 777-6363
Catalog: $1.00
Minimum Order: none
Accepts: check, MO

Mystics have been flocking to Samuel Weiser for years for their books on the occult, Oriental philosophy, and metaphysics. Weiser stocks thousands of books, including rare and out-of-print titles, reprints, publications of small presses, and foreign publications on subjects that range from alchemy to Zen.

Here you can find works by Popoff, Crowley, Blavatsky, and many others, with titles such as *Diary of a Drug Fiend, The Secret Teachings of All Ages, Finding of the Third Eye, Seven Keys to Color Healing,* and *Gurdjieff; Making a New World.* There are books here on phenomenology, the Kaballah, palmistry, astral projection, yoga, the black arts, herbalism, numerology, and every other subject related to the occult or Oriental religions available. Henry Suzuki, who runs Weiser, will retain want lists for out-of-print books not found in his rare-books department. Write with your requests.

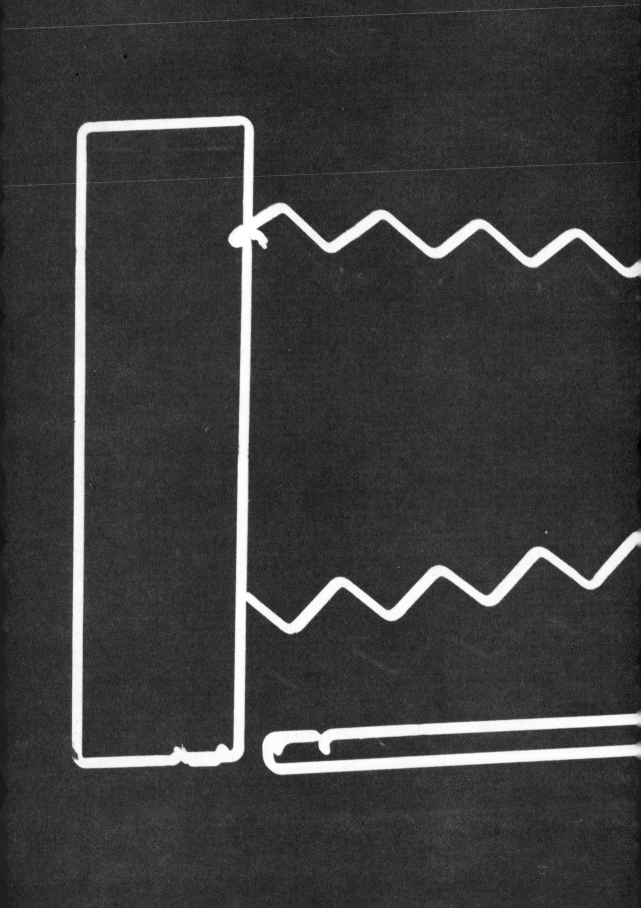

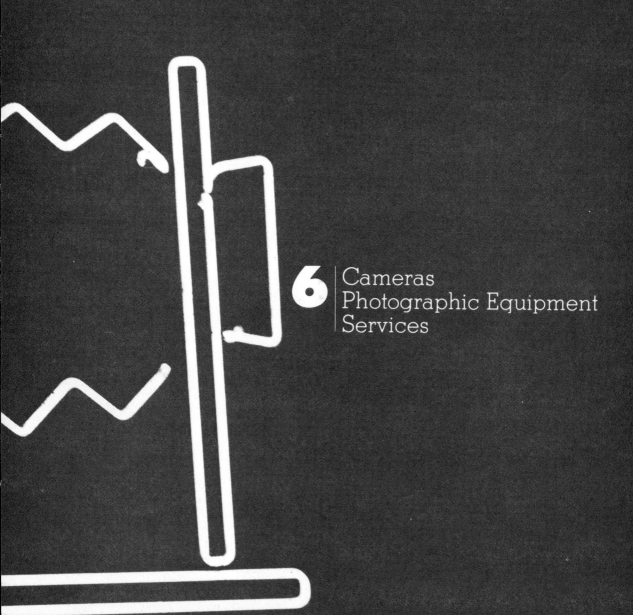

6 | Cameras
Photographic Equipment
Services

Why are cameras so cheap in New York? They're cheaper here than in Hong Kong! Japanese cameras are often cheaper than in Japan! How can it be?

Consumers benefit from the low prices created by this subculture, but you must still be careful. Often the multipiece outfits that are so heavily advertised are "stripped"—i.e., the original equipment that comes with the camera body (lenses, winders, flashes, etc.) is removed and cheaper good substituted. When buying an outfit, be sure all parts are original and made by the same manufacturer. Never bite for the "famous make" promotions—famous make is *never* famous make. If the shop is not advertising name brands by their names, you're in the danger zone. This really is a serious matter. You *can* get fantastic camera buys by mail from New York, but ripoffs are all too common. We believe all of our listings are reputable and honest—they've all been checked out. For extra confidence you might want to shop where professionals shop: Ken Hansen Photo.

B & H FOTO & ELECTRONICS CORP.

17 Warren St.
New York, NY 10007
(212) 233-9190
Information: Price quote
Minimum Order : $25.00
Accepts: check, MO, MC, Visa

B & H runs ads listing their current specials on cameras and darkroom equipment in *Modern Photography* and *Popular Photography*, but you can call or write for a price quote. They sell all kinds of cameras and darkroom equipment by Canon, Minolta, Yashica, Olympus, Pentax, Vivitar, Tokina, Bronica, Bell & Howell, Kodak, Hasselblad, Omega, Gossen, Ilford paper and film, and film only by Agfa and Fuji. B & H also carries calculators by Hewlett-Packard and tape recorders by Pearlcorder. Prices here are competitive.

BONA-FIDE NOVELTIES, INC.

Photographic Division
1123 Broadway
New York, NY 10010
(212) 242-5442
Price List: SASE
Minimum Order: $5.00
Accepts: check, MO

Better than perfect light or a model who can freeze an expression is a discount source for photographic supplies, or so say many photographers we know. Bona-Fide has some amazing bargains on camera film, enlarging and contact papers, lithographic supplies, and darkroom chemicals.

Their films include Linagraph, Dacomatic, Panatomic X, Plus X, Hyscan, Ektachrome, Anscochrome, and Vericolor II, in 16-, 35-, and 70mm bulk and sheet lot. They have enlarging and contact paper in different brands and sizes, available in sheets and rolls, and a variety of lithographic supplies.

Bona-Fide has been around for thirty years, and supplies many universities, workshops, and professional photographers. Mr. Lindt, the proprietor, knows all his materials and can answer any questions you may have.

Mail Order Tip: Never send stamps to any company, unless requested.

CAMBRIDGE CAMERA EXCHANGE, INC.

Seventh Ave. and 13th St.
New York, NY 10011
(212) 675-8600 (N.Y. orders)
(800) 221-2253 (U.S. orders)
Information: price quote, by letter
Minimum Order: $20.00
Accepts: check, MO, MC, Visa

Cambridge has just about everything you could want in photographic equipment and supplies. If you're looking for cameras by Pentax, Shinan, Nikon, Olympus, Kodak, Konica, Minolta, Elmo, Sankyo, Eumig, Chinon, Hasselblad, Bell & Howell, Leica, Canon, Bolex, and Yashica, you'll find them here, as well as Vivitar and Sigma lenses. They have film by Agfa, Fuji, Kodak, and others, and enlargers, projecters, bulbs, and a full line of darkroom supplies. The savings here run up to 60% off list prices.

CAMERA DISCOUNT CENTER, INC.

89A Worth St.
New York, NY 10013
(212) 226-1014 (N.Y. orders, inquiries)
(800) 221-3496 (U.S. orders, inquiries)
Catalog; $ 1.89
Minimum Order: none
Accepts: check, MO, MC, Visa

Shutterbugs of all varieties will appreciate the comprehensive selection of cameras, lenses, accessories, projectors, lights, and darkroom equipment and supplies that Camera Discount carries, at what they believe are the lowest possible prices.

They have all the major camera lines, plus some like Bronica, Minox, Contax, and Omega that are less common. They sell lenses by Sigma, Vivitar, Osawa, Soligar, Rokunar, Aetna, and Tamron, silent and sound movie cameras and projectors, and all sorts of accessories. There are tripods by Shik, Bogen, Vivitar, Gitzo, and Leitz, enlargers, filters, specialty lenses of every sort, and a full line of darkroom supplies. They have color analyzers and light meters, camera cases and bags, and a full line of the excellent Lowel lights. Their 30-page catalog represents the top of the stock in certain manufacturers and lines, and Camera Discount invites inquiries about items not pictured. In addition to cameras and photo equipment, they sell the Pearlcorder tape recorder and accessories, watches by Otron, Bulova, and Seiko, Zeiss sunglasses, some opticals, and a variety of how-to books.

EXECUTIVE PHOTO
120 West 31 St.
New York, NY 10001
(212) 947-5290: inquiries and NY orders
(800) 223-7323: U.S. orders only
Catalog: $3.00
Minimum Order: $25.00
Accepts: check, MO, MC, Visa, AE

Executive has *everything* in cameras, photographic equipment,and darkroom supplies. The brands they carry include Yashica, Pentax, Leica, Nikon, Sigma, Hasselblad, Minolta, Rollei, Sinar, Olympus, Bronica, Silk, Mamiya, Vivitar, Canon, Konica, Kodak, Durst, Sankyo, Elmo, Fujica—in short, just about every line currently available. Everything, including the calculators and other electronics they carry, is listed in the thick catalog they publish, and prices are up to 50% off list. Because Executive sometimes runs limited-time specials, it makes sense to call before you place an order, to make sure the camera or equipment you need isn't being sold at a better discount that week.

FOCUS ELECTRONICS
4523 Thirteenth Ave.
Brooklyn, NY 11219
(212) 871-7600
Information: price quote by letter
Minimum Order: none
Accepts: check, MO, MC, Visa

When you need a camera or coffee-maker fast, try Focus. They ship within 48 hours of receiving your order, drawing on their own huge inventory of stock, not the manufacturer's warehouse. In addition to cameras, calculators, and every sort of appliance large and small, there are TV and video sets, compact stereo systems, and watches. The camera lines include Canon, Nikon, Olympus, Yashica, Pentax, and Minolta, and watches are by Seiko and Casio.

Focus has a 14-day refund policy, provided the item is returned in its original condition and shipping container. They handle special orders and dual-voltage appliances.

47TH STREET PHOTO
67 West 47th St.
New York, NY 10036
(212) 260-4410 (inquiries and N.Y. orders)
(800) 223-5661 (U.S. orders)
Information: price quote by phone or letter
Minimum Order: none
Accepts: check, MO, MC, Visa, AE

We were told by the owner of another camera store that a guide to New York City shopping that overlooked 47th Street Photo couldn't be taken seriously. When the *competition* puts in a good word for a store, you know there's a reason.

47th Street Photo has everything in the way of camera and electronic equipment available, by manufacturers like Canon, Pentax, Olympus, Mamiya, Nikon, Rollei, Contax, Sigma, Minox, Vivitar, Minolta, Hasselblad, Leica, Asanuma, Bell & Howell, Bushnell, Tokina, and many others. They also sell film by Kodak, Agfa, and Fuji, calculators by Casio, Hewlett-Packard, Texas Instruments, Canon, and Sharp, and Seiko and Casio watches. 47th Street has gone into audio and video lines, and is selling VCRs by RCA, Panasonic, Sony, and JVC, and tapes and accessories at true discount prices, in addition to Sony Trinitrons, Sanyo cassette recorders, and Panasonic radios. They also have a large selection of business equipment, dictating and telephone answering machines by Sony, Sanyo, Code-A-Phone, Record-A-Call, Phillips Norelco, and other firms, in addition to Texas Instruments and Apple computers. They run ads featuring current specials in *The Wall Street Journal* and the "Arts and Leisure" section of *The New York Times* every Sunday, but if you don't have access to those papers you can call or write for a price quote on what you need.

FOTO ELECTRIC SUPPLY
31 Essex St.
New York, NY 10002
(212) 673-5222
Information: price quote by letter *only*
Minimum Order: none
Accepts: check, MO, MC, Visa

Foto Electric has been shipping its dual-voltage appliances and electronics to all corners of the globe for almost

The First Leica, Model A,
Circa 1929, from Ken Hansen

twenty years. Their advertising is all done via word of mouth by customers satisfied with the service and discounts of 30% and more here.

Try Foto for audio components by Sony and Panasonic, TV and video epuipment by those firms and Zenith, and appliances by GE, Amana, Tappan, Chambers, Whirlpool, Maytag, Magic Chef, Thermadore, and Sub Zero, which are only a sample of the manufacturers they carry. They also have cameras by Kodak, Eumig, Bell & Howell, Minolta, Nikon, Canon, and Pentax.

Foto's manager says that the store has "a special feeling," and that you can expect the best in service whether you're a walk-in customer or you're ordering a Trinitron to be shipped to Brazil.

GARDEN CAMERA
345 Seventh Ave.
New York, NY 10001
(212) 868-1420: inquiries and NY orders
(800) 223-0595: U.S. orders
Catalog: $3.00
Minimum Order: $30.00
Accepts: check, MO, MC, Visa

Garden's catalog has everything you could need in the way of film, cameras, darkroom equipment, and related goods. There are all kinds of film by Fuji, Agfa, and Kodak, and cameras by Nikon, Pentax, Olympus, Confax, Hasselblad, Eumig, Minox, Yashica, Bell & Howell, Minolta, Sanyo, Vivitar, Canon, Mamiya, and Leica. They also sell Seiko watches and calculators by Texas Instruments and Hewlett-Packard. The minimum-order requirement is balanced by the discounts—30% to 50% and more.

KEN HANSEN PHOTO
19 West 34th St., 11th Floor
New York, NY 10001
(212) 279-8690
Information: price quote
Minimum Order: none
Accepts: check, MO, MC, Visa

Ken Hansen is the choice among professional photographers throughout the city. He carries new cameras by Leica, Nikon, Canon, Contax, Rolleiflex, Hasselblad, Linhof, and Bronica SQ, Norman and Speedatron lighting units, and tripods by Gitzo, Bogen, Linhof, Leitz, and Majestic. In addition, Ken

Hansen maintains a large inventory of used, high-quality cameras, and rare and old collectors' items. Our photographer recommended Ken Hansen Photo above any other camera and equipment store in the city. Need we say more?

MIDTOWN FOTO
21 West 47th St.
New York, NY 10036
(212) 575-1633 (N.Y. orders and *all* inquiries)
(800) 223-9808 (U.S. orders *only*)
Catalog: $1.00
Minimum Order: none
Accepts: check, MO, MC, Visa, C.O.D.

Robert Kind (and he is) runs the advertising department at Midtown Foto. He says if you can't check out Midtown in person, you can see their ads in *Popular Photography* and *The New York Times* or write for a catalog. You can also call or write for a price quote on their cameras and photographic equipment by Nikon, Pentax, Yashica, Contax, Rollei, Konica, Vivitar, Sigma and others. Mr. Kind says that they intend stocking all sorts of "electronic paraphernalia" like video recorders in the future.

MINIFILM PHOTO
167 West 32nd St.
New York, NY 10001
(212) 695-8100 (N.Y. orders)
(800) 223-1820 (U.S. orders only)
Catalog: 50¢
Minimum Order: $25.00 on charges
Accepts: check, MO, MC, Visa

You can save up to 40% on cameras, film, darkroom equipment and supplies, and things like Canon calculators, Pearlcorder taperecorders, and Zeiss binoculars at Minifilm. They carry all the top camera and projector lines, including Olympus, Yashica, Polaroid, Canon, Pentax, Rollei, Chinon, Elmo, Hasselblad, Minolta, Konica, Bronica, Mamiya, Bell & Howell, Nikon, Minox, and Leica. They have stills, movie and bulk film by Kodak, Fuji, Agfa, and Ilford, lighting by Bowens, flashes by Ascorlight and Metz, and other brand-name enlargers, lenses, and accessory bags. If you don't see what you're looking for in the catalog, write or call, as they probably have it.

MODERNAGE PHOTOGRAPHIC SERVICES

1150 Sixth Ave.
New York, NY 10017
(212) 661-9190
Booklet of Services: free
Minimum Order: $4.25
Accepts: check, MO, MC, Visa

We asked several top New York City photographers where they go to have film developed and prints made when they don't have access to a darkroom, and they all said "Modernage." If the pros can trust them, so can we. In business since 1944, Modernage serves amateurs and professionals. The typical lineup of customers in their bright suite on Sixth Avenue includes models, actors, and actresses updating portfolios and getting publicity shots made, PR people, admen, photojournalists, hobbyists, and professionals who just don't have time to get in the darkroom and do it themselves.

Modernage does everything. Their black-and-white services run from film developing to full-scale murals of almost limitless size in black and white, pastels, or sepia. They make copy negatives, duplicate negatives, oversized and regular contacts, black-and-white slides, slides from color, enlargements, prints in sepia, Panalure, pastel shades of red, orange, yellow, green, blue, silver, and gold, exhibit and dry mounting, box framing, wood-brace mounting, and prints on photo linen and Cronapaque. Their special services on enlargements include burning-in, dodging, cropping, similar range of color services opaquing, and reductions. They offer a similar range of color services that range from simple developing to art services such as airbrushing, retouching, and hot-press lettering. All the standard services are priced in the booklet, which also includes "General Words of Wisdom," tips on making the most of your photographic efforts. The hopeful actor or actress who needs head shots can request the other Modernage brochure, *A Primer for Ordering Presentation Photos,* which gives tips on the photo session and prices for this type of photo.

Modernage prides itself on returning film processing orders the day after receipt, small print jobs within 3 working days, free negative filling services, and rush services for those who need them. Whether you're an individual who just wants your vacation photos developed, or bank that needs a 9'-by-160' wall mural made, Modernage can supply.

OLDEN CAMERA

1265 Broadway
New York, NY 10001
(212) 725-1234
Catalog: free
Minimum Order: $25.00 on charge cards
Accepts: check, MO, MC, Visa

Every camera store in town promises you a square deal on your camera purchase, but at Olden they back it up with a guarantee: Your money back on new or used merchandise, no questions asked, if it's returned within 10 days in the same carton with the same packing material and the warranty card is not filled out.

Olden has been selling photographic equipment and supplies—cameras, lenses, light meters, tripods, darkroom equipment—to serious amateur, professional, and even government photographers for forty-three years. They are known for their "oddball items," things no one else has, like a lenscap for a 1928 Leica. They carry every major brand old and new, including Nikon, Pentax, Canon, Olympus, Leica, and the rest. This store does a worldwide mail-order business, strives to ship within 24 hours of receipt of orders, and has a reputation for integrity among people who know the camera business in New York City. And they have a catalog!

SHARP PHOTO

1225 Broadway
New York, NY 10001
(212) 532-1733
Information: price quote by phone or letter
Minimum Order: none
Accepts: check, MO, MC, Visa

When we asked Morris Pillar at Sharp Photo what made him different from everyone else in the camera business, he said, "I'm much more handsome." Gazing upon Mr. Pillar's charming countenance is but one of the advantages of buying at Sharp Photo. They sell all major brands in camera equipment, calculators by Texas Instruments, Canon, and Hewlett-Packard, and European- and American-model Seiko watches. Sharp has a low overhead and is able to pass the savings on to you. They are best known for their bargains on cameras and equipment, but are planning to add audio and video lines shortly. Their ads appear in *Modern Photography* and *Popular Photography*, and they will make exchanges on defective goods.

WALL STREET CAMERA EXCHANGE

82 Wall St.
New York, NY 10005
(212) 344-0011
Information: price quote
Minimum Order: none
Accepts: check, MO

The Wall Street Camera Exchange has "everything" in professional camera equipment. They give price quotes over the phone and by letter, and are friendly and helpful.

WESTSIDE CAMERA, INC.

2400 Broadway
New York, NY 10024
(212) 877-8760
Information: price quote by letter
Minimum Order: $18.00
Accepts: check, MO, MC, Visa

A camera is usually shipped from the manufacturer with all sorts of "brand name" accessories like batteries, lens covers, and the like. Some camera discounters remove all these extras, substitute ersatz goods, sell the original parts separately, and offer the camera with its inferior extras as a "package deal"—a brand-name camera body with "famous make" accessories. The package deals are very attractive, until you find out that the "famous make" accessories are worthless offbrands and the cost of buying the original extras drives the price out of the bargain arena.

This lowdown on one of the less

honorable practices in the camera business is offered by Westside as a caveat to those comparison-shopping cameras. Needless to say, it's something Westside does not do. Their discounts of 10% to 40% on list price reflect savings on the genuine article, not a composite. The lines they carry include Nikon, Kodak, Minolta, Olympus, Konica, Omega, Bell & Howell, Canon, Ilford, Vivitar, Leica, Rollei, and Minox. They also have film by Kodak, Agfa, Ilford, and Polaroid, and a complete line of darkroom supplies and equipment. They feature a full line of accessory bags, light meters, and flashes, and Lowel lights. Write for a price quote.

WILLOUGHBY'S

110 West 32nd St.
New York, NY 10001
(212) 564-1600
Information: price quote
Minimum Order: none
Accepts: check, MO, MC, Visa, AE, DC

Willoughby's is *the* definitive camera store in New York City. They sell everything, and we mean everything, in cameras, photographic equipment, darkroom supplies, and all related goods. They buy and sell used cameras and also rent equipment. One of the nice services available here is the "buy now, pay later" plan that allows you to buy lenses and cameras on time for as little as $5.00 a month. (At finance charges of 18% and up, though, you'll negate any savings you might otherwise have gained.)

Call Willoughby's for a price quote on the camera or equipment you need. They're bound to have what you want, regardless, and their prices are competitive. They don't call themselves "the world's largest camera department store" for nothing.

SEE ALSO: Appliances, Audio, TV/Video Books, Records, Tapes, Stationery, Films, Educational Supplies

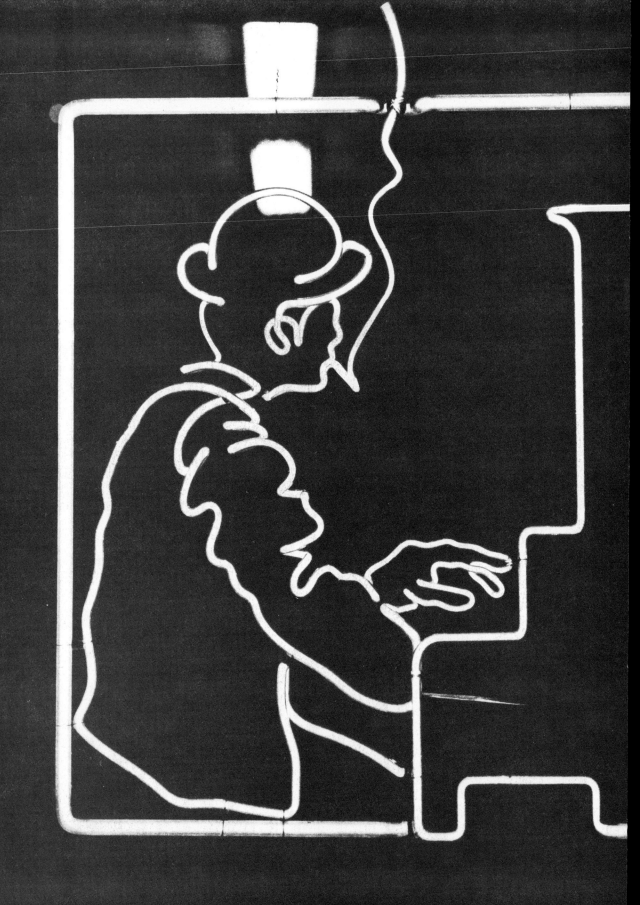

7 | Cigars Pipes Tobacco

In the city, you can do something like smoking simply by going out in the street and taking a deep breath. If you're a person who loves smoking in a more controlled way, though, you might consider living in New York, for it's a smoker's paradise. Problem air notwithstanding, harried New Yorkers love to smoke, and to smoke in style. You needn't settle for a Marlboro here. The finest and most interesting cigars, cigarettes, and supplies from all over the world are in our shops and available by mail. Places like Nat Sherman and Alfred Dunhill are meccas for serious puffers and inhalers. If you find tobacco a miraculous plant or if you've got a smoker on your Christmas list, certainly our sources are going to make life finer. You can even get Havana cigars from one of our listees—if you're a celebrity.

CONNOISSEUR PIPE SHOP, LTD.

51 West 46th St.
New York, NY 10036
(212) 247-6054
Catalog: free
Minimum Order: none
Accepts: check, MO, MC, Visa, AE

It's the habits of pleasure that serve as antidotes to the stress of city life, and the people at the Connoisseur Pipe Shop all agree that there are few satisfactions to equal a good pipe filled with a fine tobacco. They also agree that their shop has the best of both.

The typical Connoisseur pipe begins with a block of Algerian, Calabrian, or Grecian briar that is over two-hundred years old and has been cured and aged. A template of a particular bowl shape is traced on the briar, and then it is sent off to their pipemaker for execution. The grain gives each pipe an individual character, and any small flaws are left untouched. No stains or varnishes are used, insuring a sweet, dry smoke. The pipes are available in smooth or lightly carved finishes, and come with fine black English pararubber stems. Ed Burak, pipe designer and owner, has as much faith in his least expensive models as the most costly ones, and guarantees them all for life, provided butane lighters are never used—cedar matches are recommended.

The Connoisseur briar comes in scores of shapes, including the standards ($12.50 to $20.00), classics such as Oompauls, Sherlock Holmes, Bulldogs, and Dublins ($30.00 to $100.00), and one-of-a-kind and custom-made pipes for up to $250.00. Connoisseur also carries block meerschaum models with Bakelite stems ($40.00 to $150.00) and a full line of calabash pipes ($25.00 to $50.00). A range of fine accessories, from tobacco pouches of gazelle leather to walnut humidors, are available. Repairs are also done here—inquire.

The ideal complement to the Connoisseur pipe is their tobacco. There are 13 house blends, of which Scottish Ribbon ($6.50 a half pound) is the most popular, followed by Turkish Black ($10.50 per half), and Special Reserve, "the ultimate" from Havana, via Switzerland, at $27.50 a half pound. Smoking technique is as important as the equipment or materials: They recommend packing the pipe lightly and smoking it all the way to the bottom, so that the carbon is evenly distributed inside the entire bowl. When the pipe needs cleaning, a pipe cleaner dipped in vodka is the method of choice, not commercial solvents.

Between the superb selection of pipes and tobacco and the attention each customer receives, it's no wonder that their patrons will go nowhere else. One, a man of means, got to work and found he had left his pipe at home. Rather than suffer the privation of a smokeless day, he stopped in at the shop and bought a $200.00 model to tide him over. Who says there is no such thing as an indispensable luxury?

ALFRED DUNHILL OF LONDON, INC.

620 Fifth Ave.
New York, NY 10124
(212) 481-6950 (inquiries and N.Y. orders)
(800) 331-1750 (U.S. orders)
Catalog: $2.00
Minimum Order: none
Accepts: check, MO, MC, Visa, AE

Alfred Dunhill is not just another tobacco shop. This London transplant does sell cigarettes, in red and green boxes, at under $2.00 a pack. It also sells, at the other end of the spectrum, the walnut Dunhill Leap Year Pipe Cabinet, which contains 366 different Dunhill pipes of all types, including meerschaums, calabash pipes, some banded with gold and silver, and a wonderful briar pipe with its own little golden umbrella for rainy days, all for $150,000. Between these extremes are briars and meerschaums, walnut pipe rests, racks, and tobacco jars, pouches, and, of course, Dunhill tobacco. The cigar smoker is wooed with selections from Montecruz, H. Upmann, Flor de A. Allones, Temple Hall from Jamaica, Ramon Allones, Don Diego, and Partagas. They sell a crystal cigar ashtray for $45.00, and a beautiful Arginox pocket cigar cutter, Havana priced at $150.00. You can store your precious stogies in handsome humidors of rosewood, walnut, or macassa ebony, or avail yourself of the Dunhill humidor services, which include the diary order plan (regular delivery), and the contract plan (your cigars stored in Dunhill humidors until you need them).

You can light your cigarettes, pipes, or cigars with the famous Dunhill lighters in black lacquer and gold, plain gold in their criscross "barley" finish, and gold set with diamonds for $4,750.00. They sell their own stylish pens and several by Mont Blanc, signature belts, wallets and other leather goods and luggage in brown and black, jewelry and watches, desk accessories, clocks, and frames. There is even a selection of classic men's clothing: a handsome cotton trenchcoat with a separate black wool lining, a navy blazer, cashmere mufflers and sweaters, and silk ties. Dunhill completes the gentleman's toilette with the signature fragrances called Blend 30 and Dunhill Classic Blend.

Men who like to play can challenge each other on the Dunsinane Medieval Castle chess cabinet and backgammon table ($2,500.00), try their luck at the roulette wheel, or set up an impromptu poker game in the boardroom with the briarwood and pigskin case of pearlized chips and cards. Their collection of bar accessories is exceptional, especially the gold-plated bar cart that is beautifully designed, fitted with smoked-glass shelves, and seems reasonable after all the other extravagances at $375.00.

Some of the extravagances are truly excessive. The "World Time Clock," a previous limited edition, was composed of a ruby-and-sapphire-studded, gold-and-silver-plated globe that revolved slowly, indicating time in various cities all over the world. This beautiful clock, encased in glass and decorated with malachite, sold out for $13,500.00. The designer Erté has just created a set of playing cards that captures, in numerical order, scenes from *La Traviata*. A meerschaum pipe carved in your likeness is a mere $2,500.00. Just try to smoke it with a straight face.

FAMOUS SMOKE SHOP

1450 Broadway
New York, NY 10018
(212) 221-1408
Price List: free
Minimum Order: 1 box
Accepts: check, MO

The Famous Smoke Shop was established in 1939, and today boasts the largest selection of cigars and the lowest prices in the United States. While you won't find their catalog as humorous as the one J-R Tobacco puts together, you will find a comprehensive listing of cigars from West Germany, the Canary Islands, Mexico, Switzerland, Jamaica, Holland, Honduras, the Dominican Republic, and our own Connecticut Valley and Florida. The Famous Smoke Shop has direct factory arrangements with fine cigar manufacturers such as Alfred Dunhill, Culbro (Macanudo, Partagas), House of Windsor, Perfecto Garcia Co., and many more, and stores all the stock in humidified cold storage rooms.

Discounts run up to 30% on brand-name cigars, and the Famous Smoke Shop is planning to publish a leaflet on unlabeled, unbranded cigars that will represent even greater savings. The catalog gives you a few tips on choosing a good cigar, exhorting that above all, you should "let TASTE be your guide." The rest of us will go by the SMELL.

J-R TOBACCO CO.

Tuxedo Square
Tuxedo, NY 10987
(800) 431-2380 (U.S. orders)
(914) 351-4716 (N.Y. State orders)
(212) 869-8777 (N.Y. City orders)
(914) 351-5535 (all other inquiries)
Catalog: free; several times a year
Minimum Order: $10.00
Accepts: check, MO, MC, Visa, AE

What is satisfying, full of flavor, requires no paraphernalia, and doesn't "bite" or get hot in your mouth?

Believe it or not, a cigar. Every stogie-loving New Yorker worth his smoke knows about J-R Tobacco, which carries almost 3,000 different kinds of cigars to please every taste. Lew Rothman, who runs the show, does such a tremendous business that he can give discounts of 25% and 30% as a matter of course, and much more on special purchases or cigars that are "seconds" because of color. Lew gets his cigars from all over—Jamaica, Brazil, the Dominican Republic, the Philippines, Mexico, Costa Rica, Spain, and even the U.S.A. (cigars from Connecticut are considered quite choice). He puts out a free flyer every month or so listing selected bargains in his own inimitable style. At the month of this writing he had a "dynamite sale of Don Diego babies" at a third off list price, the handmade Rey del Mundos at 20% off, Royal de Jamaica, Ultimate, and H. Upmann cigars at a discount, and many more. As soon as the laws change, J-R

Bent Dublin Pipe from
Connoisseur Pipe Shop, Ltd.

will have Cuban cigars, which are reputedly the best.

Lew Rothman counts more than a few celebrities as regulars, and has a bartender's recall for his customers' preferences. He also knows which "off brand" cigars taste like the big names that cost twice as much. You'd expect that anyone this familiar with cigars, who has an inventory of millions, would love the things. Not so. Lew Rothman smokes Kent cigarettes.

NAT SHERMAN CIGARS

711 Fifth Ave.
New York, NY 10022
(800) 257-7850 (U.S. orders)
(800) 322-8650 (N.J. orders)
(212) 751-9100 (N.Y. orders and all inquiries)
Catalog: $1.00
Minimum Order: none
Accepts: check, MO, MC, Visa, AE, DC, CB, Sherman account

Mr. Nat Sherman, tobacconist extraordinaire, has been in the business since 1930. He's made it to a big, posh Fifth Avenue store that features a Spanish cedar walk-in humidor with an office that overlooks it all, but he's never lost his Lower East Side roots. He's peddled all sorts of things since childhood and is still half showman, half salesman. He passes out packs of his "cigarets"—all containing order forms—at parties, and boasts of customers like Henny Youngman, Mrs. Sammy Davis, Jr., Mia Farrow, and scores of other luminaries. It's a well-known secret that Mr. Sherman has a stash of pre-Castro Cuban cigars tucked away in his humidor. Nat won't sell them, but he does give them away—when special friends like Milton Berle drop by.

Actually, Nat Sherman is best known for his gaily colored, gold-tipped cigarettes. They come in colors like black, aqua, orange, hot pink, brown, red, and white,

and are long: the Fantasia is 6½" long and costs $2.20 for a box of 10, and Jubilee is 4" long (or queen size) and costs $2.20 for a box of 20. There are many other varieties, like Turkish Rounds, Havana Rounds, Virginia Circles, and Kojak's favorites, Cigarettellos, a blend of 18 domestic and imported tobaccos. Some are filtered, some are plain, and almost all are available in a choice of colored wrappers. These "novelty" cigarettes are made of pure, top-grade tobacco, without the molasses, saltpeter, or other additives that adulterate commercial cigarettes. Boxes of 20 run from $1.40 to $2.20.

Nat himself smokes cigars. He sells the best cigars by H. Upmann, Menendez and Garcia, Partagas, Don Thomas, Don Diego, and others, at $8.00 to $47.00 for a box of 25. They are available in double claro, English Market, and Maduro wrappers. You can become one of Mr. Sherman's cigar contract customers who have their cigars stored in the cold cedar humidor, to be drawn upon as you need them. Write for details on this service.

Pipe smokers are not overlooked at Sherman's. There are bags, cans, and crocks of tobacco with names that sound as if they were taken from the perfume counter: Black Magic, Temptation, Me Too, and Charisma. These are $1.15 to $2.80 per 2-ounce bag. Don't miss the Grecian Briar pipes, cigar cases and cutters, exquisite humidors in ostrich skin, colored suede, elephant hide, and burl inlay at $100.00 to $750.00, lighters by S. T. Dupont, Colibri, and Maruman, Lucite cigarette boxes, cigarette holders, etc. They'll even sell you a replica of a Wooden Indian, 52" tall, for $190.00.

Maybe the best thing about Nat Sherman is the line of services. In addition to cigar contracts, you can arrange for monthly, semimonthly, or weekly deliveries of your smoke via the diary system, and you can even have messages and/or your name imprinted on your cigarettes, boxes, or cigar wrappers. You only live once.

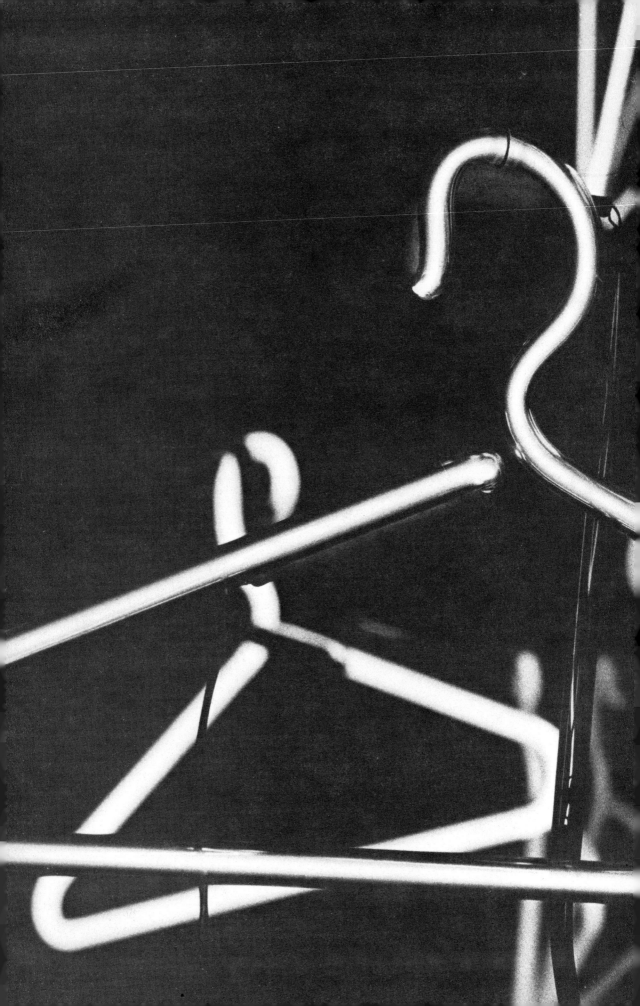

8 | Clothing
      | Furs
      | Accessories

In a capitalist society, clothing becomes a form of self-expression, of identity. What a boring world this would be if everyone wore the same plaid shirts from K-Mart—or even L. L. Bean. New Yorkers are as varied a group of people as exists anywhere, and their clothing shows it.

There's one type of clothing that's not generally sold by mail—one-of-a-kind designer dresses such as those found in Henri Bendel's, near Bergdorf's, The Plaza, and other elegant institutions. Otherwise, if you can't find the clothing you want in New York City, it probably doesn't exist. There are clothes and accessories from all over the world, clothes for every taste and budget, clothes for every activity from jogging to trout fishing, sexy clothes, demure clothes, loud clothes, quiet clothes, long ones tall ones fat ones short ones.

And we love them all.

ARTBAG CREATIONS, INC.
735 Madison Ave.
New York, NY 10021
(212) 744-2720
Information: inquire
Minimum Order: $6.75 on repairs; all
others by the job
Accepts: check, MO

You've just finished a magnificent piece
of needlepoint, but have already covered
every bare wall, throw pillow, and seat
cushion with previous efforts. What to do
with the new one?

You can send it to Artbag, where it will
be turned into a handbag or tote. The
needlepoint is lined and mounted on a
handbag frame, or sewn into a tote bag.
Artbag has different kinds of handbag
frames, can make the bags soft or stiff-
sided, and complete them with a
handbag handle, chain, or shoulder strap.

Artbag doesn't stop there. They hand-
clean said purses, make all kinds of
repairs on handbags, luggage, and belts,
and "modernize" old handbags by
adding shoulder chains or shoulder
straps. They also make bags to order.
They can make a bag in leather or fabric
to match your shoes, or use the material
you supply. Write to Artbag or call with a
complete description of what you need,
whether it's a bag to order, repairs,
cleaning, "modernizing," or needlepoint
mounting. They'll tell you whether to
send it, and will give you an estimate.
Artbag has been in business since 1935
and is thoroughly reliable.

Artbag Creations is known to New York
City shoppers for its huge collection of
bags by names like Susan Gail, Meyers,
Koret, and their own exclusive imports
(no mail order on these). The selection
alone is worth a visit.

BER-SEL HANDBAGS
79 Orchard St.
New York, NY 10002
(212) 966-5517
Information: price quote by phone or
letter (include SASE)
Minimum Order: none
Accepts: check, MO, MC, Visa

Fine handbags at 25% to 30% off list are
available here, by Christian Dior, Oleg
Cassini, Meyer, Adolfo, Pierre Cardin, Le
Tisse, Palizzio, Dorcille, and Block. Ber-Sel
also carries small leather goods and
Knirps umbrellas. Call or write (include a

stamped, self-addressed envelope) with
the style number and color for a price
quote.

BREAKAWAY FASHIONS, INC.
125 Orchard St.
New York, NY 10002
(212) 475-6660
Catalog: free
Minimum Order: none
Accepts: check, MO, MC, Visa,

A Halston is a Halston is a Halston,
whether you buy it in a Madison Avenue
boutique or on Orchard Street. The difference is, of course, the price: You can
save from 20% to 40% by buying your
Halstons downtown at Breakaway
Fashions.

Breakaway carries clothing by Harvé
Bernard, Emily, Lanvin, Charlotte Ford,
Diane Von Furstenberg, Cacharel, Tahari,
Larry Levine, John Weiss, Adolfo, Cuddle-
coat, Carol Cohen, Junior Gallery, Jack
Mulqueen, Anne Klein, Lloyd Williams,
Mary McFadden, and Kaspar. They don't
handle just anything these firms
produce, though. Breakaway culls the
best from each line with an unerring eye
for style, fashion, and taste. Because of
this, you will never walk into Breakaway
and find the "perfect dress." You'll find
five perfect dresses, two must-have suits,
and separates that are, in New York
terminology, "to die."

Breakaway is planning to open two more
stores, one with fine shoes and
handbags, and the other with *haute*
designer fashions. The catalog lists a
sample of fashions that are accessible to
the conservative budget and tastes, such
as those by Act III and Peabody House.
Price quotes are given on garments
made by firms listed here that aren't in
the catalog, providing Breakaway has
them. Write or call with model number,
color, pattern, and size.

BROOKS BROTHERS
346 Madison Ave.
New York, NY 10017
(212) 697-3131 (N.Y. orders and all
inquiries)
(800) 682-8800 (U.S. orders)
Catalog: free
Minimum Order: none
Accepts: check, MO, MC, Visa, AE,
Brooks Brothers charge

Brooks Brothers is the epitome of

conservative taste, from the dark paneling and English antiques seen throughout the store to the last stitch on their button-down shirts. They've been selling men's clothing since 1818, and over the years have added the Brooksgate line for young men, clothing for boys, and more recently, a department for women.

The button-down shirt has been revived recently, but at Brooks it was never out of fashion. In fact, the button-down was invented by Brooks Brothers in 1900. Theirs is all-cotton, available in solid colors of blue, stone, pearl, white, ecru, yellow, or pink for $24.00. There are others in graph checks for $31.00, stripes, and other shirts with plain point collars and others in cotton/poly blends. The shirts can be paired with silk rep stripe and foulard ties, which are $15.00 and $16.00. These all go beautifully with the Brooks three-piece worsted suits in pinstripes, pin dots, solids, and Glenurguhart plaids, or the herringbone tweed sports jackets and flannel trousers. Complete the suit with the calfskin belt with gold-filled monogrammed buckle, a hand-rolled Madeira linen handkerchief in the breast pocket, the handsome double-breasted trenchcoat, a khaki fur felt fedora, and English calfskin wing tips, and you're ready to brave bank or boardroom.

The Brooks Brothers "casual" wear is on a par with the rest. There are sweaters and vests of shetland, lambswool, and cashmere, worsted flannel trousers, pig suede jackets, polo shirts, lisle turtle-necks, and shirts of Brooksflannel, a Viyella-type blend of cotton and wool made in solid and tartan plaid sports shirts ($55.00). There are fine wool robes, cotton pajamas with drawstring bottoms and old-fashioned nightshirts, button front and boxer undershorts, T-shirts, cashmere and Merino wool socks, and slippers of leather and fleece.

Brooks also sells impeccable accessories, such as deerskin gloves, cashmere scarves, wrist watches and jewelry, and leather goods. They have a formal-wear section with pleated evening shirts, silk moiré suspenders, a peak lapel dinner jacket, and black patent evening pumps. The typical Brooks customer has probably been to more dress balls than discos.

Brooksgate offers a preppy version of Dad's duds, including sporty bomber jackets, snappy shirts, knitted neckwear, khaki pants, striped webbing belts with brass buckles, slickers, etc. The boys have scaled-down versions of the Brooks Brothers line, from flannel pajamas to sports jackets, in sizes from 8 to 20. Ladies can choose from camel-colored Melton coats, suits of Scottish tartans, broadcloth shirts, sweaters, shoes, gloves, hats, and a handsome bridle leather handbag.

Last but not least, Brooks Brothers sells desk accessories and stationery. These are favorites with many New Yorkers who have never worn a stitch of clothing from the store. Address books and diaries run from $11.50 to $20.00. Gold initials are free.

I. BUSS AND CO.
738 Broadway
New York, NY 10003
(212) 242-3338
Information: inquire
Minimum Order: none
Accepts: MO, MC, Visa

The only good thing to be said about war is that even a small one generates enough uniforms and equipment to keep the nation's surplus stores in business. The clothing is well made, and when combat fashions are in vogue it has added cachet. The little incidentals like canteens, mess kits, packs, and the like also have their own similar charm, besides being useful for camping. I. Buss sells all kinds of surplus military clothing and accessories in their store in Chelsea, and will sell through the mail if you know what you're looking for. Just be able to tell them the branch of the service, give them a description of the goods, and they'll give you a price quote.

CAMBRIAN FLY FISHERS
5 East 52nd St.
New York, NY 10022
(212) 752-4085
Catalog: $2.00 refundable
Minimum Order: none
Accepts: check, MO, MC, Visa, AE, DC

Cambrian Fly Fishers was established in Wales less than two decades ago, and has existed in New York City—first as a franchise in Burberry's, then in its own store—for less than two years. They have quickly gained a reputation for casual, well-designed clothing to be worn riding, fishing, and hunting. (It is interesting to note that what is called "hunting" here is known as "shooting" in the British Isles, while the term "hunting" there means "riding to hounds" in the United States. For that matter, horseriding here is called hacking there. Thankfully, fishing is fishing on both sides of the Atlantic.)

Cambrian sells the sort of clothing known as "ratcatcher" in the hunting world, the term used for less than formal hunt attire. They've appropriated the name and even a picture of the terrier used to catch rats in the stables in a multiple play on words for their logo. Cambrian's ratcatcher line begins with a handsome Tyrolean loden cloth shooting jacket, with pockets reinforced to hold the weight of a gun, and pivot sleeves that allow complete freedom of movement, for $240.00. They have a real Inverness cape—full tunic with a hip-length shoulder cape for women and men, at $265.00 and $295.00, beautifully cut corduroy and moleskin Ratcatcher trousers for men and women ($70.00 to $75.00), "breeks," or breeches of cotton moleskin, corduroy, and loden, belted tweed Norfolk jackets for $240.00, matchlock sweaters in olive, navy, and fawn with suede elbow and shoulder patches for $72.50, olive rubber "estate" boots, shooting jackets of waxed cotton with game pockets, tweed caps and Ghillie hats, tattersall shirts, and more. They even have a "rain choker," or olive terrycloth cravat, used in lieu of a towel wrapped around the throat while sporting in inclement weather, for $7.50.

In addition to selling clothing, Cambrian also takes an active role in British conservation efforts.

CERUTTI

807 Madison Ave.
New York, NY 10021
(212) 737-7540
Information: price quote by phone or letter
Minimum Order: none
Accepts: check, MO, MC, Visa, AE

Cerutti's outfits appear on the children who pour out of exclusive preparatory schools like Dalton and Horace Mann at 3:00 P.M., the sons and daughters of celebrities, and the offspring of the merely rich. Doris Cerutti runs the store with the authority of three decades in the clothing business and an unerring sense of style.

Cerutti is pricey, but those who know the top names in children's wear will understand the store's appeal. Cerutti can clothe infants, toddlers, and boys and girls up to size 18 (and the occasional petite adult who takes advantage of the superb styling and lower "children's" prices. Doris Cerutti carries Imperial dresses, Lil Filly clothing, hand-knits, and French and American snowsuits for infants. Little girls look the way little girls should in the exquisite Florence Eiseman dresses and jumpers, old-fashioned Gunne Sax dresses and skirts, and Cerutti's own line of dresses handmade in Florence, Italy, that fetch $200 each (the weekly shipments of 25 are usually gone before the new ones arrive). Girls can play in Cacharel and Olly sportswear, cavort on the courts in tennis wear by Fila, Adidas, and Little Miss Tennis, slumber in Christian Dior nightwear, and take dainty steps at dancing school in Botticelli shoes. Boys have a fabulous choice of clothing, including Ralph Lauren's Polo line, Jean Le Bourget sportswear, Calvin Klein, Imp Originals, JLB jeans, John Henry shirts, Cerutti's own button-down Oxford shirts, Pierre Gehen jeans (cut the same as the old NewMan pants), and Jeffrey Banks sweaters and coats. Cerutti has clothing for both boys and girls by Absorba and Petit Bateau, the entire Izod line, Aston Fair Isle sweaters, Sienna Designs madras shirts, skirts, and dresses in unusual shades like persimmon and royal blue, jeans by Bonjour, Gloria Vanderbilt, Lee, Levi's, Jordache, Calvin Klein, and even—mercy—unmarked, well-fitting, non-designer jeans.

Within the store there is, believe it or not, much more, and it is on this sort of quality and selection that Cerutti's reputation has been made. Mail order is done on a price-quote basis: It is assumed that you know the brands, the colors, and your child's size in those brands. Since many of the French imports are cut for the trim European body, consider these only if your child is on the lean side. If utter perfection is what you seek, consult their custom department.

Mail Order Tip: UPS must have a street address in order to deliver goods.

LOUIS CHOCK, INC.

74 Orchard St.
New York, NY 10002
(212) 473-1929
Catalog: $1.00
Minimum Order: none
Accepts: check, MO

Now that the unfair "fair trade" laws have been revoked, Louis Chock can offer all kinds of hosiery, underwear, and pajamas at discounts of 25% to 35% off list price. Chock has hosiery for women by Berkshire, Hanes, and Mayer, intimate apparel by Carter's Lollipop, and Vassarette, and Danskins for women and children. Men can pick up hosiery by Burlington and Interwoven, underwear by BVD, Duofold, Hanes, Jockey, and Munsingwear, and pajamas by Botany 500 and Pleatway at similar savings.

Louis Chock has a catalog of stock items, but if you are looking for something not listed, write with stock information for a price quote.

D & A MERCHANDISE

22 Orchard St.
New York, NY 10002
(212) 226-9401
Flyer: SASE
Minimum Order: none
Accepts: check, MO, MC, Visa

We can't tell you the brands of lingerie, hosiery, socks, and men's underwear that D & A sells because the big, prestigious department stores that have the same goods in their lingerie departments wouldn't like to know that D & A undersells them by 25% to 33%. Now that you know, you can reap the rewards by taking down the style numbers and colors of what you like uptown and calling D & A for their downtown prices. They have a flyer listing current specials, which they'll send if you forward a stamped, self-addressed envelope.

DOWN GENERATION/SYLVIA & SONS

2473 Broadway
New York, NY 10025
(212) 362-0520
Catalog: free
Minimum Order: none
Accepts: check, MO, MC, Visa

"Go down, stay down, and get down" is the motto at Down Generation, where they make down clothing for men, women, and children. They sell down coats, parkas, vests, booties, gloves, and hats, or, as they put it, "head to toe and all points in between."

Down clothing falls into three categories: fashion, ski, and classic. Down Generation sells fashion downwear by Bill Blass, Halston, Perry Ellis, Kamali, Tamala, Fox Run, Cilantano, Fairbrook, and Bibi. The ski down is by firms like Head, Sportscaster, and Levis's Gear Wear, and they carry full lines of the never-changing "classic" styles rendered in tan, navy, and brick. But you won't find pine-green classic downwear here. Michael Slepian, the advertising director at Down Generation, doesn't like the color. He says it makes New Yorkers look sick. He also says, "Green reminds me of *The Exorcist.*" While this isn't catholic marketing, Down Generation doesn't seem to be suffering. They have an inventory of almost 40,000 items and sell everything at 20% to 40% off. They even have down jackets for dogs here, plus related equipment such as backpacks, sleeping bags, tents, and hiking boots.

Mr. Slepian says that down appeals to "the healthier customer," and further, that "men today want women who are rugged and have substance." Rugged, substantial women wear down, right?

EISNER BROS.

76 Orchard St.
New York, NY 10002
(212) 475-6868
Brochure: SASE
Minimum Order: 1 dozen
Accepts: check, MO

T-shirts drip from the cubbyholes that line the Eisner Bros. store on the Lower East Side. The whole store is about as wide as a supermarket aisle, but Eisner Bros. claim that they are the largest T-shirt distributors in the U.S.A. They sell, in minimum lots of a dozen, T-shirts with long and short sleeves and different neck styles, and tank tops. Sweatshirts can be bought in quarter and half dozens. Most of the shirts are made of cotton/poly blends, although there are some all-cottons here. These shirts are made at the same mills that turn out Fruit of the Loom and Hanes, but they bear neither the labels nor the high prices. In fact, you can save up to 75% over retail prices here, just as schools, clubs, and athletic teams do. For those who want to visit the store, keep in mind that they're closed Saturdays, open Sundays.

FOOTSAVER
38 West 34th St.
New York, NY 10001
(212) 736-9081
Catalog: $1.00
Minimum Order: none
Accepts: check, MO

There are about 16 million human feet in New York City, and none of them was designed to spend their lives on concrete surfaces. Footsaver knows and cares, at least about the ladies. Their shoe store in Manhattan sells all sorts of footwear for women, with an emphasis on comfort and proper fit. The brands they carry include Locke, Oldmaine, Trotters, Audition, Hill and Dale, Penaljo, Air Step, Life Stride, Revelations, Footworks, and Decoys. The styles run from high-heeled half clogs by Revelations to conservative black oxfords on stacked heels by Locke. There are stylish dressy pumps, casual shoes, sandals, and boots. The sizes on most styles run from 5 to 12, and are usually available in narrow, medium, wide, and sometimes extra-wide widths. Prices run from under $30.00 for sandals to $75.00 for boots, and the catalog is photographed in color so you can see exactly what you're ordering. Just think of the wear and tear you'll save on your feet by sitting at home and ordering by mail.

FREDERICK FREED LTD.
108 West 57th St.
New York, NY 10019
(212) 489-1055, 1056, 1057
Catalog: $2.00
Minimum Order: none
Accepts: check, MO

Freed of London is now also of New York City, and may give the established dance supply firms of Capezio and Selva a *jeté en tournant* for the money. Freed's customers already include some of the finest dancers and companies in the world: Natalia Makarova, Margot Fonteyn, New York City Ballet, the Joffrey, American Ballet Theatre, and scores of others.

Freed's sells fine quality dancewear and shoes. The current catalog shows brochures of leotards, tights, jazzpants, legwarmers, dancing skirts, and tutus. There are no shimmering leotards slashed to the waist here, or rhinestone-studded tights. Freed's dancewear is more conservative and less trendy than Danskins, although most articles are available in a variety of colors. Freed's carries the old and new regulation leotards for the Royal Academy of Dance and the ISTD. They also have a selection of footed and footless tights, garments to warm leg, calf, ankle, knee, and foot in four knit weights, all kinds of warmup suits, and supporting underwear. Many items are available in styles for male dancers.

Freed's has all sorts of shoes for all sorts of dancing. There are pointe and soft-toe shoes of satin, leather, and canvas for ballet, men's ballet shoes, ballroom dancing shoes for men and women, stage shoes of all kinds, and jazz shoes. There are also accessories like totes, ribbon, toe taps, darning thread, and lamb's wool for pointe shoes. Freed's offers a number of services and extras on the shoes, to order, such as special sizes, wing blocks, special insoles, and more. Special orders take between 10 and 12 weeks to be delivered, but are, from what we hear, worth the wait. Prices are not low, and the price that prevails at the time of delivery, not order, is what you are billed.

FRENCH-AMERICAN REWEAVING CO.
37 West 57th St.
New York, NY 10019
(212) 753-1672
Information: SASE and inquire for price quote
Minimum Order: $10.00
Accepts: check, MO

The dying art of invisible mending thrives at the French-American Reweaving Company, which has been performing minor miracles on knitwear, woolens, linens, lace, some silks, and tapestries since 1930. They aim for—and achieve—perfection in 99 out of 100 cases, but are the first to say that not *every* fabric can be rewoven satisfactorily. Tears, cigarette burns, moth holes, and the like are best rewoven in articles of wool, raw or nubby silks, linens, and other coarse or irregular weaves. For silks, suede, leather, ultrasuede, and fine, tightly woven fabrics, they do something that the owner, Mr. Singer, calls "improvising": They repair the hole or rent, camouflage it with a decorative device such as a welt, small pocket, or seam that suits the design of the garment, and repeat the device where necessary to balance the effect. This is done only on garments that are poor reweaving prospects.

French-American has great success with their lace repairs, and specialize in bridal gown care. They offer "heir-looming"—cleaning, repairing, boxing, and sealing a wedding gown to keep it in mint condition. They also do alterations (on the premises).

If you have a reweaving candidate, send it to French-American with a letter describing the damage and what you want done. Mr. Singer will tell you whether he can reweave or if he'll have to "improvise," and give you the cost. Allow two weeks before the article is returned to you.

The saddest things Mr. Singer sees these days are the torn clothes of mugging victims. "Things happen. It's a new world," he observes. The biggest culprits, though, are still moths, lit cigarettes, and sharp objects, and French-American will do its best to right the wrong they commit to your garments.

G & G PROJECTIONS
53 Orchard St.
New York, NY 10002
(212) 431-4531, or 226-9513
Information: price quote
Minimum Order: none
Accepts: check, MO, MC, Visa

In a city where your character is evaluated by the name on the seat of your pants, you have to be picky about the clothes you wear. G & G carries furnishings for the man who likes a good label at a decent price. They carry shirts by Oleg Cassini, Egon von Furstenburg, John Henry, and Russini. There are YSL, Jordache, and Calvin Klein jeans, Bentley slacks, Adolfo suits, Stanley Blacker blazers, and Geoffrey Beene suits. Call G & G with the style or stock number of what you want and the color and size, and they'll tell you if they have it and give you a price quote. You'll save up to 35% on what you buy here, and if you visit the store you can have free alterations made. Be sure to have exact style, size, color, and brand requirements when you call or write for a quote.

LEON R. GREENMAN'S DOWN EAST OUTDOOR SERVICE CENTER
93 Spring St.
New York, NY 10012
(212) 925-2632
Catalog and Dry-Cleaning Information: SASE
Minimum Order: none
Accepts: check, MO

Leon Greenman took his first real hiking trip from his home in Queens to nearby Bear Mountain at the age of thirteen. Since then he's covered thousands of miles on foot, climbed mountains and ice, and a half century later has come almost full circle to his store in Soho, Down East.

Down East, more accurately known as "Leon R. Greenman's Down East Outdoor Service Center," is the culmination of Mr. Greenman's interests and experience in camping, hiking, trailblazing, and climbing. He had operated a camping equipment store in SoHo from 1963 to 1973, when competition from big firms forced him out of the business. When he came back after a three-year hiatus, it was in a new, much-needed incarnation: a service center for equipment used in the great outdoors.

Mr. Greenman's skill at repairing, restoring, and modifying outdoors equipment is unparalleled on the East Coast. His specialty is dry-cleaning down garments, sleeping bags, and comforters using the Stoddard process. This "leaves no harmful residue, reduces matting and clumping, and restores loft and warmth." His prices include minor patching, mending, and resealing of existing patches before cleaning to prevent down loss. Dry cleaning takes 4 to 5 days, and he can arrange to have UPS pick up and deliver the goods. Down garment modifications and full-scale repairs are another facet of the operations here. You can have comforters, bags, and garments restyled and plumped up, sleeping bags spliced together or lengthened, garments shortened and lengthened, sleeves modified, and additions of pockets, hoods, drawstrings, snaps, fur ruffs, racing stripes, and patches made. Mr. Greenman can also replace torn straps, and broken zippers, grommets, and snaps.

There is more: Your nylon tents can be cleaned, repaired, modified with "vestibules," doors, and windows, and backpacks can be repaired, altered with partitions, and reinforced with leather bottoms. Last but not least, here is the place you can send your ailing hiking shoes to have brand-new Vibram soles applied (a job only the foolish trust to their local shoe repair).

You want to make your own repairs? The goose down, nylon shell material, thread, webbing, tapes, and 100 different colors and weights of nylon are here at the store. These are being made available by mail, in addition to the Greenman line of special soft-sided luggage and travel packs. Should your hike originate in or take you through New York City, be sure to drop in at Down East for their collection of camping guides, USGS topo maps, and books on survival, canoeing, bicycling, and nature. At the very least, you'll get that rip in your parka patched, and if you're lucky you may wind up swapping trail stories with Mr. Greenman himself for an hour.

HAAR AND KNOBEL
49 Orchard St.
New York, NY 10002
(212) 226-1812
Information: see text
Minimum Order: none
Accepts: check, MO, MC, Visa

Haar and Knobel has seven floors of clothing for men and boys, managed by Herb Knobel. They carry everything from socks to coats, but offer only certain lines by mail: outerwear by London Fog, Stratojac, Sasson, Misty Harbor, Woolrich, and William Barry, Hagar slacks, slacks and jeans by Levi's, Lee jeans, and Puritan shirts and sweaters. Mr. Knobel has worked up one of the most efficient mail-order policies— without a catalog—we've seen yet. You simply find the item you need (in season) in any of the lines mentioned above in your own clothing store, copy the size, color, and model or style numbers, deduct 20% from the manufacturer's ticketed price, add $2.50 postage, and send your check or money order or credit-card data and stock information to Haar and Knobel. You can, of course, call to make sure the garment you want is in stock, but their extensive inventory almost guarantees that if you order in season they'll have what you want.

Remember to use only the preticketed suggested list price, *not* a discounted price, when you subtract 20%.

IMPERIAL WEAR
48 West 48th St.
New York, NY 10036
(212) 541-8220
Catalog: free, seasonal
Minimum Order: none
Accepts: check, MO, MC, Visa, AE, DC, Imperial Wear charge

"Imperial" is to men what "statuesque" is to women: big. Imperial Wear has been selling fine clothing designed for the outsized man for over thirty-five years, and has the largest selection of its kind in the country.

You are an imperial if you take an extra-long trouser in 32" to 54" waist, long or regular from 44" to 60", a 15" to 20" neck in shirts, and 33" to 38" sleeves. Most of the clothing Imperial Wear sells are larger versions of brand-name goods, so if you have any doubts about the style or tailoring detail of a garment (the catalog's graphics aren't that explicit), you can examine the average equivalents in a store before choosing from the catalog.

The extra-tall and extra-large man can get everything from underwear to overcoats here. Their collection of suits by designers like Hardy Amies, Donald Brooks, Ralph Lauren, and John Weitz is superb. They run from $140.00 for the John Weitz seersucker and cord suits in gray, blue, or tan to $310.00 for the simple, elegant Pierre Cardin *couture* suit in grays, blues, or browns. Light-weight poplin and casual safari suits are here, as well as designer summerweight suits. Dress pants, casual pants, and blazers and sports jackets are sold separately.

For thoroughly casual wear, there are jeans by H.I.S., Mighty Mac jackets, Jimmy Connors walking shorts, pullovers, running suits, Christian Dior beachwear, and sweat shirts and pants. The larger man can finally get shirts with tails that stay in, and sleeves that are long enough. Imperial Wear carries a wide variety that includes short-sleeved madras ($24.95), an Oxford button-down ($21.00), and a tuxedo shirt ($34.95). Pair the shirts with the extra-long ties that won't end at midchest ($8.50 to $15.00).

There are London Fog jackets and rain-coats, pajamas, robes, caftans, hand-some belts, and a full line of underwear plus shoes to size 16. One is forced to assume that the extra-ordinary man even sneezes big, because they actually have extra-size handkerchiefs!

A.W. KAUFMAN
73 Orchard St.
New York, NY 10002
(212) 226-1629
Information: price quote
Minimum Order: none
Accepts: check, MO, MC, Visa

Ladies who get their linens at Harris Levy probably buy their lingerie at Kaufman. A. W. Kaufman carries designer lingerie by Givenchy, Barbizon, Christian Dior, Eve Stillman, Chloe, Zandra Rhodes, Odette Barsa, Bill Tice, Lisanne, and Royal Robes. These top lines are sold in junior and misses sizes at 20% off and more. Even more spectacular then these are the buys on embroidered camisoles, slips, and pants of silk, robes of cashmere, mohair, and silk, silk gowns, and other similarly luxurious apparel. Those who still assemble trousseaus before the great event can save money on the best here. You can write for a price quote on any item by the brand names listed and inquire specifically about the silk underthings and nightwear.

KREEGER & SONS
16 West 46th St.
New York, NY 10036
(212) 575-7825
Seasonal Catalog: free
Minimum Order: none
Accepts: check, MO, MC, Visa, AE

When Doug Kreeger opened his store in 1972, down jackets, flannel shirts, work pants, and Vibram-soled boots were just becoming part of New York City's fashion lexicon. Almost a decade later, Kreeger offers the urban survivalist the same kinds of goods: down parkas by Sierra Designs, Kelty, Northface, and Kreeger, ragg wool sweaters, hats, mufflers, mittens, and socks, the red Doufold Union Suit, back packs, boots by Herman and Timberland, flannel shirts, hard-wearing flannel-lined chino pants, chamois cloth shirts, Coach belts, down booties, and much, much more.

Doug Kreeger outfits the serious back-packer, camper, or cross-country skier in gear and clothing—in fact, there are 3 months of weather trends for the entire United States in the current catalog. Kreeger's success, however, may be based on selling the outdoors look to people who hike the streets of Manhattan and don't even climb the stairs unless the elevator is out of order. The best thing at Kreeger's may be Doug's personal guar-antee: "If any item purchased from me ever fails to give you complete satis-faction at any time, please return it to me and I will promptly refund the full pur-chase price. If an item is in need of repair due to faulty materials on workmanship, I will promptly repair or replace, at your option, the item in question." And he *will.*

LEATHERCRAFT PROCESS OF AMERICA, INC.
54 West 56th St.
New York, NY 10019
(212) 586-3737
Information: SASE
Minimum Order: none
Accepts: check, MO, MC, Visa

One of the banes of city life is pollution. Smog breathes a shadow over all, and soot from the countless incinerators besmirches everything in sight. This fact of life creates nightmares when it comes to things like keeping white suede coats clean, which is why there is Leathercraft Process.

Leathercraft's leather garment-care services may not be cheap, but they have one priceless feature: They're guaranteed. Leathercraft has been cleaning and restoring leather, suede, and sheepskin articles for over forty years, and, as many satisfied customers can testify, they live up to their promise to return everything in perfect condition. Their unique process includes cleaning, color and oil restoration, reshaping, refinishing, and free mothballing and minor repairs. They also reline and shorten garments at a small cost.

Write to Leathercraft describing the garment or article you need cleaned, noting size, material, repairs needed, etc. They'll send you an approximate price— the estimate isn't given until you mail them the garment. Please write *before* sending anything.

Leathercraft Process sells products for the diligent who prefer upkeep to

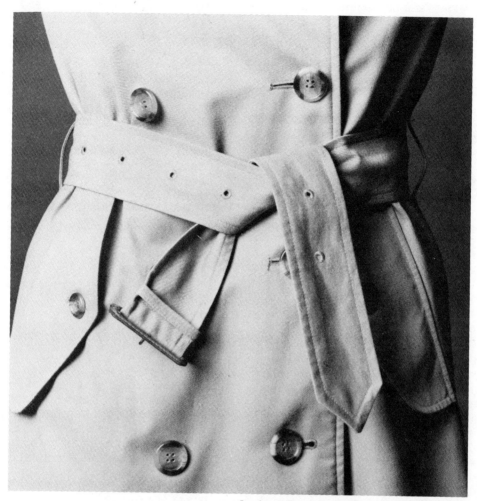

Ladies' Burberry Trench Coat
available at department stores

restoration. Suedecrafter cleans all suede; Leathercrafter cleans, nourishes, and restores smooth leather; and Suede and Leather Shield helps make both types of finish soil-and-rain- resistant. All products come in aerosol cans and are $4.00 each, postpaid, and will help your garments keep that new or just-cleaned look.

MAGIC MENDERS

118 East 59th St.
New York, NY 10022
(212) 759-6453
Information: price quote
Minimum Order: none
Accepts: check, MO

Mr. and Mrs. Novak run Magic Menders, which has been cleaning, repairing, and altering clothing and accessories for many years. So many years, in fact, that they remember repairing stockings during World War II, when shortages of synthetics made nylon precious.

Today, they clean suede and leather, clean and slim neckties, replace collars and cuffs on shirts ($12.00 each repair), repair handbags, reknit moth holes and tears in sweaters, do invisible weaving, and monogram *anything*. The Novaks' repairs are excellent, but the real feats of magic are the reasonable prices and their prompt attention to emergency repairs. The Novaks ask that you send the article if the repair is simple, or write first, describing the damage, and they'll tell you whether to send it.

MARCHELE CO.

1123 Broadway
New York, NY 10010
(212) 691-8012
Brochure: free
Minimum Order: none
Accepts: check, MO, MC, Visa

There's nothing like a good, old-fashioned walking stick to help you over the potholes, broken sidewalks, and other rough spots of New York City (or any town, for that matter). You can get help with your perambulations from Marchele, who sells walking sticks and canes from England, Ireland, Switzerland, and Germany in a variety of styles: round-handled, derby-handled, knob-ended, and straight-ended. The woods used include the very best chestnut,

rosewood, Malacca, cherry, ash, maple, hickory, ebony, beech, nilgheri, hazlewood, blackthorn, congo wood, applewood, walnut, and oak. Some of the canes are adorned with silver collars or nickel caps, and come with leather covers. All the sticks are sent with removable rubber tips, which are replaced free of charge for the entire life or the cane. Prices run from $14.00 for a simple, round-handled chestnut cane to $88.00 for the walking stick of solid ebony with the sterling collar. Marchele offers an unconditional 90-day guarantee of satisfaction or your money back.

MAYFIELD CO., INC.

303 Grand St.
New York, NY 10002
(212) 226-6627
Information: price quote by letter with SASE
Minimum Order: $5.00
Accepts: check, MO, MC, Visa

Beautiful legs at a discount! Save up to 25% on pantyhose by Kayser, Berkshire, Christian Dior, and other top manufacturers at Mayfield. Send them the stock or model number, the size, pattern, and color, and they'll send you a price quote. Remember to include a stamped, self-addressed envelope.

JEAN MERCIER

65 West 37th St.
New York, NY 10018
(212) 944-2888
Clothing Brochure and Ultra Modern Catalog: $2.50
Ultra Modern Catalog alone: 50¢ and SASE
Minimum Order: $25.00
Accepts: check, MO

Jean Mercier is a tiny, raven-haired woman who is the agent for several young fashion designers. She has innate style—she can wear a powder-blue crepe de chine blouse with a gray Shetland sweater, black leather pants, and little pointed flats and look *dynamite*—and her taste shows in the samples displayed in her showroom.

Consider Marie Baron's wine knitted sweater jacket, lined and cuffed with matching ostrich feathers. ($400.00). Or the khaki green knitted vest, lined in deep teal maribou, which is worked through the outside of the vest, creating a polka-dot pattern of maribou poufs ($260.00). There is even a coat lined with maribou (about $800.00). The ostrich and maribou creations are available in black, white, gold champagne, and silver blue, as well as in color combinations, and are as wearable as they are beautiful and unusual.

Another designer, Leslie Goldberg, makes a "cloth of gold" T-shirt, of light, almost translucent gold fabric in a one-size-fits-all design, with elbow-length sleeves: casual yet elegant, $125.00. Leslie also makes a stunning demipeplumed unlined evening jacket with full, gathered sleeves, which is made of a semisheer fabric in black, green, pink, voilet, and other pastels, worked with gold brocade roses. These are one-of-a-kind jackets, they cost $300.00, and swatches are sent upon request.

For the young and slender, Nina Chathan has designed a pure silk seersucker harem pant in magenta, handpainted it with tiny squiggle designs, and paired it with a simple black silk camisole top ($290.00 the set).

The classicist in the group is Gail Blacker. Using handwoven slubbed duponi silk, she has designed one perfect blouse that slips over the head and that has dramatic modified leg-of-mutton sleeves that can be pushed up to the elbow—or not—and the shoulders made to stand up. The colors: red, black, white, khaki, and brilliant turquoise. In description, it's absurd, but in actuality, beguiling—Jean Mercier modeled for us and looked sensational. The blouse cost $170.00. As fashion cowards but luxury lovers, our favorite was the gray duponi silk golf jacket, slightly blouson, with details like buttons and a crescent-shaped zipper pull in mother-of-pearl ($250.00).

For a touch of whimsey, there are tote bags ($30.00), T-shirts, and quilted jackets by Sweet P, all handpainted with pretty flowers. The tennis wear—visor ($16.00), shorts, and camisole ($22.00 each) painted with violets—were especially pretty. Sweet P's "skimps," short dresses with boat necks and cap sleeves, are painted with flowers, and can be worn with or without skinny pants, and cost $60.00. Last but not least, a union suit abloom with red roses, for $55.00.

Once clothed, you can accessorize yourself with goods from Ultra Modern. Jean Mercier carries their white poly-coated canvas lunch bags that are Xeroxed with artful collages of vegetables, toothbrushes, lipsticks, cows, and geometric designs ($15.00 to $30.00), briefcases screened with cows and things like sandwiches and abstract designs, and T-shirts in the same crazy vein. You can adorn your person with striped, checked, spattered, and otherwise printed plastic pins and barrettes in all kinds of shapes and sizes ($2.50 each), and the surreal cowboy can go one further with the violently colored bolo ties, closed with a printed plastic clip. And for truly spacey dining, there are "safe-t-mats," plastic mats with kindergarten-Kandinsky designs in pink, turquoise, black, and white. Hot cha, as the brochure says.

The serious clothing brochure is $2.50, and the droll Ultra Modern catalog is included. Separately, it's 50¢ and SASE. Swatches are available upon request. Jean Mercier's showroom is not open to the public as of this writing.

MIYA & YOSHI
366 West Broadway
New York, NY 10013
(212) 226-1990
Catalog: $2.00
Minimum Order: none
Accepts: check, MO, MC, Visa, AE

Down clothing has become a fashion cliché in New York City, but because winter is cold and down is warm, we know it's here to stay. Which is why Miya & Yoshi is such a find.

Miya & Yoshi are designers whose collaborations include marriage as well as the store, and who came here from Japan over a decade ago and opened the store selling clothing and furniture design. Their most successful effort to date has been a down coat that manages to be stylish *and* warm. Although the city has been saturated with "the coat" and the inevitable knockoffs, Miya & Yoshi's continual experimentation with different colors and fabric patterns keeps the coat from looking "tired." Their down and silk evening coats, with vertical quilting, pouffed sleeves, and stand-up, shawl-type collars, are sensational. They have made a patchwork version of chevron designs, in color combinations like aqua, plum, and taupe, which is dazzling. Less formal occasions warrant the zippered, horizontally quilted women's coats in colors such as plum, gold, aqua, taupe, and red, a macintosh-style smooth shell coat for men and women, two-toned down sweaters with zig-zag and checker designs, or vests. You can take the beauty of Miya & Yoshi to bed with the channel-stitched comforters, or the masterworks, Sunburst and Zig Zag patchwork bedspreads.

This year, Miya & Yoshi's collection features material that has been hand-dyed and patterned, and the colors create a quiet glow within the store. The clothing is not inexpensive—solid sweaters are $138.00, quilted coats are $295.00, and the patchwork chevron coat is $1,600.00—but no one is exactly like the next. Plain comforters come in a plethora of colors and cost $320.00 and up, and the patchwork comforters are made to order from $1,300.00

Miya & Yoshi sells light, brightly colored clothing in the summer that may or may not be featured in forthcoming catalogs.

MOONEY & GILBERT, INC.
31 West 57th St.
New York, NY 10019
(212) 355-6687, 6674
Catalog: free
Minimum Order: none
Accepts: check, MO, MC, Visa

Mooney & Gilbert sell conservatively styled ladies' shoes for the "aristocratic foot" that is long and narrow. Shoe sizes run from 6 to 12, and widths from the ultra-slim AAAAAA to the medium-width B.

The current catalog illustrates a stylish open-toed natural python dress sandal for $125.00, penny loafers for $48.00, espadrilles for $26.00, and tennis and running shoes. There are casual and dressy sandals, tailored low-heeled shoes suitable for the office, classic pumps, white work shoes for nurses and waitresses, play shoes, and slippers. Mooney & Gilbert also sell hard-to-find shoe trees designed for narrow shoes, at $9.00 a pair.

Shopping via the catalog, which is illustrated with graphics, is made hazard-free by the no-questions-asked, money-back guarantee on shoes returned *unworn* within 10 days. Mooney & Gilbert have been in business since 1932 and maintain that "you are never too hard to fit."

PERRY PROCESS CLEANERS
1050 Avenue of the Americas
New York, NY 10018
(212) 730-0220
Information: inquire
Minimum Order: none
Accepts: check, MO

The same Perry Process that gives loving care to the precious silks and suedes of well-dressed Upper East Siders will attend to your garments via the mail. They specialize in cleaning, altering, blocking, dyeing, and weaving knitwear. They are the only business they know of who can repair the crocheted bottoms of currently fashionable knitted sweaters and dresses.

Perry Process will also clean antique patchwork quilts and coverlets, and they do a big business in suede and leather. The manager, Mr. Needleman (we kid you not), asks that you mail the garment with a note describing what you want done. They'll write back with an assessment of what they can do, and a price. Your garment should be returned to you within a week after they receive your approval. The prices charged on mail order are the store prices plus UPS charges.

I. ROSENBERG DRY GOODS CORP.
70 Orchard St.
New York, NY 10002
(212) 473-0969
Information: price quote by phone or letter
Minimum Order: none
Accepts: check, MO

I. Rosenberg carries housecoats, dusters, nightgowns, pajamas, and lingerie by firms like Gossard, Velrose, Lorraine, Lollipop, and Maidenform. Their size selection is tremendous—it is here that you can get a brushed nylon gown in size 52, and the discounts run up to 25% off list price.

A. ROSENTHAL, INC.
97 Orchard St.
New York, NY 10002
(212) 473-5428
Information: price quote by letter, with SASE
Minimum Order: $20.00 on charge cards
Accepts: check, MO, MC, Visa

A. Rosenthal has been shipping

unmentionables "from here to Hawaii" for many years, usually to customers who once shopped in the store and then moved. Now they offer their savings of 20% to 25% on ladies' intimate apparel by Gossard, Maidenform, Bali, Olga, Kayser, Lilyette, Lily of France/John Kloss, Lady Marlene, Vassarette, Intimate/Huit, Teenform, Christian Dior, Playtex/Givenchy, and Poirette, as well as pantyhose by Berkshire and Burlington, to the rest of the world. Write with all pertinent stock information and include a stamped, self-addressed envelope.

HARRY ROTHMAN, INC.
111 Fifth Ave.
New York, NY 10003
(212) 777-7400
Brochure: free
Minimum Order: none
Accepts: check, MO, MC, Visa

Harry Rothman appeals to the man who wears a size 36 extra-short suit as well as the one who wears a 56 extra-long, and everyone else in between.

Rothman has been a fixture in the men's wholesale garment district for fifty years, and attracts the business of those who can afford the best as well as those who count on the discounts of 25% to 50% to help them stretch tight budgets. He sells brand-name suits, coats, sports jackets, rainwear, shirts, slacks, ties, and nightwear by mail as well as in his enormous store. You can write or call with a style number, size, and color and get a price quote on specific merchandise, or select from the items listed in the brochure. The personal service, attention, and fitting you get if you visit are hard to duplicate over the phone and by mail, but they do their best. Satisfaction is guaranteed, and returns are accepted on unaltered garments within 14 days.

A. RUBINSTEIN & SON
63 East Broadway
New York, NY 10002
(212) 226-9696
Information: price quote by letter, with SASE
Minimum Order: none
Accepts: check, MO, MC, Visa, AE, DC

Men of all shapes and sizes shop at Rubinstein & Son for their selection of

clothing by London Fog, Robert Lewis, Strato-Jac, Pierre Cardin, Yves St. Laurent, Nino Cerrutti, Oleg Cassini, Adolfo, Givenchy, Damon, Roland, Daniel Hechter, Calvin Klein, Stanley Blacker, and Cacharel, in sizes that run from 34 short to 52 long. The discounts are as good as the size range and selection: 20% to 30% off regular retail prices. Write, including a stamped, self-addressed envelope, for a price quote.

SAINT LAURIE, LTD.
Mail Order Dept.
84 Fifth Ave.
New York, NY 10011
(212) 242-2530
Brochures and Swatches: $5.00, subscription for a year, refundable
Minimum Order: none
Accepts: check, MO, MC, Visa, AE, DC

One would hardly expect the bargain blitzkrieg of the Fourteenth Street area, with its perpetual specials on hotly colored polyester garments, to yield a source for "investment clothing" like Saint Laurie, but it does.

Situated safely six floors above the melee of the street, Saint Laurie turns out fine suits and separates for men and women today as it has since 1913. The Saint Laurie suits are sold here at the factory showroom for 33% off prices they bring, under different labels, at stores across the country.

The clothes are stylish-conservative, forgoing fashion details for the staying power of classic, good business looks. The catalog illustrates four suit models for men and women, as well as blazers, pants, and skirts. They offer only a few pieces because they make them up in any of several dozen fabrics—polyester/wool blends—100% wools and silks. Colors are neutrals like navy, grays, tans, browns, and black, and the torture of guessing what "mixy gray crash weave" looks like is eliminated through the swatches.

It is the Saint Laurie attention to details that distinguishes their clothing from others. The stripes in the pinstripe suits, for example, are made of silk because rayon is too bright and wool fuzzes. They match their plaids and patterns, sew buttons on by hand, French fell the collars, and line the jackets so beautifully you could wear them inside out.

Everything is finished by hand.

The size chart determines whether you'll be able to take advantage of the good buys here. Men's sizes run from 36 to 48 suits in short to extra-long, and pants are sold in corresponding typical waist sizes. Women's wear runs from sizes 2 to 18, in petite, regular, and tall. Prices are determined by the fabric selection, and run from $167.00 to $272.00 for a man's two-piecer, and $139.50 to $199.00 for women's suits. Tuxedos are available at $195.00. (Men's extra-long and size 48 are $10.00 extra.) Returns are acepted within 2 weeks after receipt, providing the garment is unaltered and unworn. This provision makes mail order from Saint Laurie seem foolproof, although nothing beats the showroom itself, where you can choose from 25,000 garments and even tour the workrooms.

SAN FRANCISCO

975 Lexington Ave.
New York, NY 10021
(212) 472-8740
Brochure: free
Minimum Order: none
Accepts: check, MO, MC, Visa, AE

San Francisco offers a cetain sort of perfection in casual clothing for men and women—*the* raincoat, light, with timeless detail and tailoring, handknit sweaters and sweater vests in a medley of subdued colors, nightshirts of fine cotton, sash and Paul (short) ties, a handsome sporting shoulder bag of leather and canvas, tan chino pants for men, and more. San Francisco has refined the English country look with subtle, understated detail, producing classic, casual clothing. They have just begun doing mail order, offering their cotton wing collar pleated-bosom front shirt ($78.00), a Jefferson collar pinstripe broadcloth shirt ($63.00), ties, and their own watch, with 17-jewel Swiss movement, pigskin strap, and mahogany case for $390.00. The brochure will expand with succeeding seasons.

The store itself should be visited for its charm alone, and it also bears mention that the salespeople are, like the clothing, fine and understated.

Mail Order Tip: Request price-quotes on only three items at a time.

SHOECRAFT

603 Fifth Ave.
New York, NY 10017
(212) 755-5871 (N.Y. orders)
(800) 223-5542 (U.S. orders)
Catalog: free
Minimum Order: $10.00 on charges
Accepts: check, MO, MC, Visa

Shoecraft is a soft pink store with ceilings high enough to dwarf Big Foot, and there's a reason. Big feet are Shoecraft's business, and making the woman with Amazonian proportions more comfortable by scaling everything larger is one of the nice things about the store.

Ladies who wear shoes in sizes 9 through 13 are offered a large variety of shoes, boots, sports shoes, slippers, and even socks and pantyhose at Shoecraft. They have low-heeled "kilties," moccasins, and penny loafers at $47.00 to $57.00, white nurses' oxfords for $48.00, cowboy boots for $85.00, and handsome fashion and dress boots with extra-tall uppers in leather, suede, and vinyl for from $29.00 to $90.00, in addition to tennis shoes, running shoes, and sneakers. Their selection of dress shoes runs from conservative to the latest thing in fashion footwear, which is copied down to the last detail. None of the shoes are over $90.00. There are also all kinds of slippers, with names like "Poof," "Fauna," and "Spoodles" for scuffing around the house.

Every "tall gal" who has ever had a tug-of-war with pantyhose that don't make it all the up will appreciate the extra-extra-long pantyhose at Shoecraft. They carry sheer, sandalfoot, opaque, polka-dot, and queen-size styles at $5.25 to $9.90 per 3-pair box. They also have stockings that stretch to 40" long, as well as sheer knee-high hosiery, knee-high socks, crew socks, and sports socks.

Shoecraft offers a money-back guarantee on shoes returned, unworn, within 10 days. Alva Hale, their "personal shopping consultant," can help you with all your problems. If you are long of leg and big of foot, you should certainly write for the catalog.

Mail Order Tip: Most firms accept personal checks, but often require that you allow ten days to two weeks for the check to clear before they will send out the order.

J. S. SUAREZ

67 East 56th St.
New York, NY 10022
(212) 759-9443
Information: inquire, including SASE
Minimum Order: none
Accepts: check, MO

You don't usually expect bargains in bags at a store that's within a few blocks of Bendel's, Bloomingdale's, and Bergdorf's, but Suarez has them. Their selection of discounted handbags by Christian Dior, Tano, Celine, Susan Gail, and other firms is here, as well as Gucci's at less than half their normal selling prices, *sans* labels. (Are the latter the real thing or knockoffs, we wonder. Only the manufacturer knows for sure.)

Suarez is known to mail order *not* for its bootleg bargains, but for its excellent bag repair service. They can fix and remodel fine handbags of all sorts, and are able to work in evening bag materials like beads, sequins, and rhinestones, as well as silks, velvets, leathers, and other materials. You can call or write Suarez with a complete description of the bag and the work you need done. Include a stamped, self-addressed envelope with your inquiry.

R. C. SULTAN, LTD.

55 Orchard St.
New York, NY 10002
(212) 925-9650
Information: price quote by phone
or letter
Minimum Order: none
Accepts: check, MO

Feet are king at Sultan, where hosiery for ladies and men is discounted from 20% to 35% from retail prices. The brands available include Camp, Christian Dior, Burlington, Pierre Cardin, Interwoven, Hanes, and Round the Clock. The savings realized depend upon the quantity bought. For instance, Hanes Tummy Control pantyhose retail for $3.50 a pair, but sell here for $2.25 each when bought in lots of a dozen. Write or call for a price quote.

Mail Order Tip: Stamps and currency should never be sent through the mails, except in small amounts for catalog costs.

SUPERIOR REPAIR CENTRE

2 West 32nd St.
New York, NY 10001
(212) 564-2267, 2298
Information: inquire
Minimum Order: none
Accepts: check, MO

When a logo-loving lady spends $400.00 on a Louis Vuitton or Gucci handbag, she's not about to toss it in the trash when the zipper breaks, the fabric tears, or the lining wears out. For a small fraction of the initial investment, she can have her bag repaired at Superior, which also does work for Botticelli, Bergdorf Goodman's, and Tiffany's.

Superior can repair the broken locks, zippers, straps, handles, and feet of handbags and luggage, and replace linings. They can repair instrument cases, attaché cases, and tote bags, restitch camera cases, repair cuffs and the zippers on jackets, boots, and even tents. Irene Needleman (that's her name) says that Superior will also repair those beautiful antique beaded evening bags and alligator purses. She says that they're very honest and will tell you whether the repairs are worth the cost. For simple repairs, send the item to Superior, insured, and they'll send you an estimate. If the job is more involved, inquire first to see whether they can handle it.

TIECRAFTERS

116 East 27th St.
New York, NY 10016
(212) 867-7676
Information: inquire
Tips on Ties: free
Minimum Order: 4 ties
Accepts: check, MO

Ties, however absurd, are here to stay. Challenged by Nehru jackets and turtle-necks in the 1960s and tiny round collars in the 1970s, the "badge of servility" has survived intact. But the tie is still subject to the whims of fashion.

Tiecrafters, a tie-cleaning and repairs business that's been around since 1952, is receiving a lot of requests for tie narrowing. The ties of the 1970s were 4½" wide bibs that complemented the shoulder-spanning lapels of the day. When the lapels were slimmed, the ties were slimmed. Tiecrafters will take your fat ties and make them a fashionable 3", 3¼", 3½" wide. They can also shorten and lengthen ties and repair the tips, which get worn out. Any of these operations is currently $5.00 per tie. The famous Tiecrafters cleaning process, in which ties are despotted and cleaned, the edges rolled, centerpoint balanced, lining straightened, wrinkles removed, neckband adjusted, and small repairs made, is available at a very reasonable $2.00 per tie. (There is a minimum of 4 ties for either cleaning or alterations, and a $2.00 shipping and insurance charge on all orders.)

Stuart Bart, who founded Tiecrafters when he got disgusted with the way dry cleaners handled his ties, has put together some hints on cravat care in his pamphlet *Tips on Ties,* sent free on request. As far as his cleaning and alteration services go, "If we can't do it, no one can."

UNCLE SAM UMBRELLA SHOP

161 West 57th St.
New York, NY 10019
(212) 247-7163
Catalog: free
Minimum Order: none
Accepts: check, MO, MC, Visa

If any man in the world likes rain, it's Norton Simon, a.k.a. Uncle Sam. He runs the chain of Uncle Sam stores, and as lord of an inventory of over 50,000 umbrellas, he is without a doubt King of the Bumbershoots. He will tell you that the Uncle Sam shop, established in 1866, made Teddy Roosevelt's rhinoceros-covered staffs, Fred Astaire's canes, and Charlie Chaplin's indispensable walking sticks. Mr. Simon has gathered together all sorts of canes and umbrella heads with historic or antique value and will show the collection upon request if he's not too busy.

There are over 1,000 umbrella styles to choose from in Uncle Sam's stores, and a good selection of their best sellers in their 12-page catalog. They run the gamut from parasols frothy with lace to a 4-passenger model that opens to 4½ feet wide for $25.00. They carry the fine Briggs of London umbrellas, Fox of London, and the life time-guaranteed Knirps and Totes folding umbrellas. There are telescopic umbrellas, designer umbrellas, big golf umbrellas, and one that opens when you press it on the

ground and closes at the touch of a button ($13.00).

Whether you're afflicted by bursitis or dandyism, you'll find a cane is a must item. The Uncle Sam line runs from simple canes in Lucite, bamboo, cherry, Malacca, and English furtz to elegant opera canes in ebony with a horsehead or wolfhead handle worked in German silver ($19.95 to $120.00). Uncle Sam has canes that contain fishing rods, cigarette lighters, swords, umbrellas, and one that packs 5 tube-shaped flasks for surreptitious imbibing. There are models that fold to pocket size, canes that open to make seats, and fine blackthorns for the rugged Irish poet look at $15.00 to $50.00.

Uncle Sam's repertoire includes riding crops and whips, not shown in the catalog. They feature an umbrella renovation service that includes broken rib replacement, rust removal, new tips and tacking, a new tie, and new springs, all for just $5.00 to $10.00. They will cover your old umbrella frame in nylon or silk, put a new handle on an old bumbershoot, and even cover an umbrella frame with your own fabric at no extra cost. Custom-made and special umbrellas run from $25.00 to $500.00. On the whole, the prices at Uncle Sam are often lower than those at many department stores, the selection is unrivaled, and the service is superb. Need we say more?

VILLARI, LTD.

30 W. 54th St., Dept. S.N.Y.
New York, NY 10019
(212) 586-2991
Brochure: 50¢ and SASE
Minimum Order: none
Accepts: check, MO

Miss Villari's suite at the Dorset Hotel is all Old World charm and elegance, like her fine handmade Irish linen handkerchiefs. Prospective brides come here and settle on the brocade chair beneath dark old masters to order bridesmaids squares from the samples Miss Villari brings out. Their mothers order the wedding handkerchief, Villari's best seller. It is edged in French lily of the valley lace and highlighted by the names of the bride and groom and the date of the blessed event worked in pulled thread ($14.00 to $26.00), and is boxed with a flower sprig, ribbons, and the "wedding poem." Every other member of the wedding party, from the flower girl to the father of the bride, is rewarded with a special handkerchief. Should the union resist statistical pull, there are anniversary handkerchiefs and feminine boudoir anniversary pillowcases.

Villari has a fine line of handkerchiefs for men and women that they make in different designs and will embellish with one initial, a monogram, or the whole name in threadwork. Their monogrammed sheets, linen fingertip towels, napkins, kerchiefs, and cocktail aprons make perfect housewarming and hostess gifts. For those who acknowledge *every* occasion, there are handkerchiefs worked to read "Happy Birthday," "Bon Voyage," "Merry Christmas," "Happy New Year," "Best Wishes," or "Thank You." These charming remembrances are just $5.95 each.

Villari handkerchiefs are also given to mark retirements, or simply a feeling of solidarity. Miss Villari recently took an order for 18 squares that read "Capitol Hillbillies," none of which are destined to reach the Chief Executive's nose.

Villari handkerchiefs are handmade by women in the mountains of the West Indies. The art of cutting and embroidering the small squares of fine linen will die with them, making these real heirloom treasures. Miss Villari, an heirloom treasure herself, talks about everything from lace to the tax structure while she shows you her handkerchief samples. She welcomes visitors to her apartment at the Dorset—just call beforehand for an appointment.

CHARLES WEISS AND SONS, INC.
38 Orchard St.
New York, NY 10002
(212) 226-1717
Catalog: free
Minimum Order: $20.00 on charge cards
Accepts: check, MO, MC, Visa

Orchard Street is lined chockablock with stores that give the inflation-weary faith in the almighty dollar. Charles Weiss and Sons is one of its high points.

Weiss is the place to go for ladies' intimate apparel, gowns, and robes. They carry virtually every nationally advertised brand available: Vassarette, Olga, Bali, Barbizon, Warner, John Kloss, Formfit Rogers, Maidenform, Playtex, and

Kayser. They have a standard discount of 20%, and are able to offer up to 50% off on overruns, discontinued colors and styles, and other "specials." Their inventory of current styles is unparalleled—they actually have one Vassarette bra in 12 colors, and sizes from B to DD.

Weiss has been in business since 1945 and can order anything not in stock. Their catalog lists only a sample of the goods available, and if you don't see what you're looking for you can write with stock or model number, size and color, for a price quote. Weiss is new to mail order but Harry Weiss, the owner, seems enthralled with the possibility of reproducing his success in New York City across the United States, and with the combination of service, selection, and savings he offers, it shouldn't be hard.

MENDEL WEISS, INC.
91 Orchard St.
New York, NY 10002
(212) 925-6815
Information: price quote by phone or letter
Minimum Order: none
Accepts: check, MO, MC, Visa

You can reap savings of up to 25% on bras, girdles, lingerie, and loungewear by Olga, Playtex, Lilyette, Warners, Formfit Rogers, Barad, Lily of France, Pucci, Bali, Komar, Maidenform, Model Coat, and Goddess. They also carry London Fog raincoats. Write or call for a price quote.

WEISS & MAHONEY
142 Fifth Ave.
New York, NY 10011
(212) 675-1915
Catalog: $1.00
Minimum Order: none
Accepts: check, MO, MC, Visa, AE

Weiss & Mahoney, "the peaceful little Army and Navy store," is New York City's quartermaster. They've been selling all kinds of military surplus—except Jeeps and tanks—since 1924. They have uniforms and insignia for every branch of the armed service, including things like Navy bugles and swords, combat boots, parade-drill replica rifles, medals, jungle fatigues, and combat helmets. Weiss & Mahoney has an extensive flag department, and will make flags, pennants, and banners to order. Their main attraction, though, is their camping and outdoors goods department. They have cheap nylon tents, all kinds of backpacks and knapsacks, duffles, inflatable boats, sleeping bags, Coleman and Optimus camp stoves, heaters, and lanterns, knives, compasses, cookware, first-aid kits, and outerwear. There are a few things here that are such buys you'll want them even if you never use them. The height of combat chic is their camouflage jumpsuit, just $16.00. Sandwiched between a light-anywhere metal match and ammo boxes are the giant weather balloons you saw in comic-book ads as a kid. The 10' size is about $5.00, and can be used to fill your living room when unwanted guests drop by. White vinyl majorette boots are $25.00. Like all good surplus stores, Weiss & Mahoney has everything from the practical to the unimaginable.

WELLINGTEX MANUFACTURING CO., DIVISION OF SHELGO, INC.

641 Sixth Ave.
New York, NY 10011
(212) 675-6455
Flyer: SASE
Minimum Order: none
Accepts: check, MO, MC, Visa

Behind every designer label there may not be a sweatshop, but there *is* a manufacturing company. Wellingtex is the contractor for several well-known designers, and they also have their own label, Ilya. They carry playclothes, T-shirts, casuals, skirts, and dresses for women in corduroy, wool blends, and terry cloth. Their prices represent savings of up to 50% on the cost of comparable clothing sold elsewhere, and the retail prices of Ilya clothing. Send a stamped, self-addressed envelope for their current flyer.

YOUNG'S

319 Grand St.
New York, NY 10002
(212) 226-4333
Information: price quote
Minimum Order: half-dozen pairs of hosiery
Accepts: check, MO

Young's is a real find for those who want to outfit the family in no-nonsense underwear, socks, pajamas, and hosiery by Hanes and other firms, who are able to buy in half-dozen lots in underwear and hosiery, and who want to save 50% on retail prices. Write or call for a price quote.

Mail Order Tip: Always find out whether insurance is included and request it if it isn't.

SEE ALSO: Auto, Marine
Department Stores
Luggage, Leather Goods
Sports, Recreation, Toys, Games

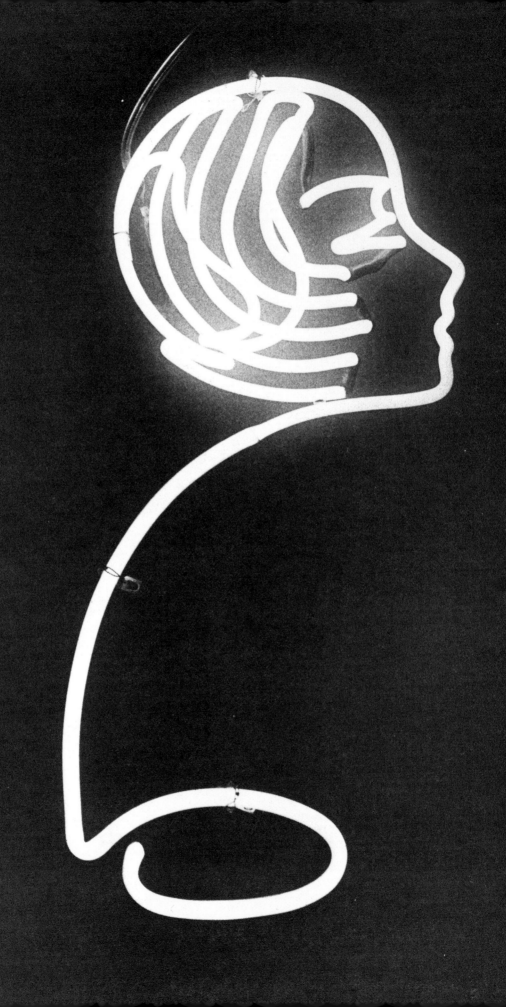

9 | Department Stores

New York City department stores run the gamut from the *very* civilized Bergdorf Goodman's, where taste is exalted above all, to the ubiquitous Bloomingdale's, which triggers fight-or-flight reactions in healthy individuals and, in the less fortunate, an adrenaline rush that propels the body forward, glazes the eyes, and creates an irresistible impulse to proffer major credit cards to salesclerks every ten minutes. Alas, not all of them welcome mail order business, so we're confined ourselves to a full accounting of those that do.

Department stores are vertical versions of the old bazaar/marketplace, and attempt to offer the ideal shopping experience, i.e., be all things to all customers. Some almost succeed. All are worthy of note.

B. ALTMAN & CO.

Mail Order Department
361 Fifth Ave.
New York, NY 10010
(212) 689-7000 (N.Y. orders and
all inquiries)
(800) 228-5444 (U.S. orders)
14 catalogs per year: any available free
upon request
Minimum Order: $10.00
Accepts: check, MO, AE,
Altman's charge

Benjamin Altman, entrepreneur and collector extraordinaire, established his store at Sixth Avenue and 18th Street in 1865. Through the early twentieth century, B. Altman & Co. supplied the finest in dress goods and ladies' fashion to the entire city. Mr. Altman's passion for art and decorative objects was reflected in the store's fine furnishings department, which has remained strong to this day. His own art collection, valued at over $15 million, was given to the Metropolitan Museum of Art before his death in 1913.

In 1906, Mr. Altman moved the store uptown to its present location on Fifth Avenue. The store continues on in the same genteel tradition—quiet, correct, and catering to the woman who observes all the proprieties. The red awnings outside and the hushed aisles within have not changed as long as memory serves most New Yorkers. Some departments, especially women's wear, are distinctly contemporary, but manage without neon and disco—what a relief!

The main floor offers a full line of cosmetics, the pet accessories shop, costume jewelry, notions, and men's apparel. The men's shop offers clothing by Christian Dior, Yves St. Laurent, Pierre Cardin, Burberry, London Fog, Calvin Klein, Bill Blass, Ralph Lauren, Cacharel, Pendleton, and Givenchy, among others. At one time, B. Altman's even featured a custom shirtmaking service. Also on one are small leather goods, hats, gloves, and scarves.

On the second floor is ladies' lingerie and sleepwear, children's underwear and nightwear, girl's clothing, the Étienne Aigner boutique, the shoe shop, and an assortment of other boutiques. Three brings us to ladies' clothing, including departments such as "Millinery" and "Sweaters." (You won't find cute titles like "That's Hats" and "Knit Bits" at B. Altman's.)

The fourth floor harbors the Bath Shop, where Altman's own toiletries—soap, lotions, even bathroom paper—are sold, in addition to bath linens, bed linens, blankets, pillows, Dyne comforters, and the like. "Gifts" are sold on this floor, as well as art porcelain and china. Altman's has one of the largest collections of Waterford, Orrefors, and other crystal this side of the Atlantic. The fifth floor features a shop devoted to baskets, other housewares, more linen, crystal, and china, lamps, small appliances, art needlework, and handcrafts.

The sixth floor has more clothing for women and juniors, shoes, and boys' clothing. The seventh floor is all modern and traditional furniture, including the antiques for which Altman's is known. The top floor offers art, gourmet goods, toys, and rare books. Their famous autograph department is also located here. This year, you can pick up a letter by John Adams, framed with a reversed portrait, for $7,500.00, among others.

Altman's publishes 14 catalogs a year, any of which are available free upon request. Catalogs are sent regularly to active Altman's card holders, and are good for one month each. The seasonal catalogs showcase a potpourri of goods from each department, while the sales catalogs highlight home furnishings, clothing, linen, and cosmetics specials.

BERGDORF GOODMAN

P.O. Box 5300
F.D.R. Post Office
New York, NY 10150
(212) 753-7300
Attn.: Direct Mail, Catalog Dept.
Catalog: $5.00, subscription for a year
Minimum Order: none
Accepts: check, MO, AE, Bergdorf's
charge, Neiman-Marcus charge

We are from the school that insists on finding the best of something, whether it be coffee, tobacco, crystal, or wallets, and staying with it. We insist that there is one perfect example of just about everything, and that palate and personal taste decide these. Having spent many hours in search of the perfect cashmere sweater, the absolutely right perfume, the best kid gloves, or the most enduring flatware pattern, we do not enjoy the aimless meandering now known as shopping, where what was seen yesterday is not there today, and will not be in stock tomorrow because the firm that makes it has gone out of business or the country from which it originates is at war. That sort of shopping is, when one knows one's mind, dissembling.

Fortunately, Bergdorf Goodman's understands. We can come back, year after year, and know that they will have the same four-button gloves waiting for us. We know that, while styles change, they can be relied upon to have classic, understated footwear in their Delman shoe salon—their own privately made designs, as well as collections by Jullianelli, Charles Jourdan, and others. We know that we will find unique papers in the stationery department, only the very best cosmetics (Bergdorf's wouldn't waste your time with less than the best), and superb linens and housewares. You wouldn't find the latest things from Copco here, but since you can go almost anywhere in the city for that, you're probably coming to Bergdorf's for a special set of French dessert plates available nowhere else. Bergdorf's provides culled designer collections for a certain sort of taste—fashion-conscious, yet not trendy. They have more distinctly beautiful and timeless pieces of clothing per square foot than any other "department" store in the city. Each department is small, but selectively stocked. Rather than offer a broad selection in a huge price and style range, they commit themselves to fewer, finer goods that are moderately to quite expensively priced—but choice.

Bergdorf Goodman was founded in 1901 by Edwin Goodman, who established his store on the former site of the Vanderbilt Mansion. He retained a sixteen-room apartment at the top of the building, and today, although the store is owned by Carter, Hawley, Hale Stores, a Goodman still lives in the penthouse: Andrew, Edwin's son and chairman of the board.

Bergdorf's draws from the finest in clothing, accessories. housewares, and gift items to fill its six floors. There are handbags by Hermes, Morris Moskowitz, Carlos Falchi, Fendi, and Judith Leiber. In addition to gems by Van Cleef & Arpels, there are baubles by Ted Muehling, Barry Kieselstein-Cord, and Christian Dior, watches by Herbelin, and fine cosmetics and fragrances. Sharing space with the hosiery, shoes, cosmetics, and accessories on the first floor is menswear. The department is relatively small, but crowed with clothing and furnishings by Trafalgar, Giorgio Armani, Gianni Versace, Ralph Lauren, Izod, and Thierry Mugler, as well as pajamas by Knote Bros., Alan Paine cashmeres, Beene ties, and more. On the upper floors, ladies can watch intimate fashion showings and then choose from the current collections by St. Laurent, Halston, Givenchy, Geoffrey Beene, Muriel Grateau, Charles Suppon, Krizia, Bill Haire, and Anne and Calvin Klein. In addition, there are lines of casual wear and sports wear by Beene Bag, Barry Briken, Perry Ellis, and Ellen Tracy, cashmeres by Lyle & Scott, silks by Jack Mulqueen, and lingerie and intimate apparel by Lucie Ann, Bill Tice for Swirl, Eve Stillman, Clovis Ruffin, Papillon, and Christian Dior.

Bergdorf's carries the imaginative furs made by the Fendi sisters, Bilston & Battersea boxes, Franco Maria Ricci papers and books, china, crystal by Orrefors, and fine linens. You can reserve your white-sale manners for other department stores—no pawing through sheets and shams here. You sit down at a desk, consult with the saleslady, and things are brought out and shown to you. The linen and certain other departments are not arranged for browsing, but if you're prepared to pay over $100.00 for one sheet, you'll probably want to sit down to do it. Once seated, you might as well have your portrait painted. Zita Davisson will capture your likeness, as she has Princess Grace, Gloria Vanderbilt, Beverly Sills, the family of John Rockefeller IV, and others, in her fourth-floor studio. You may join the hall of fame for $3,000.00 Since Zita does full-figure portraits, you may want to take a few classes at BodyWorks on the seventh floor before you make the investment.

Bergdorf's services match their goods: Personal shoppers, tailoring and alterations, monogramming, and even private showings of the latest fashions for their very favorite customers. And while the ladies shop, the gentlemen can relax in the barber shop on the mezzanine floor, where haircuts and styling, coloring, and facials are offered. Should you tire of the ardors of shopping, you can repair to the Plaza Hotel next door. Mail order is not quite so taxing, and since Bergdorf's catalogs are published three or four times a year, you can still choose from the highlights of each season's collection.

BLOOMINGDALE'S
Catalog Department
1000 Third Ave.
New York, NY 10022
(212) 355-5900
Christmas Catalog: $4.00
Other Catalogs: 12 published per year;
sent to credit-card holders
Accepts: check, MO, MC, AE,
Bloomie's charge

You live in New York City. You wonder what's new in eyeliner, chocolate, stationery, knee socks, or sheet patterns. You go to Bloomingdale's.

Bloomingdale's could only happen where there are a great number of people with an excess of nervous energy, money, and time. New York City is that place. Bloomingdale's serves as a showcase for the newest trends in furniture design, home decor, clothing styles, and general ephemera. It captures "the look" before it happens. Bloomingdale's has revolutionized the concept of the department store, and established a standard of merchandising by which all others are now judged. Consequently, Bloomingdale's has grateful and devoted followers, an avid if not fanatical group of people whose primary concern is having, or at least seeing, the latest thing. Their ardor for this "museum of the moment" is apparently so great that not only do they collect the changing Bloomingdale's shopping bags, wear "Bloomie's" perfume, observe the passing of time on the Bloomingdale calandar, and consume Bloomingdale's food, but the female fanatics wear underpants that say "Bloomie's" across the seat. (You can draw your own conclusions.) This fixation is Bloomaddition, and the Bloomaholic is the victim.

Material cravings can be satisfied on eight floors of this incredible store, not counting the subway level. The first floor is a confusion that still appears undecided even after extensive renovations, which have recently been completed. There are at least three levels to the floor, we think. On the street level are counters of scarves, bags, and gloves, and the Cul-De-Sac bag boutique. Rhinestone-studded

stockings? Silk knee-highs? Try "59th and Legs," the hosiery boutique. Step down from the street level and you enter the world of "Delicacies," the food shop that has enough gourmet cheese, bread, chocolates, and imported treats to pop the zippers of every pair of Calvin Kleins on the Upper East Side. A few steps up, and you are faced with one of the best cosmetic departments in the city. The salespeople are skilled in application and technique, and usually have the latest cosmetic collections as well as stock merchandise. Here also are the perfume complements to the cosmetic lines, and "The Perfumer's Workshop" for those who want to create their own. The innate glamor of the cosmetic department is enhanced by huge black columns of black glass, a real departure from the standard pink walls and lamps with pleated shades still seen in most beauty departments. After passing through cosmetics, we encounter the men's scent shop, the Alfred Dunhill boutique, and the men's clothing and accesories department (This is the only skimpy department in the store.) Backtracking through cosmetics, we see a flight of stairs leading to "The Loge," where the sweet fragrances of the Mary Chess and Floris boutiques greet us. Also on this level is a fine stationery department, with papers by Three Candlesticks, Crane, Fante, and other firms, a Mark Cross boutique, an excellent selection of desk accessories, and contemporary stationery and accessories.

On the second floor, we stop to admire the stylish, conservative coats in the "Plaza 2" department. Also here are dresses, bags, and all sorts of accessories, and a separate department devoted to down coats and clothing. Does your child need a new Izod in his wardrobe? Head past the "Plaza 2" dresses to "Young World," the bright red-and-orange clothing department for infants, toddlers, and growing children. You won't find understated classics here, but if you're a Bloomie's mother, your child probably wouldn't be caught dead in an Eton suit or Mary Janes. Along with the "Plaza 2" and "Young World" is the Junior department, representing young designers and youthful fashion. Juniors also have their own Cardeaux makeup concession here and can find everything from rubber cowboy boots to satin mules trimmed with maribou in the next department, Junior Shoes. (Much of the younger crowd sticks to the subway-level shop, "Saturday's Generation," which is more moderately priced and disco-oriented.)

The third floor starts to get serious with "Beekman Coats," where one glance yields three beautiful Calvin Kleins, half a wall of Burberry raincoats, and another of shearling coats. Need a sweater? Stop at "Cashmere Country" nearby and pick up a Pringle twin set. Feeling youthful? Try the Y.E.S. boutique, which features Sasson, Kenzo, and a number of other young designers, as well as one-of-a-kind things like handknit sweaters. Also on this floor is the dressier "Sutton Sportswear" boutique. (Beekman, Sutton, and Plaza are all posh New York City neighborhoods.) As we proceed past "The Beach House," a resortwear shop, we are overcome by a medley of fragrances from another "Perfumer's Workshop" on this floor. Hurrying through a cloud of tea rose, we happen upon a wonderland of designer boutiques, where the very best by Yves St. Laurent, Ralph Lauren, Nina Ricci, Calvin Klein, Zandra Rhodes, Valentino, Giorgio Armani, and Perry Ellis is available. Furs and fine leather goods are also located here.

Once properly attired, you can take the nearby escalator to four, where you are deposited in the midst of shoes by Anne Klein, Bally, Cole-Haan, Fendi, Geoffrey Beene, Guido Pasquali, Halston, Sacha, YSL, Maude Frizon, Charles Jourdan, Bruno Magli, and Joan and David. Tucked away in a little cul-de-sac on this floor is a small maternity department. At the opposite end of the store are curtain, blinds, and both dress and decorating fabrics, a huge lamp department. and in the middle of the floor, "Best bets," a novelty and gimmick department usually jammed with people trying out demonstration models of things like remote-control whistle devices that control three appliances at a time.

The fifth floor brings us to the model furniture rooms, created by Richard Knapple. They range from a Tuscany farmhouse interior to the room illuminated by kleig lights that was furnished with a few spare black upholstered pieces, and as a backdrop, a wonderful rippling picture of a dragon, done in what appears to be a mosaic of loose bits of foil, each piece fluttering,

sparkling, in an unseen breeze. Entire model rooms have been bought by people who just couldn't leave without them, but could bear to part with several thousand dollars to make the fantasy come true. Also on five is "Harry's Bar," which carries every bar tool and accessory imaginable. When we visited, a man was standing at a table outside the shop popping champagne corks—seemingly for effect, since no one was drinking.

The sixth floor brings us to "The Main Course," everything you always wanted in housewares but had no idea existed. The floor is divided into departments like "That's Entertainment," "The Pantry," and "The Cook's Cloth." There are sections devoted to the organizing plastics of Beylerian, Provencal decorative objects, and much more. "The Main Course" is where you'll find the latest addition or revision of the Cuisinart, Copco's newest color, Calphalon and Leyse pots and pans (among others), and endless arrays of kitchen gadgets. When we tire of watching Craig Claiborne or Marcella Hazan demonstrate *dernier cri* in cuisine, we pop into the radio and TV department, which whirrs, buzzes, and bleeps with the latest in home media devices. The rug and carpet department can be found on six, as well as a full luggage department, with goods by Ralph Lauren, Diane von Furstenburg, Rona, Schlesinger, Hobo, Noveau Hobo, Halston, and Valoroso. Don't leave without visiting the Diane Love boutique, unless "artistic" silk flower arrangements are not your thing.

The seventh floor is the object of our attentions every January and July, white-sale time. Here is the huge "Linen Closet" with sheets, towels, blankets, comforters, quilts, and more by every major mill and several private companies. Often, Bloomingdale's has exclusive sheet designs or colors, and the stock is tremendous. There are at least eight different pillow styles available here, not counting size, firmness, or material variations. Though the Bloomingdale's "look" is anything but fussy, this department spares no frills and even offers the line of Royal Velvet soaps that are color-coordinated to match their towels. During white-sale time, the store goes truly mad, and piles of sheets and towels are grabbed and pawed in true bargain-basement fashion. Also on seven is the book department, and "The Green House," where weary

Shalimar Perfume, available
at all department stores

shoppers can recover with health food.

Eight, the last floor, holds "The Bath Closet," with exclusive bath linens, but more importantly, toys. Since most customers use the escalators, placing toys on the top floor is great retailing strategy—Mom and Dad have to pass through every floor before they can recover Junior, and the chances of coming away without a purchase are slim.

Bloomingdale's is definitely more than a department store; it's an ongoing event. It even hosts a New York City social institution—the Saturday afternoon mating game. The privileged classes (admen, secretaries, designers' assistants, models) assemble on the first floor and stalk each other across counters of cosmetics, food, housewares, and small leather goods. The wholesale cruising must be observed firsthand to be fully appreciated.

Bloomingdale's also dabbles in foreign service. At the moment, you can't turn around without bumping into some form of *chinoiserie*, Bloomingdale's current promotion. The normalization of relations with China and that country's well-made, low-priced goods make them a retailer's dream. It's a testament to the merchandising clout of this store that, at a time when wrinkled gauze and brass elephants had long since exhausted their appeal, Bloomingdale's was able to fare decently with a promotion of India and its goods.

Bloomingdale's current manifestation is relatively new. They began in 1872 as "The Great East Side Bazaar," offering corsets and dry goods, and were just another unremarkable department store until the 1960s. Then, as the focus of business began to move uptown, Bloomingdale's seized the opportunity to improve its image, renovating every department. It hasn't stood still since.

Will Bloomingdale's survive? We couldn't say, but we do know about Siegel-Cooper & Co., another famous New York City department store. Its opening in 1896 was attended by over 150,000 New Yorkers, phenomenal in those days. "The Big Store—A City in Itself" boasted free samples of food, demonstrations of newfangled notions, and an enormous fountain illuminated with colored lights that became *the* place to meet. Siegel-Cooper saw its demise in 1914. What happened? Business moved uptown.

MACY'S

Mail Order Department
Herald Square
New York, NY 10001
(212) 971-6000 (N.Y. orders and all inquiries)
(800) 528-1055 (U.S. orders)
Christmas Catalog and Seasonal Sales
Catalogs: free on request
Minimum Order: $7.00
Accepts: check, MO, AE, Macy's charge card

Even if you haven't seen *The Miracle on 34th Street* or the New York City Thanksgiving Day Parade, you've probably still heard of Macy's. It is, after all, "The World's Largest Department Store," claiming over 2 million square feet of selling space. It once boasted the quintessential "Bargain Basement," where low prices drew crowds and general hysteria prevailed. It innovated the sale of a wide variety of merchandise under one roof, and demonstrations of new products.

Rowland Hussey Macy, a former whaler, established the store on 14th Street in 1858. He died in 1877, and the Straus brothers (of Abraham & Straus in Brooklyn) took over. As the focus of business began to move uptown, the Straus brothers sought a new location, and chose the current address at 34th Street as the site of their new building. They bought Oscar Hammerstein's Opera House, then on 34th Street, and began buying the rest of the block, lot by lot, secretly. One of the owners of two parcels of land, located on the corners of Seventh Avenue, heard of the plan and refused to sell, thinking he could hold out for more money. The Straus brothers never capitulated, and the corner lots are now occupied by a store and a Nathan's Famous hot dog concession. Macy's hangs its sign on the flattened corner of the building—after leasing air rights from Nathan's Famous below.

Macy's has been undergoing extensive renovations since the mid-1970s. The "Bargain Basement," home of the thrifty, is now "The Cellar." "The Cellar" forgoes concerns of budget for the pleasures of the palate in their gourmet food shop, where meats, fresh produce, cheese, chocolates, sweets, pastries, and other edibles are sold. Another shop in "The Cellar" sells stationery, from conservative styles by Crane to brightly colored papers priced by the pound. A thrown vase? Here in the "Pottery Shop." *Nouvelle* housewares? A pharmacy? A reproduction of the uptown P. J. Clarke's restaurant/bar? All here, as well as the "Action Down Under" clothing shop for young men on the move, Macy's answer to Bloomingdale's "Saturday's Generation." "The Cellar" is designed so that the "shops" open out onto a wide tiled avenue, like a miniature shopping mall, and provides a pleasant browsing atmosphere.

Upstairs, renovations have created new departments and invested the old with new life. In the bag department alone, there are boutiques with Gucci, Mark Cross, Étienne Aigner, Le Must De Cartier, and Coach leather goods, and lines by Enny, Meyers, Anne Klein, Halston, Morris Moskowitz, and Barbara Bolan. Macy's jewelry and watch department offers Longines/Wittnauer, Pulsar, 1928, Concord, Omega, Lanvin, and a host of other fine manufacturers. Also on this floor are women's cosmetics, including Adrien Arpel, Janet Sartin, and Lancome's Institut de Beauté clinics, Rigaud home fragrances, wigs, scarves, gloves, and men's fragrances. You don't realize just how large Macy's is until you reach what appears to be the back of the store, descend a few steps, and stumble across "The Arcade." This is a series of boutiques and concessions selling everything from "David's Chocolate Chip Cookies" to souvenirs of the Big Apple. Spotting yet another hallway, you follow and enter "Men's Furnishings," a department that is as large as another store. Every major designer is represented here, in one of the best men's shops in any of the big stores.

The second floor yields yet more men's clothing—Calvin Klein, Izod, Levi, Murgani, Oscar de la Renta, the Chaps and Polo lines by Ralph Lauren, Burberry, Aquascutum, and many other designers—plus the men's shoe shop. While he picks out jeans, you can immerse yourself in lingerie by Fernando Sanchez, Eve Stillman, Christian Dior, Blanche, Blush, Mary McFadden, Natori, Lucie Ann, Givenchy, Kayser, and many other firms. Conservative "missy" dresses (Cos Cob, Eccobay, etc.) can also be found on two, as well as Red Cross shoes.

By the time you get to three, you're ready for an espresso at Le Petit Café, where you'll emerge ready to deal with shoes by Charles Jourdan, and the latest fashions by Perry Ellis, Harve Bernard, Pinky & Dianne, Nipon, Calvin Klein, and a host of others. Here are Burberry's for rain, furs for the cold, and the "Bon Voyage" resortwear department when you decide to flee it all.

The fourth floor is shared by the women's clothing department, adult games, and coins and stamps. Half the floor is devoted to the "junior," who can choose clothing from countless racks, make-up with the glitz and glitter of Barone and Stagelight cosmetics, get shod for the evening at the "Roller Disco Shop," and take a yogurt break at Self Treat and a beauty workout at the Self Center.

Kids claim the fifth floor: clothing, toys, shoes, and even their own beauty salon, "Kenneth for Kids." Quite appropriately, maternity wear is also located here. Five is shared by "The Pet Shop," the audio department, sporting goods, luggage, calculators, and more watches. The entire family can recuperate from the venture of shopping Macy's at the "Fountain Restaurant."

By the time you reach six, your shoes may be showing signs of wear—if so, just stop in at the huge women's shoe department on this floor for a new pair. We never leave without seeing what's new in bed and bath at "Domestics" and "The Bath Shop." When money is no object, there is "Private Lives," which houses collections of linens by Pratesi, Porthault, T & J Vestor, and other fine firms. Designed as a separate shop, it is one of the new departments that has contributed to Macy's improved image.

The seventh, eighth, and ninth floors are all devoted to housewares: furniture, rugs and carpets, appliances, fabric, bedspreads, giftware, tableware, antiques, and more. Styles run from reproduction Early American to "high tech," and Giorgio Sant'Angelo and Copco to Fitz & Floyd.

Macy's is trying awfully hard, but it may turn out that it's just too big, physically, to overtake Bloomingdale's and become *the* place to shop. But no matter how chichi Macy's does become, it will never part with the red star that serves as an apostrophe in its logo. The origin of the star is true Macy's: It was taken directly from a tattoo on the arm of the founder of the store, Rowland Hussey Macy.

10 | Food
Drink

After fighting the traffic jams, the rush-hour crush in the subway, lines around the block for a movie, banks that never seem to get your checkbook balance right, the constant assault of panhandlers and winos and suspicious-looking types on the street, rushing from meeting to meeting and never quite making it on time, withstanding the scrutiny of thousands of pairs of eyes each day—after the accretion of hassles New York can impose, we escape into one of its joys: self-indulgence.

If you live in New York, or buy from New York shops via mail order, you no longer have to suffer the indignities of mass-market products and their tasteless, bland, cut-rate, unsatisfying lack of care and refinement. New York offers class! Elite pleasures! You may not be able to afford a yacht or the estate of your dreams, but you can surely treat yourself to a real cup of coffee. Nothing like a gourmet chocolate to ease those high-pressure blues.

Bored? Try top-quality Mexican treats, or Middle Eastern, or Italian, Hungarian, German, Jewish, Puerto Rican—the shops in this section will make your local Grand Union look bleak indeed, and no waiting in the checkout lines!

APHRODISIA

28 Carmine St.
New York, NY 10014
(212) 989-6440
Catalog and Price List: $2.50 by mail,
$1.50 in the store
Minimum Order: on some herbs
and spices
Accepts: check, MO

Walking into Aphrodisia is like inhaling
the breath of a magic forest. The source
of the wonderful smell is the 450 herbs
and spices that sit on the shelves in big
glass candy jars and on the floor in
wooden bins and barrels. In the back of
the store is a wood rack with testers for
over 80 essential oils, which add their
own heady fragrances. You can find their
bookshelf and handsome spice cabinets
back there too. The cabinets are made of
wood, have herb and spice charts on
both sides of the doors, and hold 16, 21,
or 30 jars. They run from $29.00 for the
smallest, empty, to $68.00 for the largest,
filled jars included.

The catalog is a folksy encyclopedia of
herbs, spices, essential oils, and
epicurean delights, with entries detailing
the history, purpose, and preparation of
many of them. Interspersed are all sorts
of recipes for things like Nettle Soup,
Herbal Moth Balls, and Tansy Pudding,
and quotes from the greats, such as
"Purge me with Hyssop, and I shall be
clean," taken from the Psalms. The last
part of the catalog is devoted to listings of
Chinese, Indian, and Indonesian
condiments and cooking ingredients, gift
ideas, and over 70 books, which include
Flower Cookery, Healing with Herbs,
and the *Witches Guide to Gardening.*

Aphrodisia begins with absinthe and
ends with zebrovka. In between is buchu
leaf, used as perfume by the Hottentots,
dragon's blood, cornsilk, deer's tongue,
crystallized mimosa, Chinese tangerine
peel, vetivert root, fleabane, bergamot,
and much more. Most of the herbs and
spices are sold in minimum amounts of
¼ pound.

Aphrodisia also sells Chinese, Korean,
and Siberian ginseng, capsules of selected
herbs, empty capsules, charcoal for in-
cense burning, Bio-Botanica herbal extracts, and Helix herb seeds. Their complete essential oils line includes styrax,
ylang-ylang, birch, frangipani, and cajeput,
as well as stock fragrances like eucalyptus,
gardenia, lilac, and tea rose. Prices run
from $1.30 to $4.20 for ⅛ ounce.

Don't miss the herbal cigarettes, soy
sauces, chutneys, and other ingredients
for Chinese, Indian, and Indonesian food,
and the line of ready-made sachets,
potpourri, and pomander balls.

Lest those who hope for better things take
the name of the store seriously, Aphrodisia
runs a disclaimer on the last page of the
catalog to the effect that their products
have no aphrodisiac properties. There's
no harm in trying to prove them
wrong.

BALDUCCI'S

424 Avenue of the Americas
New York, NY 10011
(212) 673-2600
Catalog: $1.50
Minimum Order: $15.00
Accepts: certified check, MO, AE

You'd never know it to look at them now,
but Balducci's had humble beginnings as
an Italian food shop in Brooklyn.
Balducci's moved their business to
Manhattan some years ago, where it's
enjoyed great success.

There are over 30 different kinds of
breads, many from local bakeries—Zito's
whole wheat and white loaves,
Spiekerman's Swiss Peasant bread,
sourdoughs, ryes, pumpernickels,
prosciutto and onion breads, breadsticks,
and bagels and bialies, to list a sample of
what's available—all displayed in racks
in Balducci's windows. They have a full
line of pastries, from buttery plain and
almond-glazed croissants to cannoli,
Napoleons, Italian butter cookies, tarts,
rum cakes, pies, tortes, and many other
diet breakers. If you go in early enough,
you can watch the pastry lady filling the
cannoli (and clerks Windexing the
display cases, for that matter). The pastry
counter adjoins the cheese section,
where the line of customers has been
temporarily displaced by an enormous
hunk of cheddar that weighs almost
1,500 pounds. It's no wonder that they're
putting cheese in the aisles now—
behind the counter there are over 500
varieties of every sort, from every
country imaginable. The cheese counter
softens toward the end with fresh ricotta
and cream cheese, and merges,
conveniently, with Nova Scotia lox and
Scotch salmon. The deli department has
tray upon tray of marinated olives,
kippers, pickles, baccala, prosciutto,
cured meats of every sort, smoked

chicken breasts, caviar (selected and packaged by Balducci's), patés from Les Trois Petits Cochons, white and black Italian truffles, sausages, and more. Greenwich Villagers who can't cook, stop by for the chicken curry, pizza rustica, chicken cacciatore, antipasto, and other prepared dishes, as well as homemade egg, wheat, and spinach pasta (everyone can boil water).

Ice cream fiends can find Bassett's all-natural ice creams here, as well as things like Grand Marnier sorbet. There are packaged cookies, jams by Tiptree and Crabtree & Evelyn, rare and wonderful vinegars and nut oils, a whole selection of imported candies, Lindt chocolates, Amaretto cookies, dried and glacé fruits, and canned and fresh gourmet coffees and teas. Their meat and fish departments offer everything from lamb sausage to lobster, including fresh game. But the Balducci name was made on their produce—consistently fresh, unblemished, and, except for rare out-of-season fruits and vegetables, at prices competitive with that of other Greenwich Village greengrocers. It is here that you will almost always find shallots, arugola, French morels, snow peas, hot peppers, endive, the first berries of the season, kumquats, kiwis, persimmons, and celeriac, as well as all varieties of apples, pears, citrus fruits, and things like lettuce, potatoes, and onions. The rare produce is not cheap—little red lettuces that are 50¢ a head in Europe are almost $5.00 a pound here, but no one else has them.

Bill Hyde has the Herculean task of managing Balducci's, and has decided to make his life impossible by offering *every item* in the store by mail. The catalog, which is in production, offers a representative selection of goods, but your inquiries regarding items not listed are invited. Federal Express will be used to ship the perishables, as well as UPS., and it should be emphasized that Balducci's is not for the small of wallet.

CANDY KISSES

58 Greenwich Ave.
New York, NY 10011
(212) 929-7133
Price List: SASE
Minimum Order: none
Accepts: check, MO

There is no such thing as a gracious

child in a candy shop. We watched the juvenile transactions in Candy Kisses, an old-fashioned confectionery with penny candy jars. Mr. Ashwin Sheth, proprietor, has his hands full making sales while looking out for the occasional youthful sleight-of-hand. His jars are on open shelves; now we know why candy stores of old kept everything behind the counter.

There's one thing Mr. Sheth does keep tucked away here, however, and that's the erotic chocolate. Adults only are permited peeks at the pair of solid chocolate breasts ($10.00), the "modest" *macho* man, "Dick and Jane," and the anatomically correct male and female organs (we may never eat chocolate again). Although Mr. Sheth also carries chocolate truffles, marzipan, Perugina confections, giant Hershey kisses, fudge, and other "straight" chocolates, the erotic generate the most interest. Of course.

CASA MONEO

210 West 14th St.
New York, NY 10011
(212) 929-1644
Catalog: $2.00
Minimum Order: $25.00
Accepts: check, MO

Those who think that Mexican food is summed up by the word "taco" should visit Casa Moneo. They've got all the ingredients for the fiery "chile cuisine" of Mexico and Spain, cooking tools, and the "Bazaar" upstairs that sells perfumes, colognes, soaps, jewelry, scarves, dolls, clothing, crockery, records, and tapes from Spain, Mexico, and Latin America.

The catalog lists every mailable food product in the store, plus things like cotton twine for pasteles, paella pans, parchment paper, iron tortilla presses (6½" across, $9.00), and single- and double-cast iron comals. It *doesn't* list the little meat pies wrapped in foil that you can get as a quick lunch for less than 50¢, the variety of beer and ale, the produce (fresh chiles verdes and the like), and anything from the "Bazaar"— you have to go to the store for these.

The foods in the catalog run from almonds to yerba maté teas from Argentina, Uruguay, and Brazil. The selection of chiles is staggering. There are pages of dried, pickled, sliced, and roasted serranos, jalapeños, chipotles, hot green, long yellow, chile pasilla, chile tepin, and many other chiles. There are also ground chili powders, chile relishes, and a long list of chile-based sauces. Casa Moneo has beans to go with the chile, cooked in the Cuban, Mexican, and Caribbean styles as well as dry, Mexican chocolate, coffees, flours, and meals, crackers and cookies, guava shells, hearts of palm, preserves, malt, blood sausage and chorizos, oils, mineral water, pastes of mango, guava, and sweet potato, rice, seasonings, and pages of tinned seafoods, spices, and nougats. Although the bulk of the food is from the United States, Spain, and Mexico, there are some notable exceptions, like the Danish butter, German acacia honey, Brazilian cashew juice, African palm oil, English pickled onions, and Canadian lobster meat. Some of the food is truly exotic, like the squid chunks in ink and the canned cactus.

The catalog gives the name and form of each product, and its size, brand, type of packaging, country of origin, and price. You should be able to find every nonperishable ingredient for your Mexican or Spanish recipes in the catalog, but really to experience Casa Moneo you have to visit the store.

CAVIARTERIA, INC.
29 East 60th St.
New York, NY 10022
(212) 759-7410
Catalog: free
Minimum Order: $15.00
Accepts: check, MO, MC, Visa, AE

When the old, enormous, wonderfully down-at-heel Horn & Hardart cafeteria on 57th Street was supplanted by a bookstore several years ago, few mourned the loss. After all, there was always the Caviarteria a few blocks away.

While not exactly a lunchroom operation, Caviarteria does make caviar seem a little less formidable, both to pocket and palate. Once you have acquired the taste, you know the difference between fresh American sturgeon and Caspian Beluga Imperial. At $25.00 per 3½ ounces for the former and $79.00 per 2½ ounces for the latter, your wallet knows the difference too. The Imperial is known as "the greatest and the rarest," followed by Caspian Beluga

Prime, Beluga First, and Beluga Malassol. If you're really budgeting luxuries, try the fresh salmon caviar, $10.00 for the 3½-ounce jar and "milder and sweeter than any other," or Caspian Kamchatka, vacuum-packed, bottom-of-the-barrel Beluga, at $5.95 an ounce. Those giving gifts appreciate the samplers of jars of different caviars—as little as $89.00, delivered, for 6 varieties, or $500.00 for 4 ounces of Malassol Beluga delivered in a cherry wood box with lock and mirror, plus porcelain server and spoon. The caviar spoon is a must for proper consumption; made of horn, it's $12.00. And while you're pondering the old question, "Which came first, the lox or the caviar?" you can *nosh* on said smoked salmon—Nova Scotia, Gaspé, Alaskan, Irish, or Scotch—which cost from $15.00 to $30.00 per pound. No bagels or cream cheese, though.

The folks who like caviar usually like things like paté, foie gras, truffles, morels, porcini, pfifferlings, and steinpilze. They are all here, in gift packages, as well as candies, imported cheeses, pistachio nuts, German and smoked hams, and New York City smoked deli meats— corned beef, pastrami, tongue, salami, and knockwurst.

Louis Sobol, who runs Caviarteria, says that about 80% of his business is done by mail, and he's never seen some of his best customers. He urges you to come visit if you're in the city. "I take pleasure in shaking the hands of the faces that attach to the names that I happily see again and again," he says. Pull yourself together and drop in.

CUPPING ROOM CAFÉ
359 West Broadway
New York, NY 10013
(212) 925-2898
Brochure: SASE
Minimum Order: 1 pound
Accepts: check, MO

Where do Soho gallery-hoppers go to recover from the latest art movement? The Cupping Room, of course, unless they're in need of stronger stuff, in which case they can stop next door at the Broome Street Bar.

The Cupping Room was once a wholesale tea and coffee business, and in the early 1970s they opened a retail store, and then the café. Their gourmet coffees, teas, cappuccino, and other concoctions are the attractions, plus the pies, pastries, and light fare. Those who want to reproduce the caffeine end of the experience in their own homes can write for the Cupping Room's *Gourmet Guide to Coffee Beans,* which lists several coffees we've never seen before, such as Kivi, grown in Zaïre. All the favorites are here, including French, Viennese, and Italian roasts, Mocha Java, Tip of the Andes, Maracaibo, Hawaiian Kona, five kinds of Colombian, Kenya AA, Guatemalan Antigua, and more. Prices are available upon request, and are comparable to those charged by other gourmet coffee houses.

Should you visit the Cupping Room, bear in mind that the best seats are in the back room, which is skylit, has a lovely nonworking iron stove, and what is known as a cozy atmosphere. There is always a line, but it's worth the wait.

GODIVA CHOCOLATES
701 Fifth Ave.
New York, NY 10022
(212) 593-2845
Catalog: free
Minimum Order: as stated
Accepts: check, MO

Godiva is to chocolates what Gucci is to leather goods. Godiva was founded by a Joseph Draps, who chose the name and symbol of Lady Godiva, clothed only in long tresses, to represent the firm. The lady appears—hair, horse, and all—on the gold signature boxes and on some of the chocolates. (The logo-hungry can even purchase trays, totebags, and, yes, T-shirts emblazoned with her likeness.)

Behind the status symbol are the Godiva chocolates, wickedly rich confections based on old European recipes and made with all natural ingredients. The chocolates are made in unique shapes or with imprints, and each represents a different flavor. The dark chocolate hearts conceal chocolate creams with a touch of cognac. The scallop shell has a center of praline and chopped hazelnuts, and the chocolates embossed with crossed tennis racquets hold orange cream and Grand Marnier. There are others—chocolate butter cream truffles with rum, mint parfaits, cranberry and cherry cordials in Kirsch, and many more—45 in all.

When filled chocolates are too rich, you can try the Brussels lace, an airy confection of crisp cookie mesh dipped in chocolate, or chocolate bars in milk or dark, with or without almonds. Godiva also has cooking chocolate, ice cream toppings in traditional flavors, and a line with liqueurs, a golden fruit cake, fruit preserves, and Belgian buche bars. Godiva also toys with novelty with a tennis ball can of tennis chocolates, a box of praline and chocolate golf balls, and a carton of 25 chocolate shotgun shells—no chocolate torsos or electric guitars here.

Perhaps more legendary than the chocolates themselves are their exquisite boxes. The standard container is a gold ballotin, and special occasions and holidays are honored with appropriate boxes in velour, velvet, and satin, decorated with fabric flowers, lace, ribbons, and the like. Godiva also offers a collection of very special containers (Limoges china boxes, etc.) that can be purchased and packed with their bonbons. These can be seen at their elegant blue and gift store on Fifth Avenue.

Prices here fluctuate (mainly upward) with the whims of European economy, and if money is precious to you, resign yourself to Hershey bars—Godiva's prices are, like their chocolates, a legend unto themselves.

GRACE TEA CO., LTD.
80 Fifth Ave.
New York, NY 10011
(212) 255-2935
Brochure: SASE
Minimum Order: none
Accepts: check, MO

Frank Cho, a tea importer, used to bring back samples of rare teas from his purchasing trips abroad and share them with his friends. No one could find tea to duplicate these special blends anywhere else, so in 1962 Mr. Cho founded the Grace Tea Co. as a source for fine connoisseur teas. Mr. Cho has since sold the business to Richard and Marguerite Sanders, the two personable owners of another import business, the China Bowl Trading Co. The Sanders not only honor Mr. Cho's blending secrets and use the same sources, but also retain Mr. Cho himself as a consultant so that old customers are assured of the Grace Tea "nonpareil cup quality: clarity and uniformity of color, marvelous taste, and fragrant bouquet that wafts from your steaming cup."

There are currently five black teas, an oolong and a pouchong available, but supplies are dependent on the success of the tea bush crop and tea demand. There is a Superb Darjeeling from the Himalayas in India, a house connoisseur blend that's a favorite with regular customers, a truly special Winy Keemun English Breakfast tea, a good Lapsang Souchong, and "the Original Earl Grey Mixture," a reproduction of the actual tea blended for Earl Grey by a Chinese mandarin, not the usual thing sold as Earl Grey. The Grace Tea oolong is Formosa Oolong Supreme, which is called the Champagne of Teas and possesses a bouquet that recalls peaches, and the pouchong is a wonderful Before the Rain Jasmine. Prices are currently $6.90 to $8.90 a half pound. While more expensive than Lipton, even these connoisseur teas are reasonable when you consider that 200 cups of tea can be coaxed from a pound, and the leaves can often be used twice.

Grace teas are packed in black canisters and make impressive gifts. You can have them sent to tea-loving friends, and the Sanders will add your name or message to the package. The brochure includes a guide to the ideal brewing times of each tea and hints on making the perfect pot.

THE HEALTHY GOURMET
230 Third Ave.
Brooklyn, NY 11215
(212) 624-5884
Price List: SASE
Minimum Order: none
Accepts: check, MO

The Healthy Gourmet will satisfy your sweet tooth while assuaging your nutritional conscience with their four delectable cakes: lemon nut, honey carrot, yogurt banana, and yogurt blueberry, which contain no additives, no preservatives, and 100% natural ingredients. Their cakes are on sale at Macy's but you can order them directly in two-cake packages, sent postpaid, for about $7.00 (the price is subject to change). Manager Melvin Schechter told us why the cakes are so good: One of the "natural" ingredients is sugar. Purists can go eat apples; we'll take the cake.

KRON CHOCOLATIER
506 Madison Ave.
New York, NY 10022
(212) 486-0265
764 Madison Ave.
New York, NY 10021
(212) 472-1234
Catalog: free
Minimum Order: as noted in the catalog
Accepts: check, MO, AE

An army of small purple shopping bags fills the display window of the Kron Chocolatier. The store inside is gleaming white, punctuated by displays of dark chocolates and the flat wood "crates" that are the Kron signature package. In the summer, plates of strawberries dipped in chocolate sit on the counter, irresistible to all but the most self-disciplined. Through a glass window in the store you can watch the chocolates being made.

Thomas Kron, like Florence Mondel of Mondel Chocolates, is carrying on in great Hungarian candymaking tradition, making each chocolate by hand and using old European recipes. Unlike Mondel, Kron has been doing business for less than 10 years, and has a some-what more "avant garde" selection of goodies. It is here that one can buy a life-size female leg with a ribbon garter ($60.00), or a life-size female torso ($50.00). While some records "go platinum," at Kron they go chocolate: A full-size LP of chocolate, with a message, comes in its own crate and costs $30.00. Kron has also rendered golf balls, letters, rulers, tennis racquets, and a Dom Perignon magnum ($75.00) in the dark candy.

Here Hallmark is done one better— there's no better way to say something special to a chocoholic than with the Kron card, made of and inscribed with chocolate and presented in a gift crate. Up to 10 words fit on the 6"-by-8" size ($18.00), and many more on the 8"-by-16" card ($35.00). For your beach-loving friends, there could be no sweeter gift in the middle of winter (short of a ticket to Martinique) than the seashells of chocolate, in milk, dark white, or mint, $7.50 the half pound.

Connoisseurs will forgo novelty for the apricots, prunes, hazelnuts and macadamia nuts covered in chocolate ($8.00 to $10.00 a half pound), the cherries aged in Grand Marnier, Amaretto, or cognac and dipped in chocolate, or the logs of almond paste or ground fruits covered with chocolate (a ¾-pound log, $7.00). Discriminating cooks will appreciate the Kron cocoa, baking chocolate, chips, syrup, and empty chocolate snail shells for ice cream, mousse, and the like (5 for $5.00). Every chocolate item is sold in a choice of milk or dark, and some also come in white or mint.

The real agents of ecstasy at Kron are too perishable for shipping, and must be bought at the store. These are the fresh strawberries, oranges, seedless grapes, and bananas dipped in chocolate, and the Budapest cream truffles concocted of whipped cream, cocoa, and chocolate ¾-pound for $10.00). It is treats like these that put that gleam of satisfaction in the eyes of particular New Yorkers, and make living out of the city seem like true deprivation.

LI-LAC CHOCOLATES
120 Christopher St.
New York, NY 10014
(212) 242-7374
Brochure: free
Minimum Order: ¼ pound; $20.00 on charge cards
Accepts: check, MO, MC, Visa, AE

Have you ever wondered where the Pope gets his bonbons? They're procured from Li-Lac Chocolates, a Greenwich Village fixture that's been selling their delicious hand-dipped chocolates since 1923.

The Pope sends a messenger to pick up his shipment, but notables like Doris Duke visit the violet store and choose from the pyramids of chocolates arranged in glass cases. They may decide upon light hazelnut butter truffles ($10.95 a pound), almond bark ($8.95 a pound), or nougat logs ($8.90). There is a seductive French assortment of dark chocolates filled with treats like praline, rum, truffle, and marzipan ($12.95), and everyone's favorite, fudge, in maple, walnut, chocolate nut, plain, and coconut flavors, at $5.60 a pound.

Li-Lac makes goodness better with their chocolate-covered fruits ($8.95 a pound), luscious pieces of pineapple, orange peel, apricot, figs, prunes, dates, and raisins. You can get one fruit or a mix, and they'll go heavy on your favorites.

The Li-Lac confections are made on the premises, which accounts for the

chocolate *fumes* that overcome every susceptible chocoholic who enters. If you can't visit or dispatch a courier for a few pounds, send for the brochure.

MC NULTY'S TEA AND COFFEE CO.
109 Christopher St.
New York, NY 10014
(212) 242-5351
Brochure: SASE
Minimum Order: $5.00
Accepts: check, MO

McNulty's was established in 1895 by Judge John McNulty, and has been serving discerning caffeine *aficionados* ever since. It carries on today in the same tradition of excellence that he began, featuring custom blending, rarities like Maragogype and Ethiopian Harrar, and a huge array of coffee paraphernalia and machines. The McNulty display windows often hold antique mills, grinders, brewing equipment, esoterica like pressed tea bricks, and a sleeping gray cat.

McNulty's superb gourmet coffees are listed by name and country, and described with reverence. Mocha Sanani, from Yemen, is "rare, genuine mocha, winy with chocolate undertones." The current list has 16 gourmet brews, from $4.95 to $7.00 a pound.

Colombian flavored coffees are available in tastes as subtle as almond and as strong as Jamaican rum. The staple morning beverage is represented here as "straight" coffee, in American, French, or Italian roasts. Blended coffees are also listed, and the exact proportions of straight coffees used to make them are given, so you know exactly what you're getting. If you are a true coffee devotee, you can get your cofee "green," buy one of McNulty's coffee roasters ($9.95), and do it yourself.

In the tea department, they have a full line of Celestial Seasonings herbal tea, Boston tea, Jackson's of Piccadilly, Wagner's decaffeinated, Twinings, and Rose Brand. Their black teas include a good selection of Indian, Ceylonese, Chinese, and Javanese. They have both Chinese and Japanese green tea.

Every real tea lover will have a hot pot when he sees the list of McNulty's own gourmet specialty teas. "Amorous Almond," "Gaucho's Delight," and "Apple Pie" should pique your curiosity. More reserved flavors like apricot, black

Assorted Cheeses
from Balducci's

currant, ginger, lime, orange mint, and wild cherry are also available. Prices run from $5.00 to $35.00 a pound.

McNulty's can arrange regular automatic mailings should you so desire. If freeze-dried and vacuum-packed leave you uninspired, consider this caffeine paradise.

MILAN LABORATORY

57 Spring St.
New York, NY 10012
(212) 226-4780
Catalog: $1.50
Minimum Order: $10.00
Accepts: check, MO

Along with making their own fettucine, ravioli, and pesto, many Italians in Little Italy still make their own wine. When pasta is too stiff or sticky, a little water or flour will remedy the situation, but what to do when the wine sours or goes bitter? Smart enologists have been taking their troubled fermentations to the wine doctors at Milan Lab for almost a century.

Today, Anthony Miccio, grandson of the founder of Milan Lab, stands behind the counter selling winemaking equipment, extracts, essences, herbs, spices, and baking products, and dispensing advice to would-be winemakers and diagnosing the problems in off batches. Miccio sells all the supplies you'll need to make wine except fruit and sugar. They have fruit crushers and grinders, fruit presses (which are also used for making Chinese egg rolls), white oak barrels and kegs, faucets and funnels, tubing, bungs, corks, filter bags, caps and cappers, champagne foils and lead capsules, bottle labels, malt extract, yeast, and bottles (in the store only). Once it's bottled, you can store your wine in one of their wine racks, open it with the corkscrews, and serve with the bottle pourers.

Sound like an overwhelming undertaking? Those who want alcoholic beverages without all that fuss can make instant cordials and liqueurs using Miccio's flavorings, vodka, and Karo corn syrup (recipe provided in catalog). Imagine creating Benedictine, Curacao, Drambuie, "acqua d'amore," maraschino, pineapple, and tutti-frutti liqueurs at the drop of a hat. Miccio even has flavorings for brandies and whiskies, which are made in a similar fashion. They may not give Jack Daniels and Hiram Walker sleepless nights, but the extracts offer a very cheap way to have an almost limitless bar.

The extracts can do double time in the kitchen as baking ingredients, and Miccio lists others—Sorriento cake flavor, anethol oil, clove, nutmeg, pistachio flavors, etc.—as well as herbs and spices, vanilla beans and vanillin powder, rose water, orange flower water, rock candy, and coffee beans.

Should you attempt winemaking, keep two things in mind. One, start out with the best possible grapes, raisins, cherries, apples, or other fruit. Two, if your wine sours, turns moldy, clouds up, or becomes vinegary, you can send a small soda bottle full to Miccio and they will render a "sensory evaluation." You must have at least 5 gallons to be corrected, and the diagnosis currently costs $7.95 for up to 3 samples. The cost of the diagnosis can be applied toward the purchase of Preservol or other prescribed remedy. Anthony Miccio was schooled by an unrivaled enologist, his father, and carries on in the Miccio tradition. But even he can't cure every ill, and there's nothing he can provide that will turn water—or vinegar—to wine.

NOBLE & BOWMAN

136 Seventh Ave. South
New York, NY 10014
(212) 691-4757
Catalog: SASE
Minimum Order: as noted
Accepts: check, MO

Noble & Bowman is sandwiched between Jensen's, a store of eclectic fashions and home accessories, and Montana Eve, a tourist bar that rivals the established Riviera Cafe a block away. Noble & Bowman, however, is a pure country store, with rows of big spice jars filled with teas, herbs, and spices lining the dark wood shelves, old-fashioned lighting fixtures, and all kinds of mugs, coffee grinders and tea infusers, china, and other accessories throughout the store.

Noble & Bowman currently stock over a dozen straight coffees and ten blends. These include the standard American, French, and Italian roasts, vintage Colombian aged 6 to 10 years, Maracaibo, Altura, Kona, Jamaican, Antigua, and others. Prices run from $4.50 to $5.95 per pound. In the tea department, there are straight teas from China, India, Ceylon, Japan, the East Indies, and South America, as well as blended teas, spiced teas, naturally flavored fruit teas, and herbal tea. Some of the more unusual are Rose Petal Tea from China, Moroccan Mint blended tea, Seville Orange, and Hibiscus teas. In addition to their own label, they carry teas by Jackson of Piccadilly, Twining, Hu-Kwa, Wendell, and Rosebud. Mr. Noble knows his brews and can offer assistance and advice on selecting the right coffee or tea for particular tastes.

PAPRIKÁS WEISS IMPORTER

1546 Second Ave., Dept. NYBM
New York, NY 10028
(212) 288-6117, 6903
Catalog: $1.00 per year subscription
Minimum Order: none
Accepts: check, MO, MC, Visa

Paprikás Weiss ranks with Zabar's and H. Roth and Sons as an established New York City imported-foods emporium. Paprikás Weiss began over 90 years ago with fine Hungarian paprika, which they still sell in sweet, half-sweet, and hot varieties. They now have a spice shelf with over 150 kinds of spices and herbs, from allspice to woodruff.

New York is nothing if not a city of international flavor. Paprikás Weiss really shows its cosmopolitan side in the food department. The foodstuffs now come from every corner of the globe. You can get Romanian Sibiu salami, kosher strudel leaves, poppy-seed pastry filling, raspberry syrup, canned wild boar goulash in juniper sauce, goose fat from France, Portuguese sardines, French orange flower water, 10-year-old Colombian coffee beans, and Turkish apricots here. The pastries are true Old World: Linzer tarts, vanilla kipfel, walnut roulade, Dobosh torte, and Vienna Neapolitans. For those who cook there are all sorts of gadgets like cake coolers, sausage stuffers, bean slicers, cherry stoners, spaetzle machines, and coffee roasters, as well as the more serious waffle irons, triple-coated enamel cookware, frying pans, meat grinders, and coffee mills.

Whether you've been looking for a corn slitter, Hungarian liniment, Turkish coffee, a book on Polish cookery, St. John's Bread, or crystallized lilacs, your search ends at Paprikás Weiss.

PERUGINA OF ITALY

636 Lexington Ave.
New York, NY 10022
(212) 688-2490
Catalog: free
Minimum Order: none
Accepts: check, MO, MC, Visa

Perugina of Italy is known for its light golden "Pandoro" and "Panettone" cakes, riddled with chocolate bits, which are served traditionally at Christmas, and their "Baci," or chocolate and hazelnut kisses. Perugina's store in New York City has been here for decades, satisfying the discerning chocolate, nougat, and marzipan lover.

Perugina sells its assortments in elegant, rose-decorated boxes, its cakes in conical containers with carrying ribbons, its nougat in long bars. There are solid chocolates, filled chocolates, the famous Torrone nougat, cookies, and hard candies here, and special assortments and treats for Christmas, Easter, Valentine's Day, and other holidays. Like Godiva, Perugina sells bonbonnières, china "Limoges-type" dishes, ashtrays, boxes, and vases, available with or without chocolates.

Unlike many of the new "Old World" chocolate stores in the city, Perugina is unpretentious and confident enough in its products to risk Muzak over the sound system. Their confections are European in flavor, and price. A pound of the Maître Confiseur selection of filled chocolates is $16.25, a 2-pound Pandoro cake is $12.95, and 8 "Baci" are $3.45. Their Treasure Chest, a selection of different Perugina favorites, is $49.95. According to candy connoisseurs, these are the prices of delight.

PLUMBRIDGE

33 East 61st St.
New York, NY 10021
(212) 371-0608
Brochure: free
Minimum Order: as listed
Accepts: check, MO, AE

Plumbridge is still the elegant, understated chocolate shop it must have been a century ago, when it was patronized by that breed of people known as the "carriage trade." The chocolates and confections are still made in a kitchen in the back of the store, and are still the undoing of the waistlines, if not the wallets, of every chocoholic who enters. There are truffles, whipped-creme mints, chocolate coffee beans, orange peel dipped in dark chocolate, Russian mints, and dragée, which is a mélange of chocolate-covered raisins, peanuts, orange peels, and other good things. These chocolates are well priced at $13.00 per pound. The Plumbridge nuts are equally good—the famous spiced pecans, roasted or raw cashews, peanuts, Jordan almonds, natural pistachios, and luscious mocha nuts, which are almonds and filberts, dipped in dark chocolate and dusted in cocoa ($13.00 to $15.00 per pound). Even the candy is special: ere are tiny jelly beans, black and red raspberries, French candy vegetables, and "rocket sours" at $5.00 to $7.50 a pound.

At Christmas, Plumbridge sends out a gift catalog that features assortments of edibles packed in different containers. The year of this writing there are 10 pretty tins with candy assortments that range from $10.00 to $17.00, mocha nuts in a beautiful brass cannister for $20.00, a stack of 4 wooden Shaker-type boxes filled with dragée, mocha nuts, spiced pecans, and ambrosia for $65.00, and cabinets filled with treats for $60.00 and $75.00. We must allow that mail order is ersatz compared to visiting Plumbridge, where the owner, Mr. Petrillo, provides samples of the wares and offers you a selection of antique and one-of-a-kind containers for very special gifts.

PORTO RICO IMPORTING CO.

201 Bleeker St.
New York, NY 10012
(212) 477-5421
Brochure: SASE
Minimum Order: 2 pounds of coffee
Accepts: check, MO, MC, Visa

Next to an IBM Selectric, a writer's best friend is a fresh pot of coffee. One would expect a literary watering hole like Elaine's to serve a top-notch brew, and they do. Their special blend comes from Porto Rico Importing, who also sells to the Plaza Hotel, The Friars Club, and Patsy's.

Porto Rico was established in 1907, and is still run by the same family. Peter Longo, the owner, buys his beans green, has them roasted to order, and sells the 28 varieties out of large burlap bags lined up all over the store. He has American, Viennese, French, and Italian roasts, and specializes in the dark roasts and espressos. Among the coffees listed are Altura Mexican, Hawaiian Kona, Swiss water-processed decaffeinated, Tanzanian, and Indian Mysore.

Peter Longo has two tea buyers, Chinese and Indian, who bring back the finest from their countries. Among those on the list are Russian Caravan, Assam Pekoe Souchong, Iron Goddess of Mercy, and anise. There are other flavored and herbal teas, and loose herbs and spices.

Their line of equipment includes drip pots, and espresso and espresso/cappuccino makers by Melitta, Chemex, Vesuviana, Mocha Express, Mocha Junior, La Signora, Nova, Stella, La Pavoni, and Atomic. They repair these machines and sell accessories and papers. For a price quote on supplies or equipment, send a model number with description of what you need. For an estimate on repairs, describe the machine and the damage.

SCHAPIRA COFFEE CO.

117 West 10th St.
New York, NY 10011
(212) 675-3733
Brochure and Price List: SASE
Minimum Order: 1 pound
Accepts: check, MO

At the very back of the dark little Schapira Coffee Co. store you can see the equipment that distinguishes Schapira from every other coffee emporium in the city: enormous metal roasting machines. Since they do all their own roasting, the Schapiras are able to guarantee consistency in the quality and strength of the brew the beans will produce. They also tender a fine hand in the blending of their teas.

Schapira packages their coffee and tea under the Flavor Cup label. Their current price list features seven blended coffees, including water-decaffeinated brown roast, French, Italian, and American roast, Turkish blend, New Orleans (French and chicory), and Viennese. Fine unblended coffees are also available: Java, Guatemalan, Maracaibo, Mexican, French roast, Ethiopian Mocha, Yemen Mocha, Costa Rican, Kenyan, and Sumatran Mandheling. As of this writing, prices run from $3.75 per pound for New Orleans blend to $6.00 a pound for Yemen Mocha.

We were totally infused with Schapira's tea selection. In addition to the special Flavor Cup blend of Indian and Chinese tea, there are classics like Darjeeling, Jasmine, Russian Blossom, Assam, Oolong, Lapsang Souchong, and Earl Grey. Almost all are available in bags as well as by the ¼ pound, ½ pound, or full pound. Schapira has assembled a tea bag sample, 4 bags for each of 8 varieties, a fine way to familiarize yourself with the most popular brews. Their naturally flavored black currant, raspberry, licheenut, cinnamon, almond, and apple teas are popular among those who want a refreshing drink. They also make unusual iced teas.

The Schapiras wrote *The Book of Coffee and Tea,* which they sell by mail, along with filter paper for Melitta, Chemex, and Tricolator drip makers, grinders, espresso pots, and some herbs. For a list of the equipment and herbs currently available, request the special order form.

SIMPSON AND VAIL, INC.

53 Park Place
New York, NY 10007
(212) 349-2960
Catalog: SASE
Minimum Order: $15.00 on charge cards
Accepts: check, MO, MC, Visa

At one time long ago, Maxwell House had its coffee roasting operations in Hoboken, New Jersey. The deep aroma of coffee permeating the entire area is one of the childhood memories of Mr. Harron, who owns the coffee and tea concern Simpson and Vail.

His coffees are several cuts above Maxwell House, beginning with the American "brown roast" and ending with water-decaffeinated, Kenya AA, and Mocha-Java coffees. He also sells a connoisseur line of teas, including Earl Grey, Lapsang Souchong, oolongs, jasmine, and several others, in addition to accessories such as tea infusers and dripmakers. Simpson and Vail's prices are already 10% to 15% lower than those of other stores selling comparable goods, but they will take 10% off your *first order only* if you mention *Shop New York by Mail* when requesting the catalog and when ordering.

Wondering if he had come full circle, we asked Mr. Harron whether his roasting was done in Hoboken. "Oh no," came the reply. "The EPA cracked down on

roasting in New Jersey. Maxwell House left years ago. Our beans are roasted in Brooklyn." And if the EPA shuts down things in Brooklyn? "I guess we'll be selling a lot of tea."

SULTAN'S DELIGHT, INC.

409 Forest Ave.
Staten Island, NY 10301
Catalog: free
Minimum Order: $15.00
Accepts: check, MO, MC, Visa

Sahadi's may be New York City's best-known Middle East food emporium, in business since 1895 and now located on Atlantic Avenue in Brooklyn. Sahadi's tried mail order several years ago, but found their store business occupied too much time. That's when Charles Farkouh decided to form Sultan's Delight, which carries all of Sahadi's mailable food and some cooking items, plus other imported edibles.

The catalog opens with "foul mudammas," which may sound unappealing but is actually cooked fava beans, 65¢ the 20-ounce can. Hummus can be made from their cooked chick-peas and tahini (there's a recipe in the catalog), or bought prepared from Lebanon in 13-ounce cans, $1.65 each. There are stuffed vine leaves, artichoke bottoms from Egypt, fig and date jam, and baba ghannouj, or eggplant dip. There are all sorts of grains, nuts, and mixes, including 5 kinds of bulghur, seasoned falafel filler, roasted and sugared and salted chick-peas, rice flour, jumbo lentils, Pakistani rice, couscous, pilaf mixes, red and natural pistachios, shelled hazelnuts, roasted squash seeds, and both Spanish and Chinese pignola nuts. Under the heading, "Prejarred Goods," you will find hot pickled okra, jalapeño peppers, lime pickles, chutneys, and assorted olives. The spices used in Middle Eastern cooking are here—coriander, cumin, fenugreek, saffron, ginger—even hibiscus flowers for $3.50 a pound.

Sultan's Delight has several kinds of rose and orange flower water, Turkish coffee, halvah ($2.10 a pound), dried and candied fruits, fruit leathers, honey, teas, jams and jellies, cheeses, and even breads and filo. Some of the goods are extraordinary, even for the culinary sophisticate: curry paste, grape molasses, Greek chewing gum, Swedish fish jelly candies, and canned, pistachio-filled baklava.

There is more than food: inlaid backgammon sets, Turkish coffee cups and pots, falafel molds, couscous pots, tambourines and clay drums, fezzes, and cookbooks. How to work off all the calories in hummus, falafel, halvah, and baklava? Belly dancing! You will be the sultan's delight in your gold-sequinned bra with coins along the bottom($18.95), gold-sequinned belt, chiffon skirt or chiffon pantaloons ($11.95), and brass finger cymbals. No naval jewels, however.

TEUSCHER CHOCOLATES OF SWITZERLAND, LTD.

25 East 61st St.
New York, NY 10021
(212) 751-8482
Catalog: free
Minimum Order: $5.00
Accepts: check, MO, MC, Visa, AE

It is often the tiniest containers that yield the finest jewels. It is surely so with Teuscher, whose minute shop near Madison Avenue is a showcase for what some believe are the world's finest chocolate truffles, most delectable pralines, and the richest marzipan.

Resisting temptation in the face of attractions like truffles of chocolate with walnut, vanilla, orange, nougat, and—bliss—champagne, is simply exhausting. A tariff of $18.00 a pound is levied for these pleasures which should keep all but the most indulgent away. If the truffles don't get to you, the pralines, in almost two dozen different variations on a theme of chocolate delight, will. Or perhaps you will succumb to the marzipan, flavored with walnut, pistachio, kirsch, Grand Marnier, raspberry, date, and orange, each paired with chocolate. All these treats and their well-known diabetic chocolates and those shaped like fish, crocodiles, and seahorses are flown in weekly from Switzerland.

If you can't afford to invest in these gems by the pound or even the half, you can get (and give) the whimsical gift boxes made to look like "King Frog," "Happy Donkey," "Market Girl," and other characters that contain one or several pralines or truffles, starting at $2.50. There are also beautiful anemone-topped boxes for those not inclined to cuteness. All Teuscher chocolates have

the added attraction of being free of preservatives, additives, or artificial coloring—as if you were considering your health.

ZABAR'S

2245 Broadway
New York, NY 10024
(212) 787-2000
Catalog: free
Minimum Order: coffee, 5 pounds
Accepts: check, MO, MC, Visa, AE, DC

Zabar's is without a doubt New York City's ultimate deli. West Siders queue up there on Saturday nights for Sunday morning's bagels, cream cheese, lox, and *Times*. Everyone else knows it for its Jamaican Blue Mountain coffee, available nowhere else on the East Coast, and its regular sales of cookware and kitchen machines. The lines form, however, to buy the Kashkoval cheese from Israel, egg challa loaves and croissants made by the thousands each week, ham smoked in applewood, chicken stuffed with fruit and vegetables, blood sausage, lobster salad, "black gold" truffles from France, pesto, and countless other specialties from counters loaded with smoked meats and fish, sausage, bread, cheese and gourmet cookware and appliances.

Zabar's has every conceivable comestible or condiment to go with or on: 42 different mustards for palates timid to insensitive, a vast array of spices, imported jam and preserves, crackers and flatbreads, tea, beer, coffee, nuts, sweets, and much more. Zabar's will cater almost anything and does a brisk business in the summer with their elegant picnic baskets for two, filled with rolls, fruit, cheese, cookies, and things like ratatouille, artichoke paté, and lemon garlic chicken. Their largest order ever in a single day was placed by a discerning yachtsman planning an outing, who ordered enough caviar, Scottish salmon, herring, sturgeon, and prosciutto to run up a bill of $35,000.00!

Zabar's mails only nonperishables or items with a long shelf life, including housewares and appliances, coffee, and tea. They have full lines of Celestial Seasonings, Biegelow, Twinings, Constant Comment, Wagner's, and Hu-Kua tea, to name a few. The coffee selection includes Zabar's special blend, Jamaican Blue Mountain, decaffeinated, Colombian, mocha blend, Hawaiian Kona, and Tanzanian Peaberry, in addition to other rare and common coffees.

Zabar's real forte is the gourmet cookware and housewares line, where the espresso-cappuccino machines, cookware, and kitchen appliances are often discounted 25% to 40% off list. Prices range from $3.98 for the 6-cup Melitta drip outfit to $1,000.00 for the 100-cup Olympia Superclub espresso-cappuccino machine. Zabar's also carries machines and equipment by Bunn, Wigomat, Bosch, Krups, Neapolitan, Vesuviana, Pilvuyt, Bialetti, Melior, Pavoni, and Chemex.

They sell a variety of kitchen appliances, including convection ovens by Maxim and Farberware, food processors by Sanyo and Hobart, the Hoan pasta machine, Salton appliances, and juice extractors by Braun and Sanyo. Their tin-lined copper cookware is coveted for its heavy gauge and low price, as is the selection of discounted Leyse aluminum-ware, Norwegian Polaris steel cookware, and enameled cast iron. Modern classics like the Jena glass teapot, Peugot pepper mill, Zylis salad spinner, Terralion scales, and Mouli grater are all here, at good savings over list price.

You may regret not being able to visit Zabar's if you live outside New York City, but take it from those who know—the catalog is a lot more quiet than the store, and there are never any lines.

SEE ALSO: Health, Beauty

11 | Health Beauty

In New York City, beauty is probably more important than it should be. There are so *many* people, and they are always looking at each other, all day long. The face takes on an inordinate importance. It is like living in a world of eight million mirrors. As the model capital of the country and the source of the latest trends in beauty and fashion, the city provides the most extensive collection of new and sophisticated products. Competition is keen and style rapidly changing; merchants naturally arise to meet the market. Some establish national reputations and open a counter in your local Saks which is why you won't find them here. Others, sad to tell, don't encourage mail order customers but may warrant a visit if you're passing through.

In the often gritty, dirty, odiferous air, special care has to be taken if you want to have soft, clean skin, lustrous hair, and a pleasing scent. The products New Yorkers use to overcompensate for their tough conditions ought to work wonders in more benign climes.

THE BATH HOUSE

215 Thompson St.
New York, NY 10012
(212) 533-0690
Catalog: free
Minimum Order: $5.00; $15.00 on
charges
Accepts: check, MO, MC, Visa, AE

Everything about The Bath House is
exceptional or special, including the
people who run it. Cindy Annchild and
Michael McNulty met as Peace Corps
workers in Iran, where bathing was a
social affair, and have been together
ever since. Their fascination with the
bathing rituals of other countries inspired
The Bath House, but their interests
extend to poetry, yoga, photography,
dance, the women's movement, and
caring for their son, Lincoln.

Their charming store is beautifully
colored in shades of peachy pink.
Antique washstands and bureaus serve
as props for the array of soaps, dishes,
sponges, creams and lotions, implements,
powders, and other bath preparations. At
the back is a large counter set with
colorful tiles, and above that row upon
row of large glass jars filled with perfume
essences. The Bath House features
custom scenting services, and for a
charge will perfume several of its
products with your choice of pure
essences, their own blends (Black Forest,
Now, etc.), or the Zodiac oils created by
a Greenwich Village astrologer.

Bath House soaps include ones made of
rainwater blended with camomile and
lanolin, goat milk, calendula, oatmeal,
cocoa butter, and the Bronnley soaps
made from herbs like basil and
rosemary. Their "top choice" is
Macedonia soap, an import from Spain
that is laced with mineral salts. Soaps run
from $1.10 to $4.25 a bar.

Add the lightly abrasive action of a
loofah ($1.50 to $5.00), an aloe yarn
scrub, or the Japanese "sloofah" to your
soak, or a natural sponge for gentle
washing ($2.25 to $7.50). The bubble
bath/body shampoo creates luxurious
lather and comes unscented or in apricot,
musk, mint, or jasmine, a favorite. You
can find mineral bath salts, bathing herbs,
and Culpeper's bath and foot salts here,
to name a few. After the bath, dry off with
the genuine 7'-by-5' Turkish Towel
($24.00), powder and deodorize with the
Nature de France products, and moistur-
ize with any number of lotions and
creams, including the popular French
Vanilla Lotion ($10.00 for 16 ounces).

The Bath House offers an elegant
alternative to aerosol shaving cream with
their sandalwood shaving soap in its
wood bowl, or the goat-milk soap in
sandalwood, bayberry, or musk. They
sell shaving brushes and a soothing
unscented non-alcoholic aftershave to
complete the ritual. There are a plethora
of hair-care products here, including
rosemary oil for conditioning, and Altese
brushes from France. There are also
natural baby-care toiletries, massage oils,
and implements, a complete line of aloe
vera products, Dr, Hauschka treatments,
and potpourri. Here you will find
Chinese toothbrushes with natural
bristles and bone handles at just $2.50,
quill toothpicks, sleeping masks in
several colors ($7.00), a nail file made of
the scales of the pirarucu fish (75¢),
Weleda toothpaste, bath pillows, and a
light skin peel that contains no synthetics
or acids and leaves your skin glowing
($2.50 and $10.00).

Cindy and Michael have designed The
Bath House around the specific needs of
their customers and have managed to
maintain high standards in both the
natural products and their service as the
business has grown. Theirs is a catalog
well worth writing for and a store that
merits a leisurely visit.

BOYD CHEMISTS

655 Madison Ave.
New York, NY 10021
(212) 838-6558, 5524
Catalog: $2.00
Minimum Order: $10.00
Accepts: check, MO, MC, Visa, AE,
CB, DC

One half hour of browsing near the
makeup artists at Boyd's can yield a
book full of tips. Boyd's draws models,
actresses, and aspiring beauties from all
walks of life with their makeup
demonstrations and an unparalleled
selection of professional-quality makeup,
tools, and sundries.

Carol Fader runs Boyd's which is
no mean feat. In addition to keeping
order and sanity at the demonstration
counter, she makes sure the store is
stocked with the best and the latest in
cosmetics and treatments, often hard-to-
find imports. For example, she carries
Longcils of France, Anita of Denmark,

René Gerraud of France, Renoir (Boyd's own line), and Fabriella, formerly Evermond of Italy. There are cleansers, toners, day and night creams, special treatments, makeup, body and hair-care products, and tools. Boyd's is where you go for silk cosmetic sponges, a "bottle of hair" to add fibers to your mascara, herbal eye pads, Bute eyedrops, Marc Albert sable cosmetic brushes, Barielle hand and foot products, brushes by Boyd's, Mason and Pearson, and Alexandré, wig brushes, horsehair exfoliating straps, bath sponges from Greece, and other curious beauty needs. The catalog can list only their most popular products—for example, while you'll see Feinseife fruit soaps, R. H. White soaps, and Potter & Moore bath salts, you *won't* see their full line of Guerlain soaps or some of the exotic imports from England, France, and Spain listed.

In addition to the exhaustive stock of specialty cosmetics, tools, and treatments, Boyd's sells a comprehensive line of perfume and has a prescription drug department. It is rumored that Estée Lauder drops by sometimes, but whether she's having a prescription filled, buying their cosmetics, or getting ideas for her own line is between Ms. Lauder and Boyd's. She needn't drop in—Boyds will be glad to send anything anywhere. No New York City beauty overlooks this source if she's really serious about putting her best face forward.

CASWELL-MASSEY CO., LTD

Mail Order Division
111 Eighth Ave.
New York, NY 10011
(212) 620-0900
Catalog: $1.00, twice yearly
Minimum Order: $15.00
Accepts: check, MO, MC, Visa, AE, DC, CB

If you buy your pots and pans at Bridge Co. and your sheets at Porthault, you probably get your soap and toothpaste at Caswell-Massey. This apothecary experience, established in 1752, has blended scents for no less than George Washington, P. T. Barnum, and Daniel Webster. The store is a wonderfully cool, dark, quiet place banked with huge varnished drug cabinets and immense apothecary bottles filled with jewel-colored liquids. Stacks of soaps top the

display cases, and perfume, special toiletries, and grooming implements lie arranged on shelves within. A faint and lovely scent pervades the air.

If you can't visit, the catalog is a whimsical, charming version of the store. Within the pages you will find Plisson makeup brushes from Paris made of sable, badger, or goat hair, silk sponges, swansdown puffs, Hazeline vanishing cream, Dr. Ciccarelli preparations, and Christian Gray cosmetic treatments. They also have the very gentle Rimmel's mascara ($3.00) and Eau de Bleuet cornflower water for soothing puffy eyes.

Caswell-Massey carries not only its own Vegesperm soaps in all sorts of exclusive scents but also others made of birchleaf, pine, rosewood, sweet basil, witch hazel, primrose, algae, tomato, beeswax, carrots, and lettuce. To augment the bath ritual, there are loofah mitts and straps, natural sponges, talcs, corn cutters, foot creams, manicure and pedicure implements, and sleeping gloves. Hair is treated to the macassar oil that stained countless sofa backs a century ago, as well as delights like Blue Orchid shampoo, Bearine bear grease, boar-bristle brushes, and mock-tortoise combs and barrettes. Whisker-removal equipment includes badger shaving brushes, straight razors, strops, and shaving soaps and lathers. Oral hygiene is accomplished with the aid of Walther toothbrushes ($4.00), or for true elegance, the boar-bristled, bone-handled Tilbury, which General Custer used ($8.50). The Diamant Red Toothpaste reddens gums and whitens teeth, the pastilles and cachous scent the breath with violet, rose, and vanilla, and goose-quill toothpicks give the common act a touch of grace. Even Bayer and Di-Gel have alternatives here in the English Menthol Dome ($2.50), which is rubbed against the forehead to offset an impending headache, and the Norit charcoal tablets that "quell" intestinal gas and filter away associated halitosis.

The famous CM essences, fragrances, potpourri, and pomanders will enchant you as they did Dolley Madison and Jenny Lind. These interpretations of heliotrope, patchouli, lavender, lemon & lime, vetiver, and white rose are quite special. Other classics like "Number Six," Persian Leather, and Newport have to be tried to be appreciated, and samplers of 6 to 12 scents are available

Natural Unbleached Bath Sponge
and Bath Brush from The Bath House

($12.00 to $125.00). The fragrances are sold in the forms of toilet water, cologne, shaving lotion, and bath oil. CM also sells the Potter & Moore lavender line, Lubin perfumes, and a whole range of products featuring the scent of cucumbers. You can also make your own perfumes with any of the 75 essential oils and the fixative/diluent.

Altogether, there's no end to the indulgences to be bought or created at this source nonpareil—don't forget them at Christmas!

GEORGETTE KLINGER
501 Madison Ave.
New York, NY 10022
(212) 838-3200
Brochure: free
Minimum Order: none
Accepts: check, MO, MC, Visa, AE, DC

Georgette Klinger might have been just another pretty face had she not developed a terrible case of acne right after winning a beauty contest. It was while remedying the outbreak that she developed her interest in skin care and beauty, which later became the foundation of the business.

Georgette and her daughter, Kathryn, run several salons across the country. There you can indulge yourself in facials (face treatments for men), collagen treatments, scalp treatments, or their relaxing body massage. Your skin type is also evaluated, and a skin-care regimen is formulated for you.

Even if you can't get to a salon to have a Klinger beauty routine prescribed, you can order the products from the brochure. (Certain products, such as the cleansing lotions, are made in 30 formulas, in which case you *must* know which version you want or have had a skin-care program outlined by Klinger for you. A "Skin Examination Chart" is available upon request; complete it and return it with $12.50, and they will send a two-week supply of skin care preparations and a Progress Report for further recommendations.) But anyone can use things like their massage cream (a pound for $40.00), natural rose water spray, "eight-day concentrated collagen plus elastin" ($80.00), survival kits for sun and skiing, cream for hands, feet, and elbows, mud packs for the hair, and cosmetics. Klinger has masks for dry, oily, and normal skins made of camphor,

mud, clay, herbs, gel, cod liver, and other substances, as well as night treatments, lubricating creams, makeup removers, cleansing lotions, moisturizers, eye and neck creams, and even colognes—"Georgette" and "Kathryn."

Of course, Klinger products are best used in conjunction with the regimen they devise for you. But if you don't live in New York City, Palm Beach, Beverly Hills, or Bal Harbour, or you'd just like to sample some of the preparations that help the "beautiful people" stay that way, their mail-order department provides.

NATURE DE FRANCE
100 Varick St.
New York, NY 10013
(212) 925-2670
Brochure and Price List: SASE
Minimum Order: none
Accepts: check, MO

Back in the 1950s Pierre Cattier, a naturopath, discovered the healing properties of a clay found in the Tremblay-les-Gonesse area of France. Rich in minerals, free of asbestos, it could even be used internally. Mr. Cattier found that the clay was not only nontoxic and soothing but also could cleanse and stimulate the skin and acted as a natural deodorant. He developed formulas for thoroughly natural beauty products that were not only safe but also *worked*. Nature de France uses the same clays and the same formulas to make their products, which carry a money-back guarantee.

Nature de France has products made in three clay "strengths"—white, rose, and green. White is so gentle it is used as a dusting powder and can be made into a mask for those with sensitive or delicate skin. Rose clay is the real all-purpose "beauty" clay and suits most skin types. Green clay is more astringent and is used on oily or blemished skin, and applied medicinally in packs and poultices (it is sold in bulk form for this purpose). White clay is sold in powder form for making masks and as roll-on deodorant, white clay toothpaste, and in a creamy French facial soap bar. Rose clay is available in soap, mask powder, facial tonic, skin lotion, stick deodorant, shampoo, and conditioner. Green clay comes in the form of powder, toothpaste, deodorant, cleansing masks, moisturizer, shampoo, and herbal ointment.

Nature de France makes all their products in small batches so that the quality is preserved. No dyes, mineral oils, alcohol, animal products, harmful chemicals, or artificial fragrances are used. The large color brochure illustrates the products, gives a history of their development, and describes their use. Directions for the "French Spa Facial" are given, with recipes using the clay powders with fruits, oil, tea, and juices to make masks for all skin types and purposes.

The Nature de France products really work and they cost far less than luxury skin preparations that coat the skin with perfumed lanolin and preservatives. You are welcome to call Roberta at Nature de France with any questions, and the brochure is free—send a SASE.

VITAMIN QUOTA, INC.
14 E. 38th St.
New York, NY 10016
(212) 685-7026
Catalog: free
Minimum Order: $15.00 on charges
Accepts: check, MO, MC, Visa, AE

It has been said that at any given hour of almost any day of the year you can see joggers and runners making their way around Washington Square and Central Park, undaunted by rain, snow, or muggers. This obsession with fitness and health is especially acute in cities, and has insured the success of stores that sell only running shoes, and others like Vitamin Quota, which specialize in vitamins, supplements, and a few food products.

These days, no one takes a One-a-Day and leaves it at that. The typical customer at Vitamin Quota has a shopping list of "basics" that include their B-complex Becoms 100 ($6.49), Vitamin C tablets (100 250mg tablets for $2.50), Vitamin E, and a high-potency multivitamin and mineral tablet (30 for $4.49). Other favorites are the trace element selenium, brewers' yeast tablets, lecithin granules, pantothenic acid, niacinamide, biotin, zinc (100 10mg tablets for $1.49), iron, calcium, dolomite, acidophilus, and potassium. Vitamin Quota sells several geriatric formulas, time-release vitamins and chelated minerals, digestive aids, and Vi-Kids M for children and VC Pet Vitamins.

In addition to nutrition aids, they sell cosmetic treatments and hair preparations that feature Vitamin E, bee pollen, ginseng and aloe vera, and related items like a dental buff, electric callus eraser, blood-pressure kit, Acme Juicers, wraparound heating pads, and food scales. VQ gives gifts with orders over $26.00 and $150.00 and runs regular sales, our favorite being the "buy one, get one free" that is held during the summer. This constitutes a 50% discount on prices that are already good, and there's an added plus: Their vitamins and minerals are free of sugar, preservatives, and artificial colors and flavors.

SEE ALSO: Food, Drink

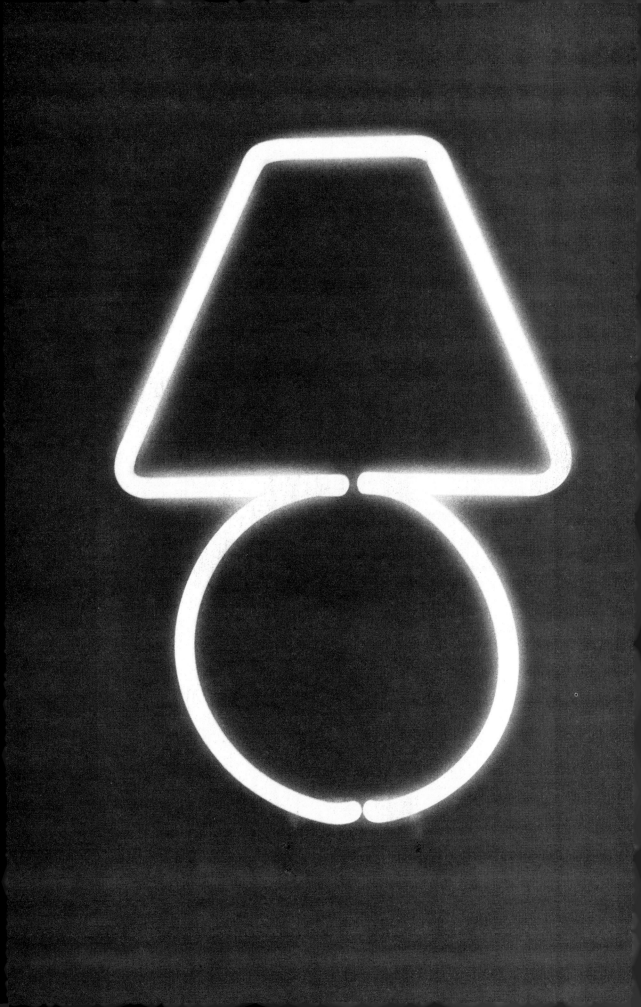

12 | Home

In New York, you don't have a yard. You have, at best, a 3'-by-5' ledge of tile, referred to as a "terrace."

Should you attempt to raise any flowers on said terrace, you will encounter a mystery of nature that defies reason: Red spiders, aphids, mealy bugs, and all manner of pests will appear on your flowers, and gradually do them in. Distance is no problem—they have traveled, somehow, to twentieth-floor penthouses and wiped out horticultural masterpieces within a few weeks. So all the energy that would go into gardening, landscaping, trim painting, and shutters goes into the small, overpriced apartment.

The apartment is a kind of fortress against the noisy and intrusive world New York can often be, an oasis, an eye in the storm. Our interiors are important because they're all we've got, and they serve as a reflection of what we are. We're fussy about them. We demand furniture that's stylish and decently priced; table linen, bedding, draperies, and carpets that are made of real cotton, wool, and down—New Yorkers consider polyester an anathema wherever it appears. And, since New York has more restaurants, more amateur cooks, and more kitchen freaks than anywhere— you'll find what you need for the ultimate kitchen here.

The catalog of the shops in this chapter will remind you of all the wonderful things you don't have inside your lovely home.

ACE BANNER & FLAG CO.

107 West 27th St.
New York, NY 10001
(212) 620-9111
Catalog: $1.00 refundable
Minimum Order: none
Accepts: check, MO

Ace Banner & Flag has been satisfying the nationalistic needs of New Yorkers and the rest of the country since 1916. Carl Calo, the owner, sells flags of every nation, yacht signals, marine flags, pennants, banners, and even tote bags and T-shirts.

Old Glory is sold in every form at Ace, from the small paper flags given out at parades ($1.00) to 20'-by-30' outdoor flags in nylon for $567.00. There are flags for poles, flags with stands, table flags, and parade flags. The foreign flags cover every nation from Afghanistan to Zimbabwe, in cotton and nylon. Mr. Calo sells a great number of these to homesick foreign students, who pin them up over their beds in their dorm rooms.

Ace makes banners and flags for schools, fraternities, bands, lodges, firms, and societies in virtually any quantity, size, material, color, or design, and will work from rough sketches. At sea, Ace signals and ensigns fly above yachts and other boats, and their international code flags relay messages across the water. Ace also makes the banners that businesses use to advertise openings and special promotions, as well as T-shirts, tote bags, buttons, and emblems.

Last but not least, Ace sells weather-vanes. They offer vanes made of aluminum in a black enamel finish, and full-bodied models of eagles, horses, roosters, owls, and other traditional symbols in black or bronze finishes, 23-karat gold leaf, or handpainted natural color. Prices run from $19.50 to $210.00. Ace also sells hand-hammered copper weather-vanes that begin at $375.00. Inquiries on the copper vanes and their custom flag and imprinting services are invited.

AMERICAN SURPLUS TRADING CO.

332 Canal St.
New York, NY 10013
(212) 966-5650
Catalog: $1.00
Minimum Order: $25.00
Accepts: check, MO

Unions and ignorance insure that every time an appliance breaks down or an outlet shorts, you'll call on an electrician. Chances are he graduated from one of those schools that advertises on matchbook covers, but he'll still charge like a neurosurgeon for his time. If you *really* want to fume about the inequity of the situation, go down to American Surplus Trading, or send for their catalog. There you'll see the strange little things like jumpers, fan blades, relays, resistors, terminals, motors, capacitors, transformers, and switches that keep the machines in your life running—all at unbelievably low prices. Many of the parts that fail us and bring on $30.00 repair bills are 10¢ and 15¢ each. Things like heating elements are $1.00, grounded cords are 50¢ each, smoke-detector chips are 18¢, and something called a "magic box" is $1.50.

Grousing aside, this is a great source for electricians and electronics hobbyists, and if you need something not listed in the catalog, it pays to give American a call. Their inventory is many times the size of this catalog, and they're always getting new parts. The prices are, of course, rock bottom.

ARTISTIC LATEX

1220 Brook Ave.
Bronx, NY 10456
(212) 293-3530
Brochure: $1.00, refundable
Minimum Order: none
Accepts: check, MO

There is something so *American* about wooden Indians made of latex. Artistic Latex makes rubber Indians, nautical figures, totem poles, masthead figures, Nativity scenes, and other Christmas decorations suitable for adorning home, business, or institution, indoors or out. The material is rigid, non-shattering latex composition.

Some of the figures have to be seen to be believed. There are bosomy ladies and founding fathers, ships' figureheads, ornate eagle plaques and figures, a set of nearly life-size Dickens carolers set up with an electrified lamppost (complete set, $615.00), a life-size madonna with child, midget-sized Nativity sets with figures and stable, a Santa with sleigh and reindeer, carrousel horses, duck decoys, and even a fake barber pole for the "olde time" look. Our favorites are the "nineteenth-century idols," a baseball player, and a "brave fireman," which are 40" tall and cost $98.00 each. The figures and ornaments are handcast in latex composition and reproduce the originals down to the cracks and the grain in the wood, are handpainted and rubbed to achieve a "mellowed patina," and can withstand outdoor display.

BACCARAT, INC.

55 East 57th St.
New York, NY 10022
(212) 826-4100
Crystal Brochure: $1.00
China Brochure: $1.00
Flatware Brochure: 50¢
Accepts: check, MO

Baccarat was founded by a bishop in 1756 in a small town in France, also called Baccarat. In the centuries that followed, Baccarat earned the title "The Crystal of Kings" by setting the tables of three Kings of France, Kaiser Wilhelm II, both Presidents Roosevelt, the great Aga Khan, and many other members of the ruling classes. And there was a reason they chose Baccarat.

Baccarat uses only the finest sand in crystal production, as well as a high proportion of lead (30% to 35%). The lead gives crystal its weight, its characteristic brilliance, and the clear note that sounds when the rim of a goblet is tapped with a fingernail. Baccarat designs, some a century old, have become standards against which all other stemware is measured. In addition to beautifully etched and cut pieces, Baccarat carries suites of goblets designed for wine connoisseurs. These are ideally clear, thin, uncut glasses with large bowls that reveal the true color of the wine and allow the bouquet to develop. Baccarat's "Perfection" and "Haut Brion" patterns were developed in 1929 and 1933 for the wine merchants of Bordeaux to fulfill those requirements, and "Perfection" is still used at the annual banquet. Both patterns are $35.00 a glass. A similar "gourmet" glass is the "Brummel," of crystal so thin it almost appears to be an open-ended bubble on a stem. At $60.00 per goblet, its fragility becomes a real consideration. Baccaret sells other uncut glasses, notably the slender-fluted "Dom Perignon," named after the Benedictine monk who created the champagne, and

"Manon," a heavy gold-banded goblet. Their cut patterns include "Nancy," a glass of classic shape cut with crisscross designs, "Paris," cut evenly with small tear drop shapes, and "Lagny," created in 1912, deeply faceted on bowl and base and at $155.00 per water goblet one of the costliest patterns here. Baccarat also sells beautiful crystal gifts, accent pieces, and animal sculptures. There are handsome square brick-cut vases for $205.00 and $560.00 and ball vases cut with swirling diagonal lines for $90.00 to $270.00, both designed by Van Day Truex. They have bar sets of flacons and glasses with deep tapering vertical cuts, square flacons with beveled edges, and commodore decanters for the yacht. There are plain wine bottles with striking rounded stoppers by Van Day Truex that are in the design collection at the Museum of Modern Art, an ice bucket with a chrome handle ($135.00), and even a handsome champagne cooler. Their plain oblong ashtray, unpunctuated by cigarette grooves, can be used for paperclips (or caviar) at $140.00. The Baccarat animals include smooth, almost abstract grizzly bears, squirrels, dolphins, and a frog, but for dramatic decorative effect nothing tops those Trylons and Obelisks, which act as perfect prisms and stand over 17" tall.

The second floor at Baccarat is devoted to china and flatware. The china is by A. Raynaud & Co. and Ceralene, Inc., two of the best firms producing china in Limoges, France. The china patterns range from the very elegant "Ambassador" china banded with two coats of gold polished with an agate stone, to the highly modern octagonal "Sorel" plates banded in china red. In between are lovely floral patterns—morning glories, irises, water flowers, crocuses, and anemones—done in brilliant color. Their "Dioraflor" is a beautiful adaptation of a floral motif found on an old Chinese vase, done by the House of Dior. This same pattern is reproduced, spectacularly, on a black background as "Dioranoir." There are gifts and accessory pieces of all sorts for most of the patterns. A breakfast cup and saucer run from $45.00 to $100.00, and the soup tureen from $335.00 to $800.00, depending on the pattern.

The ideal complement to Limoges china is Ercuis flatware. The classic, under-stated patterns suit all china, from the ornate "Dioraflor" to the plain white "Marly." Place settings run from $135.00 to $160.00, and all sorts of serving pieces are available, such as lobster forks, snail forks, ice-cream spoons, asparagus servers, rice ladles, leg of lamb holders, and grape shears.

Baccarat is to be appreciated for its civility in a city where snobbish sales clerks are usually an inevitable part of a status shop. We found them more than helpful in back-ordering a lid to a jam pot from France, to replace the broken original. The lid was relatively cheap, but they handled the transaction as if it were a service for 8.

BAZAAR DE LA CUISINE
1003 Second Ave.
New York, NY 10022
(212) 421-8028
Catalog: $1.50
Minimum Order: $10.00
Accepts: check, MO, MC, Visa

Consummate cooks and those who aspire crowd the aisles at the Bazaar, where savings of 10% to 30% can be realized on cooking tools, utensils, pots, pans, and housewares. They carry lines by Copco, Hammarplast, Cuisinart, Farberware, Melior, Calphalon, Atlas, Braun, Krups, Le Creuset, Pavoni, Henckels, Trident, Wustof, Chemex, Melitta, Sabatier, Moulinex, Salton, Masterchef, and many other firms.

The Bazaar has no catalog as of this writing, but is in the process of compiling one. Their mail-order services include copper retinning. They will accept pots and pans if you ship them insured, whereupon they will send you an estimate. Although the Bazaar caters to the professional and semiprofessional cook, the salespeople are equally attentive to gadget mavens and those who rush in for culinary gifts. Advice is always freely given.

A. BENJAMIN AND CO., INC.
82 Bowery
New York, NY 10013
(212) 226-6013, 6014
Information: price quote by letter with SASE
Minimum Order: $50.00
Accepts: check, MO

A. Benjamin and Co., purveyors of fine

china, stemware, and silver, do a thriving business among the pots and pans dealers who surround them in the city's restaurant supply district. It's not just that they carry tableware and holloware by Heirloom, 1847, 1881, Deep Silver, Community Plate, Lunt, Wallace, Gorham, Towle, Reed & Barton, Lenox, Royal Doulton, Royal Worcester, Spode, Minton, Mikasa, Fransiscan, Noritake, Giorni, Wedgwood, Val St. Lambert, Orrefors, Tiffin, Fostoria, and many other firms, in addition to pewter and stainless flatware and holloware by leading manufacturers, but also that they sell them at 25% to 50% below retail. Gold jewelry, fine cultured pearls, and diamond jewelry are also sold here, but not by mail.

Write to A. Benjamin for a price quote, include a stamped, self-addressed envelope, and be sure to mention *Shop New York by Mail*. Do take note of the minimum order.

CARDEL, LTD.
615 Madison Ave.
New York, NY 10022
(212) 753-8690
Information: price quote by letter, with SASE
Minimum Order: none
Accepts: check, MO

When you can afford the best china and crystal and don't mind paying for it, take your money to Cardel. Fine quality and selection merge in a store that's beautiful and is staffed by friendly, informed salespeople.

Mr. Rene Caraco of Cardel told us that there are 26 factories in France making what is known as Limoges. "Saying 'Limoges china' is like saying 'Detroit cars,'" he stated. Here at Cardel they carry Limoges from only 3—the best—factories. They also sell Spode, Crown Derby, Royal Doulton, Wedgwood, Royal Worcester, Minton, Coalport, Rosenthal, Aynsley, Caverswall, Charles Field, Havilland, Bernardand, Herend, and Bing and Grondhal. Their crystal lines include Val St. Lambert, St. Louis, Lalique, Edinburgh, Stuart, Rosenthal, and Riedel (no Scandinavian lines). Cardel carries the Rolls-Royce of stem-ware, Moser. Each piece of crystal they make is copper-wheel-engraved with exquisite designs, and sometimes

Watteau-type scenes and scenarios of nature. It takes a man about 2 weeks to finish each piece. Moser crystal begins at about $200.00 and goes to $675.00— a glass.

Cardel is obviously no discount store, but it is an excellent source for choice china, crystal, and giftware by the same firms. Write to them with stock information for a price quote.

EZRA COHEN CORP.
307 Grand St.
New York, NY 10002
(212) 925-7800
Information: price quote
Minimum Order: $10.00
Accepts: MO, MC, Visa

Ezra Cohen is a dry-goods emporium on the Lower East Side known for its huge selection and discount prices. They are publishing a catalog, but you can still call them for price quotes on anything for bed and bath from Martex, Spring-maid, Wamsutta, J.P. Stevens, and Cannon. They carry towels by Fieldcrest and Martex, and the superior Grand Manor all-cotton towels by Cannon. They also have shower curtains by Ames, bedspreads and coverlets by Nettlecreek, Dakotah, Masterloom, Beau Ideal, and Florentine. The Cohens will make sheets, shams, comforters, and dust ruffles to order, and sell (in the store only) draperies, throws, pillows, slipcovers, etc. Write or call for a price quote if you don't see what you want in the catalog. This store occupies three floors and is worth a visit, but remember that it's closed on Saturdays and bedlam on Sundays.

THE CONTINENTAL QUILT SHOPPE
129 East 57th St.
New York, NY 10022
(212) 752-7631
Price List: free
Swatches: $2.00
Minimum Order: none
Accepts: check, MO, MC, Visa, AE

The female eiderduck, who lives near Arctic seas, lines her nests with fine fluff she plucks from her own breast. That down is carefully plucked from the nests by eider gatherers, and finds its way to The Continental Quilt Shoppe. There it becomes the *very* precious quilt, soft beyond dreams, that is known as the eiderdown. At this moment, eiderdowns cost $1,875.00 for the twin size, $2,054.00 for the full, and $2,700.00 for the king size. A famous female rock star buys a new one every time she buys another home.

The less financially fortunate among us will have to comfort ourselves with down. Bob Scott, manager at The Continental Quilt Shoppe, points out that their quilts are made of high lofting down, which has been shown to have twice the lofting power than down found in top brand-name down quilts. They are covered in cotton cambric, 260 threads to the square inch, which is "the only down proof ticking in the world," and channel-stitched to avoid cold spots. The comforters come in camel, bone, blue, white, navy, brown, and yellow, and run from about $300.00 for the twin size to $450.00 for the king size. Reductions of $75.00 are usually available. The Continental Quilt Shoppe also sells quilts of 65% down/35% feathers and 80% feathers/20% down, at much lower prices, wonderfully firm pillows, and zippered quilt covers, pillow shams, pillowcases, and dust ruffles.

You can extend the life of your down quilt or pillow by covering it. Mr. Scott says that nothing will reduce the loft and insulating properties of down faster than repeated washings, which break the down down. They are so firm on this that they will guarantee their quilts for 3 years when they're sold without a cover, and for *10* years when sold with one.

CRYSTAL CLEAR IMPORTING CO.
55 Delancey St.
New York, NY 10013
(212) 925-8783
Information: price quote
Minimum Order: inquire
Accepts: check, MO

Crystal Clear probably has the best collection of crystal in the city, and certainly some of the finest prices: 40% and more below retail.

They import their stemware and giftware from Europe and China, and can give you a price quote if you call with a description of the crystal or the name of the manufacturer and the pattern. Crystal Clear also sells giftware of silver, gold, and porcelain.

DELBON CUTLERY, INC.

121 West 30th St.
New York, NY 10001
(212) 244-2297
Information: within listing; send shears or knives directly
Minimum Order: none
Accepts: check, MO

There are still people in New York City who remember the man who sharpened knives and scissors coming slowly down the street in a horse-drawn truck, ringing his bell. He'd pull up to the curb and women would appear from every house with hands full of dull knives and tired scissors, and the knife man would hone them keen.

The knife man and his horse-drawn truck have gone the way of all things, but you can have the same service performed via the mailman, at Delbon. Richard DeVito runs the shop, which has been in the cutlery and sharpening business since 1840. Richard sells every type of cutlery and scissors made, in the best brands. There are Wiss scissors, Henckels knives and scissors, and knives by Wustof, Dexter, and the real Swiss Army knives. Delbon also carries the most extensive line of hunting knives to be found in New York City, as well as pocket knives and manicuring implements.

The sharpening is done at the back of the store on an enormous grinding wheel. Mr. DeVito says that his wheel, which is cooled with water, will never burn the metal of knives or scissors the way a plain stone will. Delbon is recommended by Wiss and Marks scissors and is *the* service center in the East for Puma hunting and pocket knives. They also service the Embroiderer's Guild.

Delbon does a very thorough job, taking the scissors apart, cleaning and sharpening the blades, setting the points together, and oiling them before putting them back together. A pair of 7" or 8" dressmaker's shears costs about $5.00 the first time Delbon sharpens them, and $2.00 for each subsequent servicing, providing no one else has sharpened them. Delbon also sharpens and fixes knives, cuticle nippers, toenail clippers, and anything else that cuts or snips, except scissors of inferior metal or those like Fiskars, which can't be taken apart. Pinking shears can be sharpened, believe it or not, at a cost of $5.00 each time.

Richard DeVito, who really knows his blades, says that the best come from Germany, the United States, and Brazil. If yours are worth sharpening, simply mail them to Delbon and they'll send you a bill. Upon receipt of payment, they mail your things back to you. Samurai take note: They don't do swords.

DIXIE FOAM

20 East 20th St.
New York, NY 10003
(212) 777-3626
Information Sheet: SASE
Minimum Order: none
Accepts: check, MO

While most of America sleeps on stuffed and buttoned mattress and box-spring sets, New Yorkers retire on pallets of foam.

The foam mattress caught on when space-hungry apartment dwellers discovered that their loft beds gave a great night's sleep. Platform beds were developed for the acrophobic, and a whole new breed of foam mattress emerged, led by the carbamate.

If you haven't slept on high-resilience carbamate, you don't know what a foam mattress can be. This is a truly *dense* foam, at 3.2 pounds per cubic foot. That's compared to the typical marshmallow mattress of 1.2 pounds per cubic foot. Dixie's high-resilience mattress is about twice as expensive as the standard-density mattress, but it comes with a 10-year limited warranty to reassure you that its longevity claims are justified.

Dixie's mattress line includes four densities, from 1.2 to 3.2 pounds per cubic foot, in 4" and 5½" thicknesses, running from the sofa size of 30" by 75" to the king size of 78" by 80". They also have a boxspring foundation and "platform" bed foundation.

The mattresses are all covered in your choice of duck, denim, or mattress ticking. Duck makes the prettiest bed covering, in our opinion, especially the buff, cocoa, and charcoal covers edged in white. Dixie has developed a line of simple foam furniture, which they sell in their New York City store and may market by mail. Just send a stamped, self-addressed envelope and they'll send you information on everything they currently ship.

Foundations make your mattress even better.

MICHAEL C. FINA

580 Fifth Ave.
New York, NY 10036
(212) 757-2530
Catalog: inquire
Minimum Order: none
Accepts: check, MO, MC, Visa

Michael C. Fina publishes a lavish 200-plus-page color catalog that belies its reputation as a discount house for jewelry, watches, sterling and silverplate giftware and flatware, crystal, pewter, fine china, collector dolls, music boxes, brassware, clocks, leather goods and luggage, pens and pencils, typewriters, calculators, optics, and some audio and TV items. The "discounts" are established by listing "reference prices" next to the Fina prices; these higher prices are either suggested retail prices or the market prices for goods of comparable quality.

The catalog opens with a diamond bracelet of almost 200 diamonds, a total of 33 carats, for $49,500.00, and ends with the Pacific Silver cloth bags at $1.45 each. In between there are diamond wedding band sets, costume jewelry of all sorts, gold chains and bracelets, and watches by AMF, Waltham, Hamilton, Casio, Gruen, Seiko, and Omega. They sell holloware, silverplate, and flatware by Gorham, International, Paul Revere, Wallace, Reed & Barton, Oneida, Lunt, Towle, Kirk, Alvin, and Stieff. Fina sells china by Mimosa, Lenox, J & G Meakin, and Nikko, barometers and clocks by Seth Thomas, Springfield, Elgin, Casio, and Hamilton, leather goods by Amity, Bel-Aire, American Tourister, Yves St. Laurent, and Samsonite, pens and pencils by Parker, Sheaffer, and Cross.

The "discounts" are 10% to 40% lower than the "reference prices" listed. As far as price and taste go, Fina falls somewhere between an S. & H. Green Stamp Redemption Center and Bloomingdale's/Tiffany's, but the selection, especially in jewelry, gifts, and tableware, is remarkable.

HOFFRITZ FOR CUTLERY, INC.

515 West 24th St.
New York, NY 10011
(212) 924-7300
Catalog: $1.00
Minimum Order: none
Accepts: check, MO, MC, Visa, AE, DC

When we need knives or nippers or cleavers or clippers, we hurry down to Hoffritz. There we find an unparalleled selection of cutting implements, as well as a vast array of household gadgetry and charming gifts.

Hoffritz has their own line of Sabatier knives, constructed with full tangs of stainless steel, tungsten, and molybdenum, which are sold in sets and individually. They also have one of every possible kitchen knife made for them in Solingen, Germany, in addition to a variety of steak knives, poultry shears, 6 different cleavers, carving sets, kitchen shears, and barbecue implements. There are at least 14 sharpening steels, ceramic honers, knife blocks, and wall racks. There are a diversity of knife styles available, and handles to suit every taste in nylon, styrene, rosewood, stainless steel, pearlex, acetate, and Indian stag, or bone.

If it's a pocket knife you want, you're sure to find something among what they offer here. There are plain pocket knives that do *everything*, and their own Swiss Army knives that do even more, plus a stunning collection of knives for fishing, hunting, diving, and throwing.

For operations performed upon the self, there is an army of tweezers, pluckers, cuticle cutters, nail files, corn rasps, nail scissors, barber and thinning shears, scissors for the mustache and beard, angle razors, folding razors, and mustache razors, old-fashioned straight razors and stops, badger shaving brushes, and an assortment of combs, rakes, and brushes for the mustache and beard as well as head hair. Other cutting jobs are handled with the shears and scissors designed for dressmaking, trimming, embroidery, paper, pinking, silhouette cutting, buttonhole making, and thread cutting. They also carry a good folding scissors and the famous stork scissors.

Hoffritz has a huge line of gadgets, household goods, and items for travel. These include a selection of bar and wine accessories—flasks, measures, corkscrews, ice buckets, steins, and tankards—as well as things like magnifying glasses, hostess gifts of every description, an automatic cherry pitter, gardening tools, their famous clam opener, silent butlers, cheese planes and slicers, egg scissors, pickle tongs, onion holders that keep your hands from smelling, coffeemakers and thermoses, clocks, and weather instruments.

Hoffritz has a warranty on their knives that covers them against breakage, providing they're not victims of "abuse." They also fix and sharpen their own products (and only their own) for a fee. This is a great source for all sorts of things, but the choices are enough to drive a normal person mad.

INTERNATIONAL RETINNING & REPAIRING CO., INC.

525 West 26th St.
New York, NY 10001
(212) 244-4896
Information: send for estimate or calculate
Minimum Order: none
Accepts: check, MO

When the tin lining of your copper pot wears thin, you can retire it to the wall as a decoration or use it and risk copper carbonate poisoning. Or you can have it retinned.

International Retinning & Repairing not only retins copper pots and tightens the handles and knocks out dents, but also does repairs on all kinds of metal objects, from andirons to tin lamps. They do a large volume of antique restorations, but no job is too lowly: They recently repaired the mop-wringing mechanism on a bucket.

The cost or retinning is calculated by mesuring the height of the sides and the diameter of the pot or pan and multiplying each inch by $1.00. A 6" frying pan with 2" sides would cost $10.00 to retin. Teapots are estimated individually and cost $18.00 to $36.00. Add $2.50 to the "formula inch" amount for the return postage. For an estimate on repairs, send a drawing or photo and a complete description of what you need done.

International has been in the business since 1913, serving the best kitchenware shops in the city and scores of antiques dealers. These are the same shops and dealers who advertise retinning and repair services and send the work to International, but charge customers half again as much as they'd pay if they went directly to the source. Why pay more for the same thing?

Mail Order Tip: Leave space on your price-quote letter so the company can enter the price and send it back.

J & D BRAUNER BUTCHER BLOCK

298 Bowery
New York, NY 10012
(212) 477-2830
Catalog: $1.00
Minimum Order: on certain items
Accepts: check, MO, MC, Visa, AE

J & D Brauner are the people credited with taking butcher block out of the meat shop and putting it in every room of the house. They launched the trend from their store on the Bowery in the middle of the restaurant supply district. They still sell the massive chopping blocks that inspired the home furnishings, as well as cutting boards, counters, shelves, brackets, stools, chairs, desks, and tables made of the material.

Butcher block is a creation of strips of hardwood that are cured and glued together electronically, sanded, and oiled. Even when given constant kitchen use, butcher block will last forever with proper care.

You can replace your Formica counters with butcher block counters and backsplashes that run from 18" to 144" long, 25" wide (other sizes are available at the store), or use one of the cutting boards ($8.90 to $50.00) on your old counters. We like the pantry tables, heavy steel-plated wire shelf units topped with butcher block. Some have upper shelves, storage drawers, drop leaves, and casters. They run from $150.00 to $440.00. There are also rollaway carts and kitchen worktables with optional overhead storage and hanging racks of wood.

The bulk of the J & D Brauner catalog is devoted to butcher-block dining tables and coordinating chairs. You can choose from Rectangle, Circle, or Oval tabletop shapes in a variety of sizes on trestle bases, turned-oak pedestals, chrome, cast-iron bistro bases, butcher-block bases, or Parsons legs in wood or chrome. The tops not only come in different shapes and all sizes, but also in the stock butcher-block stripes, a pretty, staggered pattern of strips called Random Oak, and oak parquet. The chairs include knockoffs of the Breuer chair in cane and chrome, chrome with velvet, suede, or corduroy, and cane and wood (this version is also known as the Prague or Praha chair). There are Windsor-style chairs, reproductions of the Hitchcock seat in oak, ladder backs, Queen Anne chairs with rushed seats, folding chairs of wood, bentwood and cane side chairs, and utility stools and counter seats. Prices run from $22.50 for a folding chair with a wood seat to $129.00 for the Queen Anne armchair.

J & D Brauner runs regular specials on selected items, but you'll have to see the "Home" section of Thursday's *New York Times* to find out about these, as the catalog prices are always full retail. Delivery is available within the New York City area.

JEAN'S SILVERSMITHS, INC.
16 West 45th St.
New York, NY 10036
(212) 575-0723
Information: price quote by phone or letter
Minimum Order: none
Accepts: check, MO

Jean's Silversmiths appear here because they are such a good source for old and discontinued sterling patterns. They have hundreds of them. They also do silver replating. Their manners, however, are anything but sterling. The manager himself was rude and impatient over the phone, which we find a real detraction from the whole shopping experience. If you really need a silver pattern that you can't find elsewhere, you can call or write with pertinent information for a price quote. Just remember: You're dealing with silver snarks.

JENSEN-LEWIS
156 Seventh Ave.
New York, NY 10011
(212) 929-4880
Catalog and Price List: $1.00
Minimum Order: none
Accepts: check, MO, MC, Visa, AE

There was a time when canvas was known only to artists and sailmakers. Then came the director's chair, the canvas tote bag, and espadrilles. And Jensen-Lewis.

Jensen-Lewis *is* canvas. They use it to slipcover the ubiquitous director's chair, upholstered sofas, chairs, sleepers, room dividers, all sorts of totes, and even drawer units. They also sell canvas by the yard: heavyweight and lightweight. Heavy comes in 28 colors, including California blue, and can be used for upholstering, tote bags, screens, and tents. Lightweight is available in a dozen colors and can be used for draperies, bedspreads, clothing, and accessories.

Jensen-Lewis sells the director's chair in 6 different styles, slipcovered in your choice of canvas, Naugahyde, linen, a fake suede, or genuine leather. The chairs can all be folded, and are available with a matching stool-table. So many of these chairs are sold to residents of Soho lofts that they may be renamed "the artist's chair."

Jensen also sells a streamlined version of the British officer's chair and matching ottoman, butterfly chairs, and a variety of "easy" furniture in rope, leather, and canvas, including hammocks and the Kennedy rocker. The newest ventures into the land of "real" furniture include upholstered sofa beds, modular units, gate leg tables, parquet-top Parsons-style tables, and bentwood chairs.

New York is a city of inveterate *schleppers*, who can be seen carrying everything from goldfish to windows through the streets. Jensen-Lewis makes canvas containers to accommodate all but the largest of loads. There's a heavy-duty ice bag, a mailbag, a backpack, a script bag that fits over the arm of a director's chair, duffel bags, and even a briefcase, all in canvas. About the only things Jensen-Lewis doesn't carry are sails and espadrilles!

HOWARD KAPLAN FRENCH COUNTRY STORE
Dept. NYBM
35 East 10th St.
New York, NY 10003
(212) 674-1000 (inquiries and credit-card orders)
Catalog: $2.50
Minimum Order: $5.00
Accepts: check, MO, MC, Visa, AE

The French have a knack for incorporating enough grace and playfulness in something as common as a cup and saucer to make it pleasing yet not tiresome. Howard Kaplan has collected a storeful of these "little French somethings," which he sells next to his store of French country armoires, hutches, beds, tables, chairs, and mysterious pieces vital to life in a French farmhouse.

The Kaplan catalog showcases a variety of practical and decorative items that run from the antique pedanque ball for $68.00 to the large Louis XV-style parquet table in oak veneer at $1,195.00. Object-obsessed New Yorkers looking for the perfect accent delight in the genuine grape carrying baskets of different designs, available by mail for $195.00 each. The 9-bottle wine rack made of lashed twigs is a sturdy, rustic alternative to high-tech chrome shelves and costs $68.00. There are iron sausage hanging racks from Alsace and pot racks from Provence, and flowered enameled signs that read "Salle de Bains," "Cuisine," "Prive," and "Occupé/Libre" at $15.00 each. The light fixtures run from a 9½-inch-tall brass wine cellar oil lamp to a striking Louis XIV 8-armed black iron chandelier, electrified ($350.00) or candle-burning ($295.00).

Kaplan sells Provencal, Normandy, Brittany, Lorrain, and Picardy-style armchairs and side chairs in oak and cherry with rush seats that are much more affordable than the originals at $210.00 to $295.00 each. The marble-topped tables and bentwood chairs that charmed you in Paris cafés are here, as well as dainty forest-green folding garden chairs of wood and iron.

Of course, if you're just looking for a special cup and saucer or that little touch or a gift, Kaplan has just the thing. Few can fault the heavy white porcelain bistro dishes banded with blue, the "workingman's" glasses (French jelly glasses), or the simple cotton *petit carreau* dishtowels in green, blue, red, or yellow and white checks, at $4.50 each. There are café au lait and smaller espresso cups in heavy porcelain with subtly chiseled sides, perfect simple wine glasses (8 for $10.00), and the wonderful reproduction bistro match strikers that advertise Dubonnet, Apollinaris, Cassis Quenot, and the like at $12.50 each. For absolute whimsey and a touch of the barnyard, you can't beat the white hand-molded faïence geese, pigs, hens, and rabbits, with glass eyes, iron feet, and blue and white gingham bows ($28.00 to $195.00). And for the person who has everything, there's the 39" Celsius thermometer that not only measures the temperature but also tells you the ideal or actual temperatures of Orléans in 1879, Paris in 1830, the Sahara, a sickroom, the maturation of grapes, the incubation of chickens, a hot bath, deep snow, Upper Volta, the freezing point of milk, wine, vinegar, and urine, and more, for just $125.00.

For all these things and a host of others, like bakers' smocks, glass-stoppered vials of bath preparations in unusual fragrances, old copper pots and pans, and totes and umbrellas in Provencal prints, be sure to visit the Kaplan store on East 10th Street or their smaller version at 400 Bleecker Street when you're in Greenwich Village.

LAMP WAREHOUSE
1073 39th St.
Brooklyn, NY 11219
(212) 436-8500
Information: price quote by letter with SASE
Minimum Order: none
Accepts: check, MO, MC, Visa

A Light Shines in Brooklyn could be the story of the Lamp Warehouse, where you can get "any lamp from any company," says the manager, Mrs. Aim. They carry every lamp imaginable, from swags to those for wall, table, and desk. Write with the model or stock number of what you want and include a stamped, self-addressed envelope and they'll send you a price quote.

LÉRON
745 Fifth Ave.
New York, NY 10022
(212) 753-6700
Catalog: free
Minimum Order: none
Accepts: check, MO, MC, Visa, AE

Those who like frogs, mushrooms, butterflies, fruit, hearts, and flowers appliquéd on their bed and bath linens will like Léron. This elegant boutique is lit with chandeliers and presided over by the soft-spoken Mr. Foster. Each year he introduces a new collection of the finest linens appliquéd with animals and flowers, holiday sets for the table, romantic bed ensembles in pastel shades with scalloped trim, embroidered and flowered sheets and cases, and boldly trimmed "contemporary" styles. Léron also sells classic trousseau linens of cotton, beautiful blankets of wool, pillows, linen towels, placemats, cocktail napkins, and much more.

Léron whimsey extends only to its linens. The price tags are deadly serious, the sort that make sacred acts of sleeping, bathing, and dining. The lovely "Bravissimo" tablecloth of white Bisso bordered in green and hand-appliquéd with tulips is $375.00 in the 6'-by-9' size. Matching napkins are $175.00 a dozen. A scalloped, monogrammed bathmat is $49.50. Their all-cotton sheets embroidered with beautiful roses are $150.00 per twin sheet, *on sale.* And for your holiday table, you can buy a set of 4 placemats of Bisso appliquéd with appropriate scenes plus matching napkins for $295.00. The quality and workmanship are, of course, the best, and Léron is thriving after half a century, even at these prices.

HARRIS LEVY

278 Grand St.
New York, NY 10002
(212) 226-3102, 3103, 3104
Information: price quote
Minimum Order: $15.00 on MC and Visa
Accepts: check, MO, MC, Visa

We've always fantasized about a place like Harris Levy, but didn't believe it existed until we visited the store on the Lower East Side. There they sell "softgoods"—linens and accessories—for every room in the house, ranging from the middle-quality goods produced by the big mills to the most beautiful things usually found on Madison Avenue in linen boutiques. *Everything* is sold at substantial savings.

For the bedroom, there are sheets, pillows, blankets, comforters, and dust ruffles. There are towels for the bathroom and bathrobes, throw rugs and wall-to-wall carpets, scales, toilet seats, mirrors, hampers, and baskets. In the kitchen department they have towels, potholders, mitts, and aprons, and there are tablecloths, placemats, and napkins for the dining table.

Harris Levy doesn't stop here. They make blinds, shades, throw pillows, bedspreads, curtains, dust ruffles, and even sheets to order. Mr. Kaplan, the manager, told us that they make a lot of "boat sheets." It appears that the beds on boats are often oddly shaped, and the sheets must be custom-made. Harris

Levy also does monogramming and Swiss stitch embroidery on sheets (this takes three weeks).

What distinguishes Harris Levy from other dry-goods stores is the quality range. They have bed, bath, and table linens by Springmaid, Wamsutta, Fieldcrest, Martex, Dan River, Burlington, and J. P. Stevens/Utica (or everyone but Cannon). They also have exquisite imports from England, France, Italy, China, and Switzerland. We tested their reputation for carrying the very best. Did they have all-cotton sheets? Yes. Egyptian percale? Yes. *Linen?* Yes, and at a good third less than what was being charged uptown.

You can call or write to Harris Levy with the name of the mill and the stock number and color, or a description of what you want, and they'll tell you if it's available and give you a price quote. This store is a must on any tour of the great bargain sources of the Lower East Side.

MAIL ORDER PLASTICS, INC.

302 Canal St.
New York, NY 10013
(212) 226-7308
Catalog: free
Minimum Order: $50.00
Accepts: check, MO

Just about everyone we know in New York City has "parts control problems," a technical term for not being able to keep track of small things. Mail Order Plastics has a solution.

Organize your nuts, bolts, hairpins, desk supplies, crafts materials, or what-have-you with their modular cabinets. These units are 18" wide, have heavy-duty steel frames, and come with anywhere from 3 to 36 polystyrene drawers. These units are designed to stack together and/or hang on the wall. MOP has lighter versions of these that feature carrying handles, and have 9 to 50 drawers. Those who want to take their parts with them can choose from many different polystyrene boxes with hinged lids, the sort sold packed with nuts and bolts in the hardware store. There are also cylindrical containers of all sizes, and transparent boxes for storing shoes and sweaters.

Since MOP is industrially geared, they have all kinds of polystyrene jars and vials, polyethylene and polypropylene scoops, mixing spoons, tongs and

Crystal Goblet from Baccarat

spatulas, measuring cups, funnels, bottles, and jugs for lab use. There is also a good selection of trays perfectly suited for darkroom use. Most of the jars, bottles, boxes, and other containers could serve a multitude of purposes within the home, such as storage of spices, buttons, vitamins, hardware, puzzles and games, construction sets, cosmetics, jewelry, etc. While the prices on the plastics are low, the heavy-duty modular storage units aren't as cheap. But they are good solutions to all kinds of parts control problems.

METROPOLITAN TELETRONICS CORP.

134 West 18th St.
New York, NY 10011
(212) 594-4030
Catalog: $2.00
Minimum Order: $10.00
Accepts: check, MO

Now that it's legal to own your own phone, telephone and equipment boutiques have begun springing up all over the city, giving Ma Bell's "PhoneCenter Stores" some serious competition.

Metropolitan Teletronics, also known as The Telephone Shack, has a full line of rotary-dial and push-button phones, including standard desk and wall models in white, black, brown, beige, gold, and green, as well as gold French boudoir styles, old-fashioned models with separate earpieces, bathroom extensions, and hands-free speaker phones. You can get weatherproof outdoor phones and jacks, boxes that convert your conventional connection box to a modular unit, 4-prong adapters, extension lines, chimes, and headsets. They also have phones with "universal dialing," which are push-button phones that operate on rotary-dial systems. These are now legal, and pay for themselves in less than two years by saving you the extra charges the phone company makes for the push-button (Touch-Tone) system.

In addition to selling telephones and equipment, Metropolitan Teletronics repairs antique phones. Just write with a description of the phone and the disorder, then they'll tell you whether or not to send it.

THE SHOP IN THE NEW YORK BOTANICAL GARDEN

Bronx, NY 10458
(212) 220-8705
Catalog: free
Minimum Order: none
Accepts: check, MO, MC, Visa

When you get through with the lions and tigers and bears (and bats and apes and snakes) at the Bronx Zoo, you can amble over to one of the New York Botanical Gardens, located behind the zoo. There, the acres of blooms will leave you speechless, and if you visit in winter or between seasons, the greenhouse is always lush with its collection of rare flowers.

The Botanical Garden's shop now offers to the general public the same bulbs that produce the spring glories in their gardens. Choose from 77 different dwarf or giant tulips that bloom late or early, with single or double flowers. There are daffodils and narcissus to plant in the fall or force during the cold winter, hyacinths in white, yellow, blue, scarlet, and pink, early-blooming crocuses, alliums, anemones, iris, gladioli, and other flower bulbs. The bulbs run from about $1.25 for a dozen small yellow allium bulbs, to $9.75 a dozen for the spectacular parrot tulips. Members of the Botanical Garden receive a 10% discount on all purchases, and the bulbs are shipped in the fall with planting instructions.

NORSK

114 East 57th Street
New York, NY 10022
(212) 752-3111
Catalog: free
Minimum Order: none
Accepts: check, MO, MC, Visa, AE, DC

Someday, it's said, Danish Modern will see a revival. When it does, Norsk will be ready to furnish the movement.

They have all the teak, walnut, and rosewood pieces you'll be looking for, and at good prices. A streamlined teak 3-drawer chest is $229.00, a spare gateleg table in walnut is $259.00, and an 11-foot wall in it is $899.00. They carry the Stressless Chair from Norway, upholstered in leather for $409.00 (ottoman, $139.00), bookcases, desks, dining sets, tubular steel and canvas chairs, chrome and glass occasional and cocktail tables, plain sofas in Haitian cotton, and more. The furniture is simple, functional, and unobtrusive, and so are the prices.

PINTCHIK
478 Bergen St.
Brooklyn, NY 11217
(212) 783-3333
Catalog: free
Minimum Order: none
Accepts: check, MO, MC, Visa

They supplied the paint for the recent recoating of the Manhattan Bridge, and are responsible for the stripes running down the center of part of the Connecticut Turnpike. Pintchik is the place New Yorkers and their neighbors go to get paint, whether they're doing a bathroom or a bridge. Nathan Pintchik began the firm seventy-one years ago, and it is now in its third generation, being run by Nathan's grandson, the handsome and charming Michael Pintchik.

Pintchik sells nothing at list price. They do such a huge volume that they can offer discounts of 20% to 40% as a matter of course. This is the place that most of New York comes when it's time for painting, wallpapering, new blinds, and floor treatments. They sell paint by Benjamin Moore, Pittsburgh, Pratt & Lambert, Red Devil, Luminall, and Imperial Finishes (their own line; Michael likens the quality of this paint to Benjamin Moore Regal Wall Satin, and uses the shade "Linen White" in his own home). Color chips for all the paints are available upon request. Pintchik has Minwax finishes and varnishes, Flecto Varathane, Rustoleum, Klanks epoxy finishes, DAP and USG caulks, glazes and paints, and the superior Emalj Swedish finishes.

Those who don't paint can wallpaper. Pintchik has over 2,000 patterns in stock and can provide virtually any paper made in or imported into this country if you supply the pattern name and number. A sample or the brands they sell includes Schumacher, Imperial (their own line), Katzenbach & Warren, Mary McFadden, Marimekko, Laura Ashley, Diane Von Furstenburg, Walltex, General, and Venilla. Institutions can send for samples and special prices, and Pintchik will even custom-print patterns, logos, and colors to order with a minimum order of 6 rolls.

Floors aren't neglected at Pintchik, where you can buy carpeting and linoleum in tile and roll form made by firms like Bigelow, Armstrong, Kentile, Amtico, Lee's Kane, World, and Empire. You can even buy the floor itself—Hartco oak flooring in convenient tile form. Window problems? Levolor solves all with their Levolor blinds (40% off here) and Louverdrape vertical draperies. They come in over 200 colors, aluminum, vinyl, mirror, macrame, and fabric finishes. If this isn't enough, you can have the Louverdrapes laminated with your choice of paper or fabric.

In addition to all of this, Pintchik also sells Swivolier lighting fixtures, shelving hardware, soft bathroom seats, drapery fixtures, imitation brick facing, DC Fix Swedish self-adhesive vinyls, and much more. The catalog can't possibly list everything, so if you want an item you don't see they urge you to write or call for a price quote. They do their best to help solve every kind of paint problem. They are working on a brownstone paint for the New York Landmarks commission at the moment. As Michael Pintchik puts it, "No request is too strange."

PLEXI-CRAFT QUALITY PRODUCTS CORP.
514 West 24th St.
New York, NY 10011
(212) 924-3244
Catalog: $2.00
Minimum Order: none
Accepts: check, MO

You can pay hundreds of dollars for Lucite furniture through decorators and in posh furniture stores. Or you can go to the source, Plexi-Craft Quality Products, and buy it wholesale. Here you will find tables, chairs, pedestals, planter display units, cubes, telephone caddies, magazine racks, étagères, desk accessories, bathroom fixtures, and even a Lucite footlocker trunk and backgammon board. Everything comes in clear Lucite, and some items are also available in smoke and tortoise shell. To ensure that your acrylic plastic objects are still gleaming when the oil reserves are gone and plastics are precious, clean them only with Plexi-Kleen and Plexi-Polish, both sold here. (Window cleaner and ammonia will eventually cloud the surface of the material.)In the unlikely event that they don't have what you want, tell them—they can probably make it for you.

D. PORTHAULT, INC.

57 East 57th St.
New York, NY 10022
(212) 688-1660
Catalog: $2.50
Minimum Order: none
Accepts: check, MO, MC, Visa, AE

A bed should not simply be clothed, it also should be decorated—with scattered posies, with lavish embroidery, with conservative geometrics—and above all, it should be a pleasure next to the skin. Such could be the philosophy of D. Porthault, linen purveyors to the titled and the merely wealthy. This French firm specializes in the pure cotton sheet with scalloped hem that is sprigged with mistletoe or blooms with wildflowers and tulips, violets, and daisies, and is very, very costly. A set of typically Porthault sheets, in white with a ribbon and bowknot pattern, is $915.00 in queen size, with pillowcase. A pair of utterly white cotton voile queen-size sheets, with cases, is $530.00. The most popular Porthault sheet patterns are commonly adapted to lines of accessories, accounting for toast warmers, teapot covers, coffee pots, egg cups, creamers, sugar bowls, cups, and saucers, and even vases appearing in patterns of lavender hearts, for example. The sheet patterns also lend themselves nicely to luncheon and tea tablecloths, but when a formal dinner is to be served, don't spare the linen. There are enough cloths, mats, and napkins here that are simply appliquéd and embroidered (often in gold) in geometrics and scroll designs to alleviate the irritation produced by all those busy floral patterns. A truly grand cloth, of white cotton voile embroidered in white and gold, 6' by 12' long, costs $1,850.00, including napkins. Prices run up to $5,500.00 for another cloth that is appliquéd as well as embroidered, and of course, the sky is the limit should you choose to have anything custom-made.

Not everything is Rothschilds-priced. For a mere $8.00, you can own a bath mitt with the Porthault bowknot pattern. Its status value is negligible if kept in the bath, as no one sees it, but you *could* use it to wash the car and impress your neighbors (providing they recognize the pattern, of course). Seriously, Porthault has an extensive line of handsome bathrobes, matching mats and towels, and even wildly patterned beach towels. Porthault designs are seen at their best on the delicate negligees and matching nightgowns, which are tucked, flounced, and lace-trimmed just enough to be sweetly feminine.

Porthault's New York City store is managed by Mr. Albert Aferiat, whose charming presence and attentiveness can dissolve all but the strongest price resistance, which is why shopping Porthault via the catalog is so much safer. You won't, however, see the laminated fabric eyeglass cases, picture frames, tissue boxes, address books, and even wallpaper, all in the Porthault patterns. Perhaps it's just as well.

THE POTTERY BARN

231 10th Ave.
New York, NY 10011
(212) 741-9122
Brochures: free, 4 times a year
Minimum Order: none
Accepts: check, MO, MC, Visa, AE

Thirty years ago an enterprising family drove down to a local china factory, loaded up on china seconds, and brought them back to sell to neighbors from their garage. Business was great and they soon outgrew the garage, which is when The Pottery Barn was born.

The Barn still sells seconds, but its focus now is clean, modern design in housewares at affordable prices. The Barn introduced the Colorful French Connection extension cord, white wire shelving, and grid systems, and popular French jelly glasses to New York, where they became instant best sellers. When hi-tech was in, they had not only the book on it but also civilized adaptations of the look for home use: white-enameled folding chairs, clean chrome-and-white waste receptacles, 18-gallon polystyrene garbage pails in red, blue, yellow, and white, moving pads in all sorts of colors, and industrial shelving in sparkling white rather than the typical dead gray.

The bulk of their business is done in glassware. There are delicate pousse glasses, big cheap bubble glasses from Poland, beer mugs, all sorts of different drink glasses, vases, glass baking pans, glass ashtrays, and much more. The Pottery Barn is also known for its heavy, simple glazed earthenware crockery and sleek eating utensils, kitchen gadgets, strainers, teapots, welcome mats, roll-up tatamis, baskets, Heller plastics, and special things like herbs from Provence, imported cooking oils, blank books from China, and quaint grass brooms from the Philippines.

The Pottery Barn is committed to reasonable prices and quality standards, and will discontinue items when the value declines or the devalued dollar forces their costs up. Which means: If you like it, stock up on it, as it may not be there when you go again. Both mail-order and store customers wait for the famous Barn sales featured in brochures in *New York* magazine, which are also sent to those on the mailing list. Sometimes it's "Good Stuff," things you want and need, "Glass," "Frames," or "Before Christmas," the time when you need a sale most. Real bargains on seconds, close-outs, and specials are always available at the warehouse store on 10th Avenue, which makes it worth a detour on any housewares shopping trip.

ROBIN IMPORTERS

510 Madison Ave.
New York, NY 10022
(212) 753-6475
Information: price quote by letter
Minimum Order: none
Accepts: check, MO, MC, Visa, AE, DC

Robin Importers may be the undoing of Madison Avenue, selling fine kitchen tools and housewares at discounts of up to 50%. We found knives by Henckels, Wustoff, Oxford Hall, Sabatier, and Marks on a recent shopping trip. They have Mellior coffeemakers, tea kettles of every description, and all sorts of gift items. They also carry stainless flatware by Lauffer, Frasier, Lunt, Dansk, Supreme, Stanley Roberts, Georgian House, Towle, and Reed & Barton, as well as china by Denby, Mikasa, Thomas, Arabia, Block, Arzberg, and Fitz & Floyd. Set your table on the "Carefree" table linens, in Dacron/cotton blends, all sizes, available in 16 colors. Write to Robin with specific information (style number, color, pattern, name, etc.) of what you're looking for, include a stamped, self-addressed

envelope, and they'll send you a price quote.

ROGERS & ROSENTHAL, INC.

105 Canal St.
New York, NY 10013
(212) 925-7557, 7558
Price List: SASE; also price quote by phone
Minimum Order: inquire
Accepts: check, MO

Rogers & Rosenthal has beautiful things like china, stemware, silver, and pewter at beautiful prices—sometimes up to 65% off list. They carry all the top manufacturers, including Wallace, Gorham, Lunt, Towle, Reed & Barton, International, and many more. In addition to table settings, they also stock giftware from the same firms. Send a stamped, self-addressed envelope for the current price list, and if you don't see what you want, give them a call because they probably have it in stock or can order it for you.

JAMES ROY, INC.

15 East 32nd St.
New York, NY 10016
(212) 677-2565
Brands Flyer: SASE
Minimum Order: none
Accepts: check, MO, MC, Visa (charges on deposits only)

New York furniture design is just getting over an attack of high-tech, but at James Roy you'd never know it. Their showroom is filled with beautiful, comfortable, traditional furniture and accessories made by manufacturers who don't think "upholstery" is a dirty word: Heritage, Broyhill, Pennsylvania House, Lane, Thayer Coggin, Sealy, Henredon, Stiffel, Simmons, and Drexel, to name a few of the 66 firms they carry (send a stamped, self-addressed envelope for the complete list). Everything sold here is one third or more off manufacturers' suggested retail prices. Since James Roy doesn't have a catalog, you must obtain the style, model, or stock number and color of the piece you want, and write or call them for a price quote. Furniture is shipped from manufacturers' warehouses, not directly from New York City. Take note that charge cards are honored only on *deposits*. All final payments must be made by check or money order.

RUBIN & GREEN, INC.

290 Grand St.
New York, NY 10002
(212) 226-0313, 0314, 5015
Information: SASE
Minimum Order: $5.00
Accepts: check, MO

There are New York City matrons who buy their handbags from Hermes, their furs from Fendi, and their cold cuts from Fay and Allen's, but when it comes to sheets, towels, and bedding they brave the Lower East side to search out sources like Rubin & Green.

It's not really strange when you consider that the bed and bath collections of Calvin Klein, Mary McFadden, Bill Blass, Christian Dior, and Marimekko are represented here. The mills include Martex, Dan River, Springmaid, and Wamsutta. They carry shower curtains by Bloomcraft, bath carpeting by Carter Bros., Dakota Handicrafts and Bates bedspreads, towels by Avanti and Faribo blankets. They have a custom-order department and do a brisk trade in bedspreads, dust ruffles, pillow shams, bed ensembles, and draperies made to order. They even *make* down pillows and comforters!

One of the features of Rubin & Green is their emphasis on natural materials. They carry the 200-thread Wamsutta Supercale all-cotton sheets in every size, gorgeous 100% wool blankets, down comforters, and the complete line of 100% cotton towels by Martex, in 3 grades of lush. Recently sighted among the sheet samples in their busy store was the exquisite Bassetti collection of dacron cotton-blend linens.

Rubin & Green sell only first-quality goods at a substantial discount on list prices, and manage to be polite and attentive to everyone. You won't suffer for your savings here.

J. SCHACHTER

115 Allen St.
New York, NY 10002
(212) 533-1150
Catalog: $1.00
Minimum Order: none
Accepts: check, MO, MC, Visa

Whether you call it a quilt, comforter, eiderdown, or duvet, if you live in New York City chances are you've called Schachter's when you needed one.

Schachter's can make quilts to order stuffed with down, eiderdown, feathers, synthetic material (Dacron), or lambswool, stitched in 1 of 14 designs, using your fabric or theirs. They also restyle, recover, and sterilize comforters (sterilization takes from 2 to 5 weeks). Another Schachter specialty is pillows. They have them ready-made or can stuff them with feathers or down in the density you desire, in a creamy white ticking that doesn't read "Bloomingdale's" or "firm." Old pillows can be recovered, too. Their other customer services include pillow shams and dust ruffles to order and monogramming.

Schachter's also sells bed linens, towels, shower curtains, and mats by Burlington Mills, J. P. Stevens/Utica, West Point Pepperill, Cannon, Wamsutta, and Spring Mills. They carry all-cotton sheets and wool blankets in addition to the blends and synthetics commonly available. A catalog of services and prices is available, and price quotes on the dry goods are given by phone or letter when you provide the pattern or stock number and brand of the goods you need.

JOHN SCHEEPERS, INC.

63 Wall St.
New York, NY 10005
(212) 422-1177, 2299
Catalog: free
Minimum Order: as listed
Accepts: check, MO

It seems incongruous that flower bulb specialists are located amid the concrete of the financial district, but when Scheepers was founded over seventy years ago, Lower Manhattan was the center of all trading, not just shares and stocks.

Assuming the carriage trade had gardens behind their townhouses and mansions, Scheeper most likely supplied the bulbs for fall plantings, and live plants in the summer. (They still leave a blank on the order sheet for the name of your superintendent or gardener.) Their bulbs are the classics of proper gardens, with emphasis on gladioli and dahlias in the spring, and chrysanthemums in the summer and fall. There are almost 20 pages in the current spring catalog on gladioli alone. Scheepers has them in every possible color and tint, from the pure white of Cascade, to the deep violet of Blue Isle, with all shades of pink, yellow, peach, mauve, orange, and green in between. Some of the exhibition bulbs grow to 7' tall, but for smaller gardens as well as good cuttings, Scheepers offers miniature glads. The orchidlike Montbretias are cited as the ideal companions to gladioli, but dahlias could be considered as complements. Scheepers has lovely open-faced anemone dahlias, the daisylike New Holland collarette types, glovelike pompom dahlias, and both large and miniature traditional varieties.

Scheepers carries tuberous begonias with blossoms that resemble carnations and roses, lilies of the valley from Germany that grow dense with bells and heady with the sweet fragrance, irises in the usual white, yellow, and violet varieties and sky-blue, blush-pink, mahogany, and ruby-red types, tuberoses, plantain lilies, calla lilies, ground cover of all kinds, ferns, bleeding hearts, garden lilies, and wildflowers like columbine and jack-in-the-pulpit. In the summer, Scheepers' chrysanthemums are available as pot plants. The varieties include the big football type with blooms 5" to 7" across, daisy-faced mums, cutting varieties, fine cushion mums, and harvest giants, which flower in September and October.

The bulbs and plants run from $2.90 for 10 to $6.00 each, and prices drop with quantity purchases. Coax the most from your plants with Scheepers' own bulb food, which is virtually all organic. A 5-pound bag, good for about 250 bulbs, is $4.50. Since New York City is not noted for its rich soil, Scheepers also sells "Native Wood Soil" at $10.00 per 50-pound bag, shipping extra. The catalogs available throughout the year include the spring and fall catalogs, the forcing catalog, and specials on mums and irises.

THEEMA
10 Christopher St.
New York, NY 10014
(212) 242-8693
Information: SASE
Minmum Order: none
Accepts: check, MO, MC, Visa

Rick Barberio does voice-overs on ads when he's not running Theema, a home-furnishings store on Christopher Street.

He is thoroughly unsentimental about the business and home design in general, telling us in two breaths that his typical customer is a person between 25 and 35 with more taste than income who is newly married or just moving, and that hi-tech was the brainchild of self-serving designers who profited handsomely from the fad.

The furniture and accessories at Theema reflect Barberio's no-nonsense attitude. Everything is sleek and simple, yet comfortable. The Theema be is the best example. It is made of oak that is finished with oil and wax and hand-rubbed, or in a black or white formica-type finish. This bed combines the clean design of a platform on a recessed base with the warmth of a good hardwood. The platforms are sold on plain and storage drawer bases, and can be bought with a simple headboard or headboard/end-table combination, in full, queen, and king mattress sizes. These beds are beautifully built, reasonably priced, and covered by a 3-year warranty. Free delivery and installation are available in the 5 boroughs of New York City, and are arranged at customers' cost FOB New York City for points elsewhere. (Boston area residents can get Theema beds at the Hooper-Ames furniture stores there and save the trucking charges.)

Theema carries all sorts of other furnishings and accessories, only beds are sold by mail.

THOME SILVERSMITHS
328 East 59th St.
New York, NY 10022
(212) 758-0655
Information: see text
Minimum Order: none
Accepts: check, MO

The best way to judge a business that offers a service is by its clientele, and Thome's customers include the Plaza Hotel and the Metropolitan Museum of Art. Thome cleans, repairs, and replates antique and contemporary silver pieces for them, and will do it for you. They can repair and replate gold articles, clean and repair pewter, polish copper and brass, lacquer and refine different metals, put new handles of ivory and ebony on metal objects, cast feet, and replace parts. Thome also buys and sells silver objects and flatware, and can match patterns.

This firm has been in business since 1931 and is considered the best by those who can't afford less. Jean Ralph, who runs Thome with her husband, asks that you send objects in need of repair directly to Thome, insured, with a description of the work you need done. She will send you a receipt for the article and an estimate for the work. She'll wait for your verification before doing the job, and simply return the item if you decide against having it done. If you're trying to match a flatware pattern or want to sell silver, write first with complete details and rubbings, pattern names, or photos.

GARRETT WADE CO.

161 Ave. of the Americas
New York, NY 10013
(212) 695-3360
Hand Tool Catalog: $1.00
Swiss INCA Machinery Catalog: $1.00
Minimum Order: none
Accepts: check, MO, MC, Visa AE

If a fine tool inspires its craft, Garrett Wade could perpetuate woodworking single-handedly. Their catalog is 132 color pages of exquisite woodworking tools and equipment, photographed beautifully and supplemented with discussions of the relative merits of different kinds of tools, their construction, care, and use. For instance, the Pax saws from Sheffield are perfect for general use, but when you are cutting dovetails, veneer, flooring, plywood, joints and tenons, logs, or slots, you should use a tool suited to the job. Specialized saws for all of these functions are available at Garrett Wade, in addition to bow saws, fret saws, and the fine Cowells jigsaw and piercing saw. Those who want an excellent hand-held power saber/jigsaw need look no further than the Swiss-made Bosch tools, sold here in three models ($149.00 to $226.00).

After the wood is cut, smoothing the surface can be accomplished with any of scores of planes, ranging from the Record Multiplane that has 24 *standard* cutters for all types of work ($259.00) to the tiny 1-inch finger plane originally designed for violinmakers, now used in cabinetry and modelmaking ($33.50).

Finer woodworking and carving are accomplished with chisels, knives, and gouges, represented here in every possible shape and size, specialized and plain drill bits, and files, rasps, and rifflers. The best efforts can go awry if your workshop doesn't have the proper clamp for the job. Garrett Wade has clamps and vises for the lightest jobs and those requiring tons of pressure. And if you treat your tools with care, they'll repay you with indefinite good service. You don't hang these tools on pegboards—you place them in the magnificent, felt-lined walnut craftsman's toolchests ($190.00 and $245.00). Keep a pry bar ($4.75) in the shop and avoid the temptation of using a screwdriver or other tool and ruining the blade. Line your toolbox with "rust preventative paper" to prevent oxides from forming on steel tools, and keep your shop clean with the horsehair bench brush ($10.60). Of course, a dull tool thwarts all attempts at fine work, and Garrett Wade has a complete selection of natural and synthetic benchstones, slipstones, and strops, plus the necessary honing oil (unless you're using the Japanese stones, which are lubricated with water). Use your tools on a good workbench. Garrett Wade has, simply, the finest we've ever seen, from just over $200.00 to just under $1,000.00.

Not everyone has occasion, or skill, to use many of these tools, but everyone can measure. Once you've seen Garrett Wade's 6-inch stainless folding ruler, calibrated in 64ths and fitted with two Sheffield knife blades, you'll wonder how you ever did without it. Our favorite is the Splendid Folding 36" Boxwood Rule, with a built-in protractor of brass and a spirit level, which costs $20.50. You may be inspired to collect the squares, made of steel, brass, and rosewood.

The tools are a pleasure to the eye and hand, and Garrett Wade is so assured of their superior performance that they offer a money-back guarantee on any purchase, within 14 days. The firm also carries the excellent Swiss INJECTA INCA stationary woodworking saws and joiner planers, which are cataloged separately.

SHERLE WAGNER

60 East 57th St.
New York, NY 10022
(212) 758-3300
Catalog: $5.00
Minimum Order: none
Accepts: check, MO

There are as many ways of disposing of

money as making it in New York City. Sherle Wagner makes it possible to sink tens of thousands of dollars into home decor and never leave the bathroom.

Sherle Wagner has supplied people like Frank Sinatra and Princess Grace with opulent bathroom fittings that are the stuff of fantasy. Consider their shell pedestal washbasin in pink onyx with rose quartz and gold faucet and taps, the rose aurora carved marble toilet and bidet casings, and the marble tub facing. At $19,784.00 you may want to reconsider. Add the cost of rose quartz wall tiles (6" squares at $117.00 each), coordinated gold towel racks, bars, soap dishes, paper holders, towel rings, lighting fixtures, knobs and door handles, switchplates, hinges, and mirrors, and you have enough for the down payment on a respectable home.

Sherle Wagner does have a few inexpensive items, such as the 8"-by-8" tiles, in white, at $7.00 each. Its reputation rests, however, on things like their platinum and gold tiles, which are priced at the time of shipment only. The predominating style at Sherle Wagner is High Ornate, with just a few modern tap and faucet designs punctuating the pages of gold, crystal, lapis lazuli, onyx, amethyst, malachite, and tigereye sets, many adorned with swans, cherubs, dolphins, and shells. If you can appreciate these things and towel bars, switchplates, soap dishes, tumblers, tiles, and wallpapers all designed to match the handpainted interior of your washbowl, you'll love Sherle Wagner.

THE WORKBENCH
1320 Third Ave.
New York, NY 10022
(212) 753-1173
Catalog: $2.00
Minimum Order: none
Accepts: check, MO, MC, Visa

Workbench furniture is a combination of simple design, function, good materials, and excellent construction—at reasonable prices. What it lacks in knockout style it makes up for in comfort and practicality. This is the kind of furniture that appeals to indecisive Early Marrieds or Young Professionals hedging their bets.

The Workbench sells sofas, love seats, sectional furniture, convertibles, and easy chairs in three lines: stock upholstery, knockdown construction, and custom upholstery. All are variations on the Tuxedo design. The stock upholstery is Haitian cotton, corduroy, velvet, and a tweed blend. The knockdown furniture is identical in appearance, comes in tweed upholstery (other fabrics are available on special order), and can be bought with butcher-block arms. It assembles without tools. In the custom upholstery department, the same Tuxedo style is offered with options on length, height, depth, seat firmness, arm style, and fabric. The sectional sofas come in several different styles, 2 of which have sections that open to form beds. Prices run from $150.00 for a sectional ottoman in cocoa cotton velvet to $1,645.00 for a 74" custom sleep sofa.

You can assemble a wall unit/storage system from the white-lacquered Swedish sections that come in separate drawer, shelf, cupboard, and bookcase units. There are other sectional units in teak and elm veneers, classic Danish bookcases, an open oak and glass étagère, and a simple country hutch in pine veneer. There are also "music benches," low units designed for housing stereo components and records efficiently, in a choice of finishes. The all-purpose painted polystyrene Palaset cubes from Finland are also shown, grouped to form wall units and the base of a kitchen work island.

For the dining room there are butcher-block tables on beech or chrome bases, an array of simple dining tables in maple, and oak, and veneers of pine, teak, and walnut, dining chairs that range from Breuer copies in cane and chrome to white molded polypropylene seats by Joe Columbo, and stools. They have the Kennedy rocker, airy Italian summer furniture in steel wire coated with PVC, lovely occasional tables in wood, laminate, chrome, and glass at $60.00 to $290.00, sleek bedroom storage systems of oak and walnut veneers or lacquer, platform beds, simple juvenile furniture, desks and posture chairs, and a line of Kartell plastic accessories.

The catalog is updated periodically with price lists, and includes specific measurement information for every piece of furniture, and complete descriptions of the construction of the upholstered furniture. Delivery is free with orders over $400.00 within the store area. Order from the Workbench closest to you—there are stores in New Jersey, Connecticut, Pennsylvania, and Massachusetts.

WORLD ABRASIVES CO., INC.

1866 Eastern Parkway
Brooklyn, NY 11233
(212) 495-4300
Catalog: SASE
Minimum Order: varies
Accepts: check, MO

World Abrasives is in the gritty business of sandpaper and grinding discs. They sell cloth sanding belts for wood, metal, plaster, rubber, and plastic, waterproof belts for ceramics and wet glass, sanding discs, sheets of sanding paper, rolls, and grinding discs. They buy the sandpaper in huge rolls and convert it to the finished product, and are consequently able to offer custom abrasives at decent prices if you need them. Belts are sold in lots of 10, sanding discs in lots of 10 and 25, sheets in packs of 25, and the grinding discs and rolls of sanding paper individually. You can get a belt that sells in a hardware store for $1.89, for 89¢ to $1.29 here, depending on the grit. They also have lawn mower sharpeners, oil stones, and related products. World Abrasives can help you with any of your sanding problems and offers good advice.

ZIP-JACK

P.O Box 352, East Station
678 Central Park Ave.
Yonkers, NY 10704
(212) 299-0288 or
(914) 423-5000
Brochure: SASE
Minimum Order: none
Accepts: check, MO

Envied are those with terraced penthouses, for they shall be cool when it's hot. The gentle breezes that barely ruffle the feathers of the madding crowd below become buffeting winds far above, an advantage that does have its drawbacks. The gusts can not only knock over plants and chairs, but also they'll eventually rip up the coverings on the garden umbrellas that shade the tables used on the terraces. That's when Zip-Jack is called in.

Zip-Jack will launder, refringe, recover, and repair those big umbrellas used on terraces, patios, at the beach, and outside cafés. They handle conventional, pagoda, and 2-tier shapes, with 8 or 12 ribs. They make vital mechanical repairs, including new lifting cords and mechanisms. Their complete recovering is done in vinyl-laminated nylon in solid colors or, for an additional cost, cotton duck, cotton/poly, or decorator fabric. Refurbishing and servicing an umbrella isn't cheap, but it's far more economical than buying a new one.

That alternative is also offered at Zip-Jack. They sell café umbrellas advertising Smirnoff, Perrier, Bolla, Salada, Campari, Fiorello's, and Cinzano. These are made in vinyl-triple-laminated nylon, or can be custom-made in cotton duck, mesh PVC, "Sun Fade Proof" woven acrylon, or your own fabric. Stock umbrellas are $55.75 each. There are also golf and rain umbrellas with 40" to 53" diameters, from $14.00 to $25.00. Our favorites are the large designer umbrellas, made of oak and unbleached canvas or other fabrics. The striking square umbrella, 6' across, is $280.00. The 8-sided umbrella, 9' across, is $350.00. There are sliding discounts of up to 50% on all the umbrellas, depending upon the quantity purchased.

If you need repair services, you may have wondered how you'd get your umbrella to Zip-Jack. They provide details on how to get prelabled shipping bags from UPS, or to have them pick up the umbrella at your home (there are charges for these services). Send a stamped, self-addressed envelope to Zip-Jack for the brochure and current rates.

SEE ALSO: Appliances, Audio, TV/Video
Art, Antiques, Restoration Services
Auto, Marine
Clothing, Furs, Accessories
Department Stores
Food, Drink
Office Supplies
Unusual, Rare

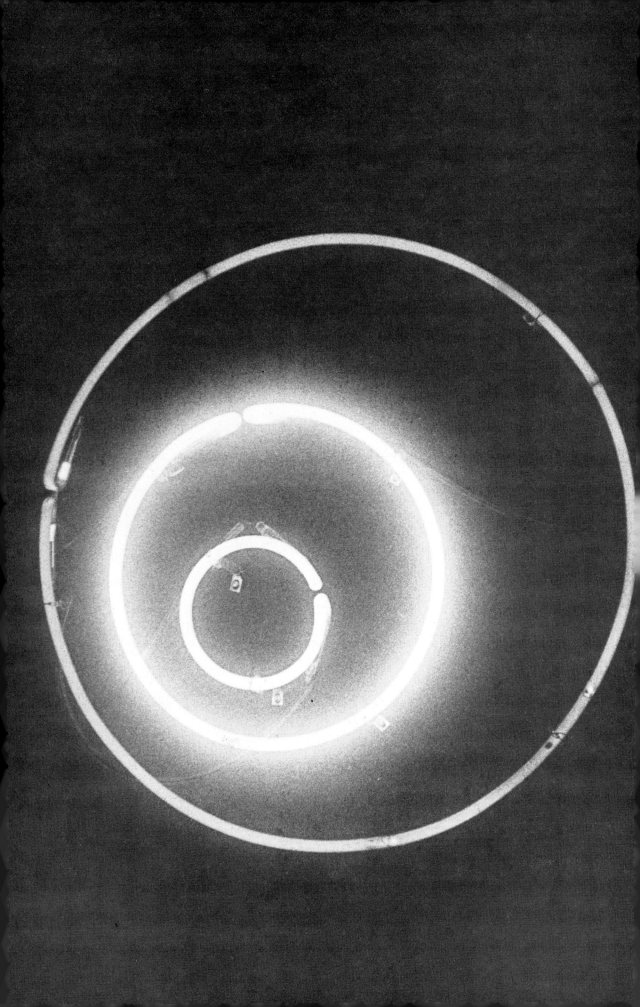

13 | Jewelry
Gems
Watches

After hearing Rennie Ellen's lecture (see listing) on various practices in the diamond and jewelry trades, we decided to list in this section only sources with a solid reputation for integrity and honesty. That's why the chapter is a little on the thin side. In this area of merchandise, the warning *caveat emptor* could not be more appropriate. A tip: When New Yorkers want to buy, and they don't want to mess around, they go to Tiffany's.

CARTIER

609 Fifth Ave.
New York, NY 10022
(212) 753-0111
Catalog: $5.00
Minimum Order: none
Accepts: check, MO, MC, Visa, AE, DC

"Understated ostentation" seems a contradiction in terms, until you've been to Cartier. Goods may be kept under glass, and salespeople might sit behind antique desks, but the store is relaxed and short on pretension.

Cartier was founded in 1847, but its most seminal designs in jewelry and bibelots emerged in the 1920s and 1930s, under the auspices of Louis Cartier. The "Jeweled Clocks," made of jade, coral, citrine, rock crystal, black onyx, gold, and vermeil date from this period. They are magnificent: The dial of the Citrine Mystery Clock is 1,800 carats of citrine, under which the diamond-studded hands seem to float. The pedestal is of rock crystal, the base decorated with mother-of-pearl, and the numerals marked in diamonds. The price is an enigma, but not that of the platinum panther brooch, studded with pavé diamonds, onyx, and set with emerald eyes. The brooch is $57,000.00, and takes a year of work to complete.

At the other end of the spectrum is the "Three Gold" collection of rings, necklaces, earrings, and bracelets, made of bands of white, yellow, and rose gold. Anything but baroque, their contemporary design belies the fact that they were created in 1925. The "rolling ring" of three interlocking bands, a popular "status" wedding band, is $260.00. Those who want to formalize the feeling can give the object of their affections the "Love Bracelet," a heavy gold band decorated with screw heads. The bracelet comes complete with a screwdriver, and is fastened on the arm of the beloved. While not as effective as a chastity belt, it does express territorial prerogatives.

Jewelry represents but one facet of Cartier. Their semiprecious evening bags of silk lamé brocade, velvet, and calfskin, with clasps of pearls, zircons, onyx, and gold are exquisite, and begin at $320.00. Their "Gift Salon" offers everything from frosted crystal tennis balls to one-of-a-kind English and Chinese antiques. They also have silver flatware by Christofle,

Old Newbury Crafters, and other firms, in addition to their own crystal tableware and giftware, Bilston and Battesea boxes (including one that features Snoopy), Limoges porcelain, gold and sterling picture frames, and some spectacular vases, boxes, and bowls of curving, ribbed sterling.

Cartier is best known to the general public for "Les Must de Cartier," a boutique that has branches in several department stores across the country. "Les Must" burgundy leather goods, with the interlocking "CC" initials, are the least vulgar and best-made status accessories we've seen yet. The pens and lighters in this collection are adorned simply with the "rolling ring" motif, and look rich without being flashy. But the Cartier talent for achieving elegance without excess reaches its zenith in the "Tank" watch, whose rectangular face, Roman numerals, and 18K gold casing induced enough people to part with $2,600.00 to give it the reputation of a classic.

Needless to say, "Les Must" are necessities only to those who believe that living well is the best revenge, and are able to afford to retaliate in style. Those who can may also be interested in knowing that Cartier does engraving (including family crests on blazer buttons), custom engraved stationery, repairs jewelry and timepieces, restyles and designs jewelry, and will provide discreet personal shopping services with pleasure.

DIAMONDS BY RENNIE ELLEN

15 West 47 St., Room 401
New York, NY 10036
(212) 246-3930
Catalog: $1.00
Minimum Order: none
Accepts: check, MO

There are hundreds of dealers in the diamond district, but there's only one we know and trust, and that's Rennie Ellen.

Rennie is a tiny dynamo of a woman who learned how to cut and manufacture diamonds after retiring as a dancer, and embarked upon her second career: diamond dealer. She was the first female dealer to set up shop on 47th Street, and has met with resistance from other dealers all the way down the line. After over fifteen years in the business, the Diamond Dealer's Club, a very male enclave, has finally extended membership to a few women.

We suspect that the issue is more than sex discrimination. Rennie Ellen is not only female, she's also scrupulously ethical. Known as the "Mayor of 47th Street," she's constantly monitoring the block and bringing the shills to the attention of the police. Any person walking down 47th Street alone can be literally propelled into a store by one of these "solicitors." Walk down the street with Rennie Ellen, and the only signs of corruption you'll see are the blue lights in the shop windows that make yellow or off-color diamonds look colorless, or more valuable.

Of course, Rennie Ellen's business is run with integrity, and since she's a wholesaler, her prices represent savings of 50% to 75% on regular retail prices for gems of the same weight, color, and clarity. Rennie Ellen has a line of engagement rings, bracelets, pins, diamonds-by-the-yard, wedding bands, and diamond watches she sells in her fourth-floor offices (by appointment only) and by mail. She has and cuts diamonds in every shape, size, and quality, priced to suit every budget, and sets them in platinum or gold. Custom orders (monograms and special designs) are accepted. All the work is guaranteed, and refunds, less mountings and labor, are made on anything except custom work within 5 working days.

Rennie Ellen invites you to call person-to-person or write, and she'll discuss your requirements. She's in the process of putting together a catalog that lists her services and the range of jewelry she sells. If you're in the city and are shopping for jewelry, be sure to see Rennie before you buy elsewhere. She'll probably bring out her album thick with cards and letters from young marrieds and other customers, whose appreciation of their diamonds is rivaled by their fondness for Rennie Ellen herself. On the flawed block of 47th Street, Rennie stands out as a real jewel.

Mail Order Tip: Complaints—if you have a complaint about the goods or the firm, the first thing to do is write that company a letter stating the problem and what you would like done about it. Be clear, concise, and civilized.

B. HARRIS & SONS, JEWELERS
25 East 61st St.
New York, NY 10021
(212) 755-6455
Information: inquire, send SASE
Minimum Order: none
Accepts: check, MO

The Harris family has been selling traditional jewelry since 1898. Their antique and contemporary pieces are always in good taste, and they have a charming collection of jewelry for babies and children that ensures the business of godparents, friends, and relatives who want to give a gift to the child that's utterly proper and bound to be appreciated by the parents.

Since even the best jewelry can suffer damage, the Harris family also offers repair services. They can clean, repair, and restore old jewelry, modernize antique jewelry with new settings, recut and repolish stones, and do appraisals. The services don't stop there—B. Harris also repairs and restores antique and modern watches and clocks. Write to them describing what you need done and include a picture if necessary, plus a stamped, self-addressed envelope. They may give you an estimate then or ask to see the piece. They also make offers on your jewelry (costume jewels excepted) and do estate buying.

KANE ENTERPRISES
15 West 47th St., Room 401
New York, NY 10036
(212) 246-3930
Brochure: $1.00
Minimum Order: none
Accepts: check, MO

Rennie Ellen is our choice among the diamond dealers on 47th Street (see "Diamonds by Rennie Ellen"). Even at wholesale prices, though, diamonds are still out of the reach of many people. That's why cubic zirconium is so apealing.

This synthetic material can be cut into a "diamond" that's flawless, colorless, and so similar to the real thing that jewelers have been fooled. Better yet, a cubic zirconium (imitation) "diamond" costs only a fraction of what a diamond of identical size and quality would. Best of all, Rennie Ellen has opened a division within her diamond business called Kane Enterprises, which sells cubic zirconium

Piaget Watch from
M & I Haberman, Inc.

jewelry. She sets the fakes as if they were real gems, in 14-Karat white or yellow gold, with the same guarantees that she offers on diamonds. Write for her brochure.

M & I HABERMAN, INC.
380 Lexington Ave., Suite 521
New York, NY 10168
(212) 697-5270
Catalog: free
Minimum Order: none
Accepts: check, MO, MC, Visa

You can save from 15% to 40% on watches by Seiko, Pulsar, Longines, Wittnauer, Bulova, Accutron, and Borel at Haberman, as well as Cross pens. Just write with a model number for a price quote if you don't find what you want in the catalog. If your watch should conk out, their repair department will come to the rescue at very reasonable rates.

RISSIN JEWELRY CLINIC
4 West 47th Street
New York, NY 10036
(212) 575-1098
Information: see text
Minimum Order: none
Accepts: check, MO

Joe Rissin is that phenomenon known as a one-man operation that "does what they call the impossible." "They" are other jewelry repair shops and craftsmen who turn down work because they lack the ability to conceive of a solution to the problem. These jobs come to the Jewelry Clinic. Mr. Rissin, who does not cloak his talents in modesty, tells us that he can design, sculpt, and carve, and that he possesses great mechanical ability and ingenuity. He was trained in the European manner and comes from a family that seems to have artistry "in the blood": One of his ancestors designed furniture for the Russian Czar. Mr. Rissin is able to look at a jewelry problem that others can't solve and, applying his design training, backtrack mentally from the finished piece through all the stages of construction until he sees where the repair can best be made. This approach apparently works, because Mr. Rissin has his hands full just with the work he does for dealers, jewelers, and museums. Since he's a qualified gemologist, he does appraisals and also designs unique

pieces himself, which have to be seen to be appreciated.

The services of the Rissin Jewelry Clinic are available by mail, and you are invited to send your jewelry, insured, to Mr. Rissin and he will send you an estimate. He can do alterations on jewelry—describe what you want done. If the piece you send is not worth the cost of the repair, or won't look good no matter what he does, Mr. Rissin will tell you. Some of his services—cutting jewelry off people—can't be rendered by mail, but are good to know about if you find yourself in New York City with a jewelry emergency. Joe Rissin's been asked to do everything once, and *nothing* fazes him.

TIFFANY & CO.
727 Fifth Ave.
New York, NY 10022
(212) 755-8000
(212) 759-9110 (orders)
Catalog: $3.00
Minimum Order: none
Accepts: check, MO, MC, Visa, AE, DC, Tiffany's charge

Few stores have generated as many references, associations, and stories as the legendary Tiffany & Co. The firm was founded in 1853 by Charles Lewis Tiffany, who is also responsible for adopting the standards of English silver and establishing the designation "sterling." Mr. Tiffany's store was frequented by the rich and the famous, including Abraham Lincoln, who bought pearls for Mary Todd there. Founding Tiffany & Co. would have been enough to ensure Charles Lewis a place in history, but he went one further and fathered Louis Comfort Tiffany, the famous Art Nouveau designer.

Tiffany & Co. apparently started off well, but while the business was respectable, it wasn't the institution it is today. A man named Walter Hoving changed all that. Hoving had been vice president of Macy's and Montgomery Ward and president of Lord & Taylor and Bonwit Teller before he became chairman of Tiffany & Co. twenty-five years ago. Mr. Hoving's winning combination of merchandising genius, taste, and boundless energy proved the key factors in Tiffany's success. His attention to details, for instance, is exhausting. The famed Tiffany boxes of azure lacquered paper are wrapped without tape and fastened with knotless bows. The crystal cigar ashtrays do *not* have notches ("vulgar," he says). Men can look elsewhere for diamond pinkyrings, and you will never find anything made from Lucite in his store.

Outlawing Scotch tape doesn't guarantee sales of $100 million a year, though. Hoving also had the instinct and foresight to know that the designs of Angela Cummings, Elsa Peretti, Jean Schlumberger, and Paloma Picasso were worth display space before they'd made their names as jewelry artists. He possessed unerring good taste, and such assurance about his choices that he once proclaimed, vis-a-vis Tiffany's: "There's not a thing ugly. Nothing." All this contributes to the feeling that a gift bought at Tiffany's can be given without anxiety, and it's proven by the things themselves.

The current Tiffany & Co. catalog has over 200 pages of jewelry, watches, silver, china, crystal and glass, clocks, pens, bibelots, and stationery. It opens with the elegant designs of Angela Cummings, which include a "spider's web" necklace of 18K gold woven with 291 diamonds, simply faceted gemstones set in diamond bezels and strung on gold chains, a twisting choker of 11 strands of different-sized pearls, and even a silver choker and bracelet executed in softened rectangular pieces. Elsa Peretti, who gave us Halston's cosmetic containers and the much-copied "Diamonds by the Yard," follows. Her diamond-studded gold chain was an instant success, and Tiffany's was hard pressed to keep it in stock. Peretti offers the same jewelry formula this year, using amethysts, chryoprase, moonstones, and sapphires, as well as the diamonds. Her gold sculptured credit-card holder (one card, please) dangles from a black silk cord. Peretti's rock crystal mango pendant could become as popular as her famous asymmetrical hearts and tear-drops, this year offered as earrings and necklaces in coral, gold, and lapis. For the seamstress fantastic, the sewing kit: a case of rock crystal, a green jade needle case shaped like a pea pod, 18K gold needles, and spools of gold and jade.

Mr. Hoving just introduced the jewelry of Paloma Picasso, and the collection is almost sold out. Her heavy necklaces of minerals and semiprecious stones, pavé diamond balls set into gold rings and on snake chains, and chain link chokers of 18K gold are stunning pieces designed for a vibrant, contemporary woman. Jean Schlumberger's jewelry is showcased in the mezzanine, where the pearls, emeralds, sapphires, diamonds, and brilliant enamels cast a light all their own.

The designers' works run from $12.00 for a black metal pen by Elsa Peretti to $52,500.00 for a Schlumberger sapphire. These are small potatoes next to the Tiffany diamonds, which run—in the catalog—up to $1,750,000.00 for a large marquise diamond. (The Tiffany Diamond, a 128-carat dazzler, has its own wall case. Offers of up to $12 million have been refused). Tiffany & Co. has one of the largest diamond band collections in the world—*thousands* of rings set with sapphires, emeralds, rubies, and others made of gold and semiprecious stones.

Those people who can tear themselves away form the baubles on the first floor will find clocks, silver, and bibelots on the second. Every silver object, down to the last heart-shaped picture frame, tape dispenser, pen, and paperclip is made of sterling silver. Inventiveness prevails in this department: Imagine a sterling Shaker box, complete with fastenings, priced at $2,650.00. The Tiffany flatware is superlative, comes in over two dozen patterns, and ranges from the ornate to the modern (request the flatware booklet separately).

The third floor yields hand-painted, richly colored French table settings that are the perfect complement to the silver. Tiffany's carries Limoges reproductions of the blue, yellow, and white porcelain that Claude Monet designed for use in his home in Giverny, as well as other exclusive Limoges patterns in tableware, cachepots, trinket boxes, vases, and service pieces. Prices range from $5.00 for a white and gold dessert plate to $152.00 for a hand-painted "Private Stock" dinner plate. The finishing touch is provided by the proper stemware. Tiffany's offers it all, from cut crystal goblets to The Tiffany All-Purpose Glass, *the* bubble glass, which is also a bargain at just $7.00.

Tiffany's has been known to push the limits of common sense (what exactly does one do with a sterling frying pan?) but can always be relied upon for good taste. Their engraved stationery is unquestionably correct, and one simply couldn't cheat while playing bridge with the Tiffany deck. The store is almost always jammed with tourists, browsers, and customers. This is, after all, the Tiffany's that charmed Holly Golightly in *Breakfast at Tiffany's*. It's the Tiffany's of the faultless blue box, of the now retired Walter Hoving, of affordable extravagance. We can't imagine New York City without it.

We like the understatement of tiny cabochons, found here in stud earrings, rings, bracelets, and necklaces of many types of stones, such as lapis, malachite, opal, jade, amethyst, agate, onyx, moonstone, and tigereye. Prices are reasonable —small rings begin at about $14.00— and the jewelry suits everyone. Not so with Van de Lune's cast "mask" pin and earrings, high-heeled shoe earrings, or grape necklace, but then, half the fun at Van de Lune is the unexpected.

VAN DE LUNE

118 Prince St.
New York, NY 10012
(212) 966-3354
Catalog: $2.50
Minimum Order: none
Accepts: check, MO, MC, Visa, AE

How small is small? If you blink while passing Van de Lune, you'll miss it. The store is the showcase for the jewelry designs of Claude Vande Lune, who rearranged his last name for the business "because it looked better."

In the jewelry business, one develops an eye for detail. Claude developed his over the years, studying with artists and learning the fine points of casting from Italian craftsmen in Rome. Surprisingly, his jewelry is anything but avant-garde. The most popular pieces are in the Wildflower series—violets, irises, gardenias, lilies, poinsettias, forget-me-nots, bud sprays and leaflets, roses—all in plain brass and gold- and silver-plated brass, or colored enamel, which is lovely. Van de Lune uses the lost wax process for casting, which creates fine detail not usually seen in inexpensive jewelry. The necklaces are strung on silk cords, and the bracelets are wire bands set with the flower or leaf. Prices currently run from about $12.00 for earrings in brass to about $45.00 for a vermeil seed pod necklace. All prices are subject to change.

WELLINGTON JEWELS

General Motors Bldg.—Plaza
767 Fifth Ave.
New York, NY 10022
(212) 751-8633
Brochure: free
Minimum Order: none
Accepts: check, MO, MC, Visa, AE

Rich ladies buy fakes so they can leave the good ones in the vault, and poor ladies buy them to look rich. Both have been buying them from Wellington for over fifteen years. Wellington give their fakes beautiful gold or platinum settings, and sometimes adds genuine diamonds, sapphires, rubies, emeralds, opals, and garnets to enhance the deception. They sell classic solitaires with pear, emerald, marquise, round, and oval-shaped "stones" in Tiffany mountings, cluster "cocktail" rings, heart and marquise earrings, drop earrings, studs, a ring set with 3 rows of "diamonds," and a band bracelet studded with 17 "Wellingtons." Prices run from $110.00 for a pair of pierced ear studs, to $675.00 for the bangle bracelet. Rings can be made in sizes up to 20 carats for those who like the Liz Taylor look, and almost anything can be made to order.

Satisfaction is guaranteed, and they give you 15 days to decide whether you'll keep your "jewels" or not. Remember: Only your insurance agent will know for sure.

SEE ALSO: Clothing, Furs, Accessories
Department Stores
Unusual, Rare

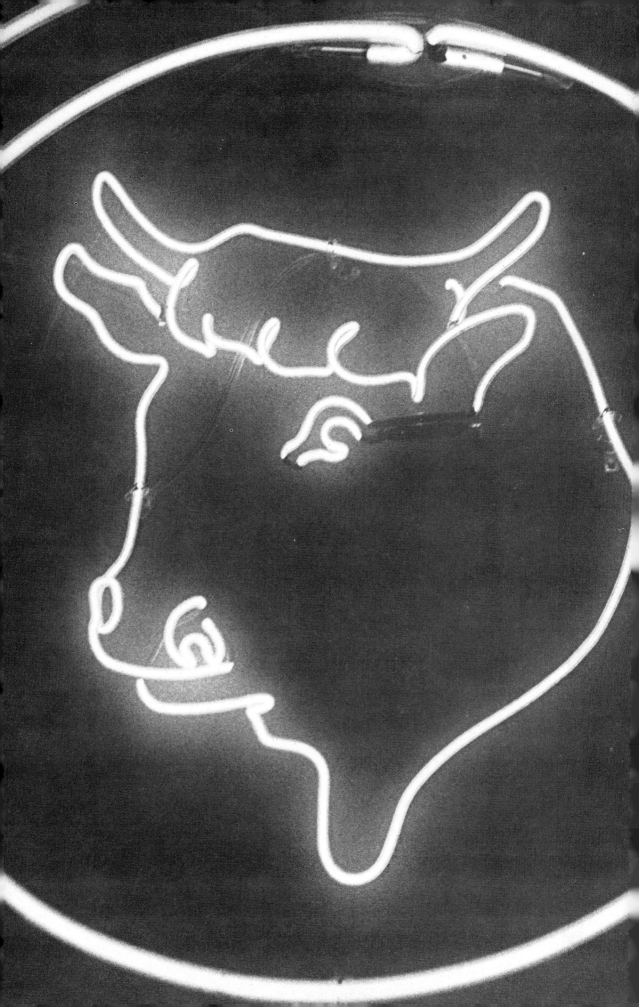

14 | Luggage
Leather Goods

If you spend a little time watching people in New York City, sooner or later you will come to realize that everyone is carrying something. The image of lines of ants, each lugging a crumb, comes to mind. People are carrying books, things they've bought, attaché cases, briefcases, shopping bags, lumber, umbrellas, animals, whatever. It's the rare pedestrian who has nothing in hand. One of our favorite sights is the quintessentially New York image of a svelte young beauty, a fashion model, crossing the avenue with a huge leather art folio, her showcase full of photos.

In this chapter you'll find sources for things in which you can carry your things.

ACE LEATHER PRODUCTS
2211 Avenue U
Brooklyn, NY 11229
(212) 891-9713
Information: price quote
Minimum Order: none
Accepts: check, MO

Ace Leather has been going strong since 1919 selling *every* brand of luggage and leather goods you can think of at prices they guarantee are unbeatable. Call or write for a price quote with the style number and color of the luggage you need. If you have a discount price from another store that you want Ace to better, be sure to mention the store and the price.

A TO Z LUGGAGE CO., INC.
4627 New Utrecht Ave.
Brooklyn, NY 11219
(212) 435-6330
Information: price quote by letter
Minimum Order: none
Accepts: check, MO, MC, Visa

Luggage is sold here as briskly as Big Macs, often because the customers' old luggage has been terminally mauled by the airlines' baggage carriers and they need a "fast suitcase" for an unexpected trip. Whether you're buying your first piece for camp or college, or are a business traveler on your fourth 2-suiter, you can get it much cheaper at A to Z Luggage—at up to 70% off list price. They sell full selections of Lark, Ventura, Hartmann, American Tourister, Amelia Earhart, Samsonite, and other major brands. They accept only written inquiries for price quotes that include model numbers, colors, and sizes of the pieces needed.

BETTINGER'S LUGGAGE SHOP
80 Rivington St.
New York, NY 10002
(212) 674-9411
Information: price quote by letter, with SASE
Minimum Order: none
Accepts: check, MO, MC, Visa, AE

The Bettingers have been running their luggage shop for about seventy years, selling top brands at incredible (read 30% to 50%) discounts. They have lines by Christian Dior, Ventura, Wings, Fulton of France, American Tourister, Samsonite,

Lark, and other manufacturers too numerous to mention. Ray Bettinger seems to be able to put her hands on any piece of luggage or one of the 200 different kinds of attaché cases, instrument cases, and camp trunks at a moment's notice, an incredible feat in this tiny store that's a no-contest winner of the Chaos of the Year Award. Bettinger's has appeared in shopping guides and TV specials on bargains sources, and business is booming. Ray, a little overwhelmed by the success, points out, "You can't eat with two spoons, can you?" When things get too good, she'll probably shut up shop and move to Florida. Until then, you can write or call her with the model numbers of the pieces you're interested in and she'll give you a price quote.

CARRY-ON LUGGAGE
97 Orchard St.
New York, NY 10002
(212) 226-4980
Portfolio Brochure: SASE
Information on other luggage by price quote by phone or letter
Accepts: check, MO, MC, Visa

Carry-On is one of the few luggage discounters that will allow the brands they carry to appear in print. They sell luggage and leather goods by Ventura, Land, Tumi, Amelia Earhart, Samsonite, Anne Klein, Diane Von Furstenburg, Invicta, St. Thomas, Pierre Cardin, Verde, Harrison, Michael Scott, Rolfs, and Pax at savings of 30% and more on suggested retail prices. They also have a collection of portfolios that is featured in the brochure they'll send if you forward a stamped, self-addressed envelope. Write or call with stock information on any of the luggage or leather goods.

MARK CROSS
645 Fifth Ave.
New York, NY 10022
(212) 421-3000
Catalog: $2.00
Minimum Order: none
Accepts: check, MO, MC, Visa, AE, CB, DC

Mark Cross originated as a saddle and harness shop in Boston, and was established by Henry Cross in 1845. When his son Mark joined the business, the firm began to manufacture trunks. After Mark Cross died, the repertoire of luggage and leather goods was refined and expanded by members of the Murphy family. Today, Mark Cross is run by the Wasserbergers, who ensure that "MC" will continue to be known for its fine leathers and impeccable craftsmanship.

Indeed, Mark Cross surpasses classification as "just another" leather goods shop. They are responsible for bringing the Thermos bottle, Sheffield cutlery, golf clubs, cocktail sets, and cigarette cases to America. They also introduced the wristwatch to the United States. Their current version boasts a gray pinstriped dial, a total of 30 grams of gold, a quartz movement, sapphire crystal, lizard strap, and a lifetime guarantee. You wouldn't want to have to buy another at $2,400.00.

The emphasis at Mark Cross is on leather. Their Signet collection of mocha calf trimmed with brown pigskin ranges from $45.00 for a zippered coin purse to $900.00 for the stunning "business companion," and extra-large attaché case designed for overnight business trips that is even fitted with its own briefcase. Several classic handbag and shoulder-bag styles are available in Signet at $280.00 to about $500.00. These are also made in black calf or the Mark Cross cinnamon Signature fabric trimmed in brown pigskin. Mark Cross has just introduced "Pannier," scuff-resistant calfskin embossed with a basket-weave texture that's altogether more subtle than actual woven leathers. The current Pannier collection includes a key case ($35.00), shoulder bags, a zippered satchel bag ($250.00), and a folio ($195.00), all in warm tan or black.

Mark Cross also excels at extravagance. A wine-colored lizard shoulder bag lined in calf, suspended from a gold-plated chain, is perfection at $600.00. Desk accessories finished in nutmeg calfskin and brass fairly gleam. A simple whiskey-colored billfold of farm-bred ostrich elicits $250.00 for softness alone. (No endangered species are used here. You *will* find lizard, napa, calfskin, pigskin, and lambskin, and farm-bred ostrich, though not crocodile, elephant, or pin seal.) The Mark Cross reversible belt, in black/brown calf, black calf/brown pigskin, and Signet represents a bargain at $75.00, since it's actually two

belts in one. And their special line of accessories for the working woman includes an evening briefcase in red or black silk or black suede for $500.00, which can also be made to order in other materials.

In addition, Mark Cross sells luggage, silk scarves, folios, miniaudieres, manicure sets, toiletries kits, photo albums, scrapbooks, jewelry rolls, lighters, tool kits (fitted in calfskin cases), and their own "woodsy, clean-smelling" cologne and toiletries for men. And finally, there is the car. David Wasserberger has styled the interior of an Imperial in what seems an acre of rich, burgundy leather. The car is available from your Chrysler dealer.

The Mark Cross catalog is elegant, but until it is executed in Carpathian elm burl, beveled glass and mirrors, a soft carpet, and installed with a glass elevator, it can't hold a candle to the store. Even the store is diminished by the services: Gold initialing and gift wrapping are *de rigueur;* their luggage registry aids in recovery of lost Mark Cross pieces; repairs are made on all Mark Cross goods; and their personal shopper is always available to help in your selections. Last but not least, the Mark Cross staff should be commended for their courtesy and manners, which are especially welcome if one has just come from Gucci.

INNOVATION LUGGAGE
487 Hackensack Ave.
River Edge, NJ 07661
(201) 487-6000 (orders and inquiries in N.J.)
(800) 631-0742 (rest of U.S.)
Catalog: free
Minimum Order: $15.00
Accepts: check, MO, MC, Visa, AE, DC

What you save on luggage here could actually pay for a vacation. Innovation's 12 outlets in the metropolitan area boast "the lowest prices" on leather goods, handbags, Timex watches, and jewelry, in addition to luggage.

Innovation is America's largest independent Samsonite dealer, and also sells lines by American Tourister, Amelia Earhart, Ventura, French, Hartmann, Skyway, Invicta, Lark, Land, Le Sportsac, U.S. Citation, Tumi, and designers like Christian Dior and Bill Blass. There are

Ladies' Wallet from Mark Cross

the lovely leather handbags by Coach and Étienne Aigner and others by Halston, Enny, Dior, and Le Sportsac. Small leather-goods brands include Prince Gardner, Buxton, Ross, Swank, Coach, and St. Thomas, and there is jewelry by Monet, Trifari, Napier, Cardin, and Swank.

If you don't see what you want in the catalog, write or call with a picture or a model or stock number, as they probably have what you're looking for.

LEDERER

613 Madison Ave.
New York, NY 10022
(212) 355-5515
Catalog: free
Minimum Order: none
Accepts: check, MO, MC, Visa, AE

Lederer has been selling fine leather goods for seventy-five years, and has shops in Paris and London. With these credentials, you'd expect prices in the Gucci-Mark Cross range, right?

Surprise! Good luggage and accessories need not sport phenomenal price tags. Lovely attaché cases of top-grain calf are $250.00, and on sale for $149.50 at this writing. Sturdy cases of brown Irish "hand leather" with 24K gold-plated locks are $210.50 to $279.50. There are several other styles, ranging from under $50.00 to under $350.00. A particularly beautiful organizer in wine, black, or brown Italian calf has slots for business cards and pens, and is under $190.00.

Small leather goods are also well priced: Long wallets that hold checks, change, cash, and cards and fasten with a bit are

just $29.95. A burgundy business-card case is $18.50. Lederer's accessories include a digital clock pen, and "status" watches. (One appears to be an attempt to imitate Cartier's Tank watch, and although it wouldn't fool a hard-core snob, it's as close as you'll come for $19.95. At that price, you can buy 150 for every *one* Tank watch—and they both tell time.)

The Lederer catalog captures only a fraction of the goods available in the store, but will have to suffice when you're not in Paris, London, or New York City. The bargains in their sales catalogs should take your mind off what you're missing, though.

MODERN LEATHER GOODS REPAIR SHOP

11 West 32nd St.
New York, NY 10001
(212) 279-3263
Information: inquire
Minimum Order: none
Accepts: check, MO

Injured leather handbags, luggage, belts, and clothing have been getting second lives at Modern Leather for forty-five years. The skilled repair people here can do almost anything to return damaged, worn, and broken articles to service— everything except replate handbag hardware.

Mr. Paul runs the shop and invites you to send the article you need fixed to the shop, insured, with a description of what you want done. He'll send you an estimate. If your problem is out of the ordinary, write or call and make sure they can do the job before sending it.

SEE ALSO: Appliances, Audio, TV/Video
Clothing, Furs, Accessories
Department Stores
Jewelry, Gems, Watches

15 | Music

It sometimes seems that in New York, you can barely take a longish walk without bumping into at least one street musician, set up in front of an office building, playing folk guitar or steel drums or classical violin, with his instrument case set open on the sidewalk to receive donations from frequently spellbound listeners. In warm weather, rock groups set up along Sixth Avenue with battery-powered amplifiers, and Haitians play mysterious drums in Riverside and Washington Square Park. Street music is a happy and long-standing tradition. *Bob Dylan*—and many others—first revealed their talents to the world on a park bench in Greenwich Village.

The best jazz musicians play in the city's clubs, the best classical musicians in its concert halls. We know several people who have moved from the suburbs into New York just to be closer to the music.

And as with the graphic arts world, New York has become the country's mecca for musical instruments and equipment. On West 48th Street alone, there are perhaps a dozen musical instrument stores, each of which would be the largest shop in any other city. And, because of the competition, everything is sold at discount. Note that sometimes mail order is a bit on the slow side— these shops are kept extremely busy meeting the needs of the hundreds of major bands and individual musicians who patronize them regularly.

ACCORDION-O-RAMA
16 West 19th St.
New York, NY 10011
(212) 675-9089
Catalog: free
Minimum Order: none
Accepts: check, MO, MC, Visa

"Accordions are not weird," states Peter Shearer, which settled our doubts. Mr. Shearer, mail-order director for Accordion-O-Rama, also pointed out that only accordions combine bass, melody, and accompaniment in one instrument.

Accordion-O-Rama, also known as Alas Accordion, has been selling, tuning, servicing, and repairing accordions since 1950. They carry new and reconditioned accordions by Farfisa, Leslie, Accorgan, Arpeggio, Avanti, Alas (their brand), Hohner, Polytone, Roma, Ferrari, Hagstrom, Sonola, La Prima, and many other firms. The catalog consists of brochures on the different Alas services, and several cards with color photos of popular models that are currently in stock. All the accordions they sell are discounted a minimum of 30%, and run from $145.00 from $225.00 list for the Roma beginner's model to $2,800.00 from $3,800.00 for the Arpeggio "Super" with case and strap. Alas is an authorized Cordovox dealer, sells the Bandoleer invisible strap, Gerry accordion stands, concertinas, electric pianos, and organs.

The Shearers will be glad to demonstrate any of the accordions hanging on the showroom wall. Catalogs will be sent only to people out of New York City and New York State, as they assume that if you live within the state, you can visit.

SAM ASH MUSIC STORES
301 Peninsula Boulevard
Hempstead, NY 11550
(516) 485-2122 (N.Y. orders, inquiries)
(800) 645-3518 (orders and price quote out of N.Y.)
Information: price quote by letter or phone; brochure once a year
Minimum Order: $15.00; $25.00 on parts
Accepts: check, MO, certified check, MC, Visa

The first thing that hits you in the 48th Street Sam Ash store is the low-level cacophony, created by a score of musicians trying out electric guitars and equipment simultaneously. The Sam Ash easygoing "try before you buy" policy has helped make them one of the leading retailers of musical instruments and accessories in New York City. Paul Ash, of the Ash family, told us that they carry more name brands than anyone else in the business, that *every* brand is available to them, and that they carry everything except "home" instruments (pianos and organs). This includes classical and band instruments, electric keyboards and sythesizers, sound (PA) equipment, effects boxes, fretted instruments of all kinds, and things like parts and sheet music.

As if the stupendous selection weren't enough, Sam Ash offers great discounts. Sam Ash is large enough to import student drums directly and pass the savings on to you. They feature "lowest prices" on Gibsons and Fenders, and discounts of 30% to 50% on list price are common. They buy and sell used instruments at all of their 6 retail stores, and feature a guaranteed trade-in policy that credits a percentage of the cost of a Sam Ash instrument (prorated on the basis of time and wear) to the purchase of a better instrument from them. Sam Ash guarantees and services what it sells, which is enough to keep their battery of specialized repair men busy. Whether you're buying clarinet reeds or a synthesizer, don't miss Sam Ash.

CARROLL SOUND, INC.
895 Broadway
New York, NY 10003
(212) 533-1003
Catalog: free
Minimum Order: $25.00
Accepts: certified check, COD

After having worked under Toscanini, Stokowski, and Mitropoulos, played with the New York Philharmonic and the National Symphony, and taught at the Peabody Institute, Carroll Bratman opened Carroll Sound to offer professionals and students the most comprehensive range of specialty percussion instruments and nonelectric sound effects possible. There's no doubt, glancing around Carroll's "Gallery of Sound" at Moroccan dumbeks, ghungroos, frogmouth almglockens, and Chiness nipple gongs, that he's succeeded.

Today, Mr. Bratman and his son Garry

run the business, and are committed to furthering the range of instruments and effects. Their beautifully photographed catalog opens with a quote from Walter Pater, "All art constantly aspires to the condition of music." But does it aspire to the sounds of jaw harps, tom-toms, and cowbells? Aesthetics aside, the instruments and effects are extraordinary.

There are all sorts of drums, including Indian Tabla drums, Chinese tom-toms, dumbeks from Israel and Morocco, a full range of steel drums, boing boxes, and log drums, a musical saw, kalimbas, bell trees, gongs, crotales, finger cymbals, tambourines, jingle sticks, triangles, chimes, Khartals, and other percussion instruments. More intriguing are the various devices used to create sound effects. With Carroll's help, you can simulate the sounds of marching men, industrial warning horns, bosun's pipes, cuckoo calls, a baby's cry, taxi horns heard in Gershwin's *American in Par:* train whistles, champagne corks popping, dogs barking, lions roaring, horses' hooves, a hammer on an anvil, and even the NBC radio chimes. Carroll even has a device that captures the sound of disco, which is available in small, medium, and large shakers. Prices run from $1.00 for a replacement pop-gun cork to $1,500.00 for a set of steel drums with stands.

Carrol has everything from the triangle and sleighbells used during kindergarten music hour to the newest percussive instruments found in experimental music today. No professional percussionist should miss this source for the truly eclectic. Visits by appointment.

GIARDINELLI BAND INSTRUMENT CO.

151 West 46th St.
New York, NY 10036
(212) 575-5959
Mouthpiece Brochure: SASE
Minimum Order: none
Accepts: check, MO

Giardinelli specializes in screw-rim mouthpieces for trumpet, flugelhorn, French horn, trombone, cornet, tuba, and sousaphone, and they also make one-piece models and custom duplications. The screw-rim mouthpiece allows a musician to try out different kinds of cups and underparts and achieve different

sounds without switching to an unfamiliar rim. Giardinelli stocks many different cups in different bore sizes, and has on file hundreds of impressions and specifications for custom mouthpieces, as well as templates and specifications for well-known models. Current prices run from $15.00 for a silver-plated one-piece cornet/trumpet mouthpiece to $95.00 for a custom mouthpiece (duplication) for a tuba/sousaphone (plating is extra).

Giardinelli also alters, restores, and repairs all sorts of instruments. They sell band instruments and accessories by manufactures from Alexander to Zuleger. Write with a complete description and model/stock number of what you're looking for, and include a stamped, self-addressed envelope.

MANNY'S MUSICAL INSTRUMENTS

156 West 48th St.
New York, NY 10036
(212) 757-0577
Information: price quote
Minimum Order: none
Accepts: check, MO, MC, Visa

Manny's is the poshest of the "big three" musical instrument stores on West 48th Street, with its candelabras, autographed photos of famous musicians, and the two levels of instrument display. Like Sam Ash and Silver & Horland, Manny's has been around for fifty years and "sells everything for the musician."

This covers the electronics of rock 'n' roll woodwinds, brass, and percussion. They sell the instruments by mail on a price-quote basis, as well as instruction manuals, which you should request by name. They don't repair or rent, and their guarantee on mail-order instruments is elusive, so we recommend buying only new instruments from them sight unseen. The discounts of 30% to 50% on many instruments should make this condition more bearable.

SILVER & HORLAND MUSICAL INSTRUMENTS AND ACCESSORIES

170 West 48th St.
New York, NY 10036
(212) 869-3870
Information: price quote
Minimum Order: none
Accepts: check, MO

Silver & Horland is as modest and

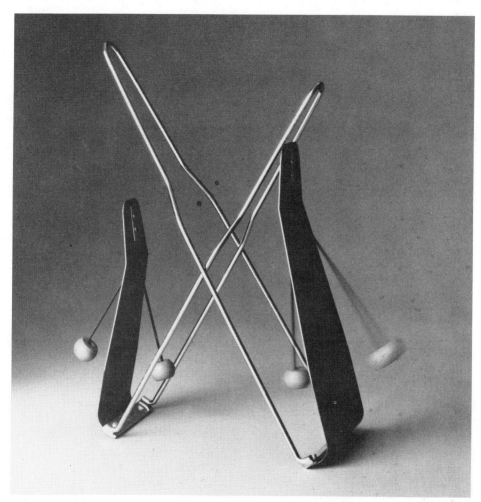

Flex-A-Tones from
Carroll Sound, Inc.

subdued as Manny's is grand and Sam Ash is noisy. Lest appearances deceive, we are reminded that in the music world the instrument's the thing, and Richard Silver has an excellent selection, including vintage, used, and new equipment.

Silver & Horland sells brasses, woodwinds, percussion, fretted instruments, and even accordions, or everything but pianos and organs. They also sell parts and supplies such as stands, straps, strings, and reeds. The specialty here is used and vintage instruments, of which their stock ranges from the common to the rare. They will sell used instruments under the same sort of policy that Sam Ash uses (returns within 48 hours in the same condition as shipped), and will retain want lists if you're looking for something special that they don't have.

Call or write to Silver & Horland with model or stock numbers or a complete description of the instrument or supplies you need for a price quote. They also buy used equipment; call or write with a complete description.

TERMINAL MUSIC
166 West 48th St.
New York, NY 10036
(212)245-5249
Information: price quote
Minimum Order: none
Accepts: check, MO, MC, Visa

Terminal Music is definitely no last resort in the instrument world. They carry classical, band, fretted, string, keyboard, percussion, and Latin instruments—in fact, just about everything except double-reed and home instruments. They specialize in acoustic guitars, recorders, drums, small PA equipment, amps, and effects boxes. They have the less common Sigma, Madeira, and Suzuki guitars, instruction books, accessories for everything, and "metronomes for everybody." They sell only new instruments by mail, which carry the manufacturer's warranty. Write for a price quote.

Larry Nitka, the Terminal vice president,

dispenses advice on all aspects of music with a great sense of humor. He says he prefers as customers 16-year-old kids to rock stars any day. Larry is also the only person we've met who *knows* that his business will be around in 2010. How can he be so sure? "It has to be, I've just signed a 30-year mortgage," says he. We didn't know it was that simple.

WE BUY GUITARS, INC.
159 West 48th St.
New York, NY 10036
(212) 869-3985
Information: price quote
Minimum Order: $200.00
Accepts: certified check, postal MO

We Buy Guitars finds its roots in the pawnshop that Larry Friedman's father ran. The cameras and watches are gone, but the counters are still leapproof and most of the merchandise is displayed behind them, hung on white pegboards. While we were visiting, a raven-haired punk musician brought back a Rickenbacker he had bought there a few months before. He had paid $350.00, wanted $300.00, was offered $250.00, and settled at $275.00, in the classic pawnshop dickering style.

Mr. Friedman not only buys guitars and other musical instruments but sells them, too. They have accordions, mandolins, violins, cellos, zithers, lutes, brasses, amps, and things like stands and bows. They also rent instruments. Mr. Friedman is interested in buying good used electric guitars and violins by mail. Write or call with details of what you want or have to sell, including the make, year, any custom work, finish, special details, and things like original case if you have or want that. He will tell you if he has what you want or wants what you have, and give you a price on the former or ask to see the latter (be sure to pack instruments well and have them liberally insured.) If you buy by mail, you have 24 hours after receipt of the guitar to try it—returns must be received in the same condition as shipped and you pay postage both ways.

SEE ALSO: Appliances, Audio, TV/Video Books, Records, Tapes, Stationery, Films, Educational Supplies

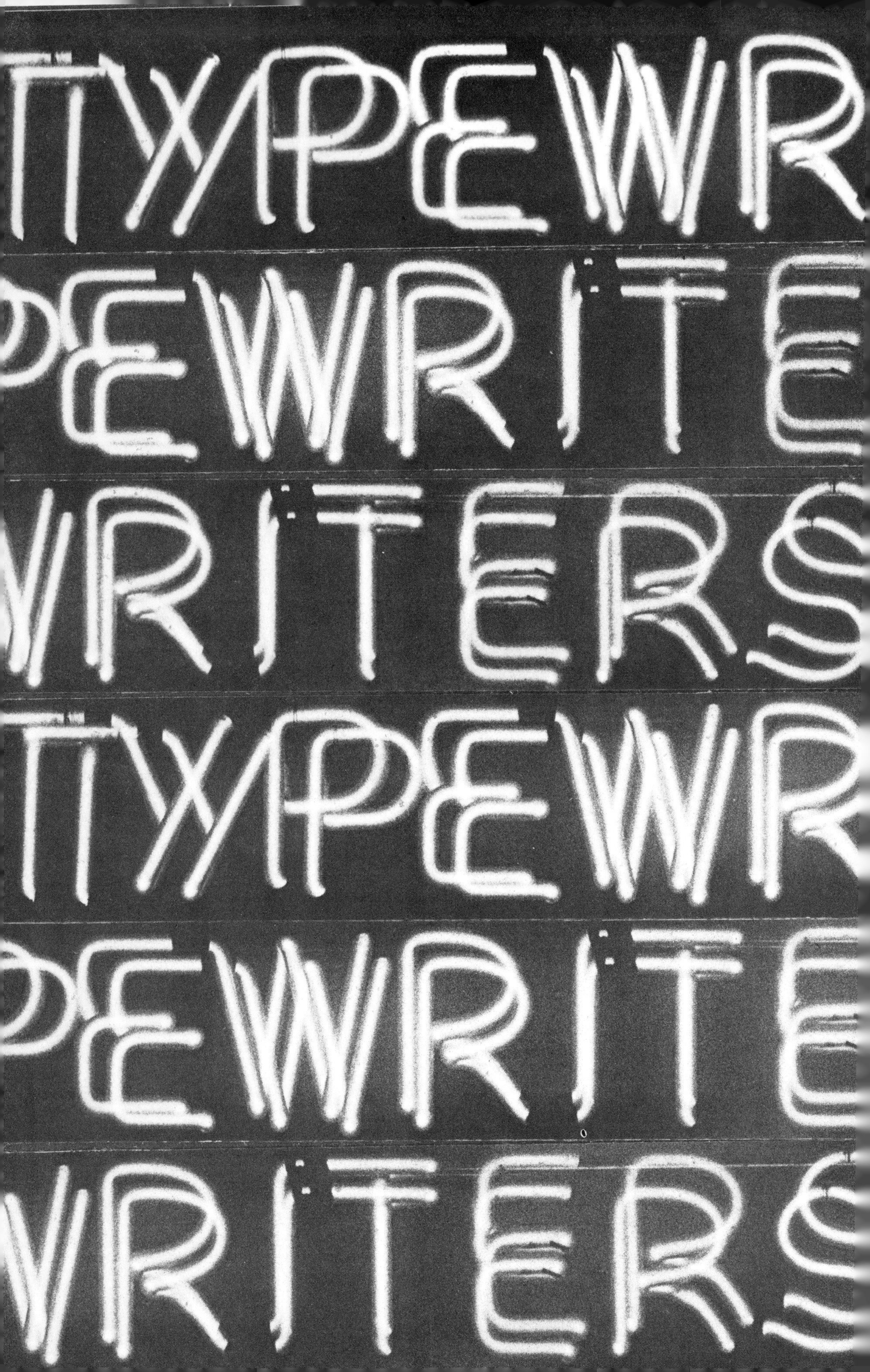

16 | Office Supplies

If you didn't want to call New York City "The World's Largest Shopping Center," you'd surely have to call it "The World's Largest Office Building." New York is also the answer to that famous old Zen koan, "How many secretaries can you fit on the head of a pin?"

Obviously, it's a great place to buy supplies and machines. Go ahead, order yourself some wonderful crystal, designer skirts, gourmet tea, and some nice five-part forms—for *him*.

A & B BEACON

36 West 32nd St.
New York, NY 10001
(212) 736-1440
Information: price quote by letter
Minimum Order: none
Accepts: check, MO, MC, Visa

A & B Beacon carries all kinds of typewriters, word processors, and calculators by Sperry, Sanyo, Olympia, IBM, Remington, Adler, SCM, Olivetti, Hermes, Norelco, and Casio. They also have typewriter ribbons, cartridges, and other accessories. A & B will save you up to 20% (sometimes more) on everything, add their own warranty to the manufacturer's, and service what they sell in their own repair shop.

ABALON OFFICE EQUIPMENT CO.

227 Park Ave.
New York, NY 10169
(212) 682-1653
Information: price quote by phone or letter
Minimum Order: none
Accepts: check, MO, MC, Visa

We asked Mr. Singer at Abalon what they sold there. "Typewriters, calculators, and adders," he responded. By which manufacturers? "All brands," he said. What kind of prices? "Reduced." You'll have to take it from there. Mr. Singer will give price quotes over the phone as well as by letter.

ADIRONDACK DIRECT

Dept. GS85
219 East 42nd St.
New York, NY 10017
(212) 687-8555 (N.Y. orders, inquiries)
(800) 221-2444 (U.S. orders)
Catalog: free
Minimum Order: varies
Accepts: check, MO, MC, Visa, AE, DC

Adirondack Direct has been selling "furniture for business institutions"— church pews to bicycle racks—since 1926. They have wholesale catalogs for schools, churches, and institutions, in addition to the general catalog of office and institutional furnishings. The general catalog features the sofas and chairs that you seen in waiting rooms and lounges, in a range of styles and prices, modern desks in Formica and walnut, bookcases,

"VIP" executive swivel chairs for the boss, and posture chairs for the secretary. There are places for *everything* in the nonsuspension, suspension, and fireproof lateral, flat, and standard files, lockers, book trucks, literature and magazine racks, safes, and wastebaskets. You need bleachers, lecterns, coatracks, conference tables, picnic tables, or cafeteria tables? They're all here.

Much of Adirondack's stock is well suited to home purposes. Their basic folding chair is $8.45 (less in quantity), comes in 5 colors, and features a four-hinge construction that makes it twice as strong as ordinary folding chairs. The free-standing room dividers of vinyl and chrome are sturdy and an ideal way to partition a child's room. Many of the chairs and tables incorporate design features that make them much more durable than other office furniture. Adirondack offers an "ironclad guarantee" against defects, good for 2 years on most items. They ship from 10 cities across the country, which helps keep costs down, and have a showroom open to business buyers at their New York City address.

ALL LANGUAGES TYPEWRITER CO., INC.

119 W. 23rd St.
New York, NY 10011
(212) 243-8080
Information: inquire
Minimum Order: none
Accepts: check, MO

All Languages Typewriter has a stuffed, 2-headed calf in the display window next to an old Pitney-Bowes mailing machine, a ten-foot-tall mountain of office machines in front, and a clock at the back that doesn't keep time. New York City writers are willing to brave the eccentricity of the store for the stock: typewriters of all sorts, including ones with characters in Arabic, Armenian, Bulgarian, Chinese, Czech, Dutch, German, Greek, Hebrew, Hungarian, Japanese, Polish, Russian, Spanish, and many other languages. The symbols of music, chemistry, mathematics, medicine, pharmaceuticals, astrology, and engineering are also available. Write with a description of the language or symbols for a price quote.

Jacob Sachs, the owner, has been in the

office machine business since he came here from Russia in 1939. He buys, repairs, rents, and rebuilds machines, in addition to selling new and used equipment. The typewriters are his only mail-order items, but he also sells adders, checkwriters, mimeo machines, photocopiers, duplicators, time clocks, offset machines, and Pitney-Bowes mailing machines (but no two-headed calves) in the store. If you stop in you may be able to pick the brains of the man fixing typewriters, who will tell you what makes the IBM "B" better than the "D" and why you rarely see an Underwood or Remington in an office these days. Best yet: They accept machines for trade-in even if they are in poor condition or irreparably damaged. The prices here are excellent on everything.

FRANK EASTERN CO.

625 Broadway
New York, NY 10012
(212) 677-9100 (N.Y. orders, inquiries)
(800) 221-4914 (U.S. orders, inquiries)
Catalog: free
Minimum Order: $40.00 on Frank Eastern charge
Accepts: check, MO, Frank Eastern charge

You can't live in a closet-sized apartment or work in an office with the dimensions of a shoebox without using the survival tactics of organization. One of New York City's great weapons in the fight against chaos is Frank Eastern.

This office supply source has everything you need to order your life when it comes to the home or business office. There are lateral suspension files in 2-, 3-, and 4-drawer models, literature racks, bookcases and book trucks, shelf units, desktop pigeon hole organizers, blueprint cabinets, transfer and data printout transfer files, and all sorts of modern office furniture. Their famous Tidi-Files (6 for $9.95) will straighten out magazine clutter in a jiffy and you can put them all in lateral files designed just for them. There are hanging and plain manila file folders, BiC pens, Pentel markers, IBM Selectric balls, IBM film ribbons, calculators, phone machines, Xerox paper, tape, rotary stamps, and more. You can save up to 50% here if you buy in quantity. What better excuse for organizing your office and your life?

GERSTEN

103 Fifth Ave.
New York, NY 10003
(212) 255-4700
Information: price quote by phone or letter
Minimum Order: none
Accepts: check, MO, MC, Visa

Gersten sells, services, and rents all kinds of office machines—typewriters, calculators, paper shredders, checkwriters, minicomputers, etc. The brands include IBM, SCM, Remington, Olympia, Olivetti, and Hermes, to name a few. We asked Sam, who manages Gersten, about prices. "When we run ads, we get calls from all over. No one can believe how low we are." You can see how low by calling or writing for a price quote. Reconditioned IBM machines are sold here.

GRAYARC

882 Third Ave.
Brooklyn, NY 11232
(212) 788-2204 (inquiries)
(800) 221-0618 (U.S. orders)
(800) 522-5105 (N.Y.S. orders)
Catalog: free
Minimum Order: none
Accepts: check, MO

The next time you (shudders) receive a collection notice on an overdue account, take a look at the fine print along the bottom for the name of the printing firm. Chances are it's by Grayarc. They not only make collection forms and statements, but also reply messages, speed messages, memorandum forms, sales slips, register forms, invoices, sales orders, and purchase orders. Some are available in carbon or carbonless versions, and all come imprinted with your firm's name and address. They also have self-inking stamps for business and mail use at $4.98 each that read "paid," "rush," "for deposit only," "air mail," etc. They sell price marking systems and sales tags, shipping and mailing labels, advertising labels, mailing envelopes, sealed-air shipping bags, and pens and pencils. The home office could be set up in any of their Unifiles file cabinets, one of which has a fold-down work area, 2 file drawers, 2 shelves, and costs about $120.00. There are 3M dry copiers for home office use, first-aid kits, typewriter ribbons, Rolodex-type files, tape, paper, file folders, and calculators.

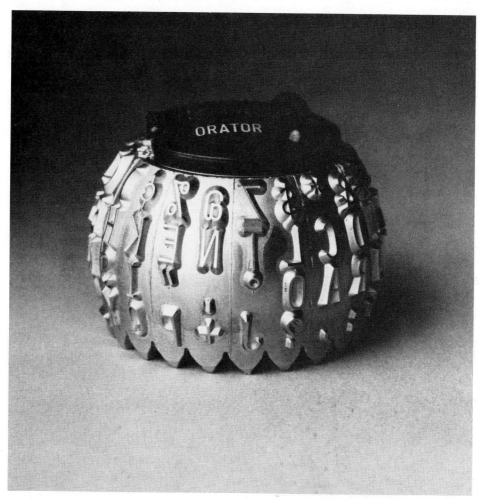

IBM Selectric "Orator" Type
Element from Frank Eastern

Grayarc runs periodic "warehouse sales" on selected items that take 30% to 50% off the original prices. They also offer an unconditional money-back guarantee on goods returned in 30 days.

GROLAN STATIONERS, INC.

115 W. 57th St.
New York, NY 10019
(212) 247-2676
Products Catalog: $10.00, refundable after $200.00 in purchases
Minimum Order: $10.00
Accepts: check, MO, MC, Visa

Grolan's Mr. Gross said that their not-large stationery store sold everything, a claim often made by New York City merchants. He then backed it up with a 615-page catalog, which doesn't even represent everything Grolan and their associate, Standard Office Equipment, sell. This encyclopedia of office supplies covers everything from Abco hand trucks to Zip Code directories, and its $10.00 cost is refunded after you've bought $200.00 in goods from Grolan.

A sample of brands available includes Avery, Smead, National, Oxford Pendaflex, Dennison, Ampad, Rhodia, Liquid Paper, Steel Master, Sheaffer, Cross, Pilot, BiC, and Rolodex. Bargain hunters with foresight know Grolan for their half-off summer sales of Christmas cards, held every year (not available by mail). They also offer imprinting and rubber-stamp services.

According to Mr. Gross, you don't have to cough up $10.00 for the catalog. Just write to Grolan with a complete description, picture, and/or manufacturer's stock number (or a sample if available) and the number of items you want, and they'll send you a price quote. Not only is the selection unbeatable, but since Grolan doesn't feel compelled to charge list price for everything, you may even save some money!

JILOR DISCOUNT

1178 Broadway, Room 305
New York, NY 10001
(212) 683-1590
Information: price quote by phone or letter with SASE
Minimum Order: none
Accepts: check, MO

You won't find Jilor Discount in a big flashy storefront with miles of display and scores of salesmen. They save all kinds of overhead by operating from one room, but still sell only factory-sealed goods, and at up to 50% off list prices. They specialize in office machines and in odd items such as Soft-Touch tone dialers, which permit the conversion of a rotary telephone to a Touch-Tone simply by changing the mouthpiece. Some models feature automatic redial and automatic dialing of up to 80 preprogrammed numbers.

Jilor carries dictation equipment by Pearlcorder, Craig, and Sanyo, automatic phone dialers, speakerphones, and cordless telephones by Panasonic (including the Muraphone, with ranges of up to 1,500'). There are telephone answering machines by Code-A-Phone, ITT, Phone-Mate, Sanyo, Record-A-Call, and Pansonic, typewriters by Olivetti, SCM, and Olympia, and calculators by Hewlett-Packard, Sharp, Texas Instruments, Casio, Victor, Toshiba, and Unitrex.

LINCOLN TYPEWRITERS AND MICRO MACHINES

100 West 67th St.
New York, NY 10023
(212) 787-9397
Information: price quote by phone or by letter with SASE
Minimum Order: none
Accepts: check, MO

Lincoln sells typewriters, calculators, ribbons, and cartridges. Their typewriter lines include IBM, SCM, Olivetti, Royal, Olympia, and Hermes. They will give you a price quote over the phone or by letter (include a SASE). They sell both new and used machines in their store but mail-order only new goods, and back up their own warranties with a complete repair service. You can save up to 40% on new machines here, depending on the model.

LONGACRE OFFICE MACHINES CO., INC.

20 East 40th St.
New York, NY 10016
(212) 684-2471
Information: price quote by phone or letter
Minimum Order: none
Accepts: certified check, MO, MC, Visa

You can get typewriters, checkwriters,

adding machines, and calculators here, and repairs and service on all of them. They have machines by SCM, Hewlett-Packard, Texas Instruments, Sharp, and used and reconditioned IBM equipment. Longacre can save you up to 30% on list prices on the new office machines, and will quote prices over the phone.

PEARL BROTHERS
476 Smith St.
Brooklyn, NY 11231
(212) 875-3024
Information: price quote
Minimum Order: none
Accepts: check, MO

In Arthur Pearl's opinion, Adler manufactures the best affordable type-writer on the market today. He carries Adler/Royal typewriters, as well as lines by Olympia, SCM, Remington/Rand, Olivetti/Underwood, and the IBM recon-ditioned machines. Pearl Brothers also sells Olympia and Adler copying machines, Paymaster checkwriters, and calculators by Sanyo, Sharp, Olympia, Toshiba, and Casio—all at discount prices. Call or write for a price quote.

TYPEX BUSINESS MACHINES
149 Madison Ave.
New York, NY 10016
(212) 683-0557: inquiries and N.Y. orders
(800) 223-1528, 1529: U.S. orders
Information: price quote by phone or letter
Minimum Order: none
Accepts: check, MO, MC, Visa, AE

Mr. Eizikovitz, manager at Typex, will give you a price quote by phone or letter on any small office machine that he carries. He sells typewriters by Olivetti/Underwood, SCM, Olympia, Adler/Royal, Remington/Rand, and reconditioned IBM machines. Mr. Eizikovitz will sell you an IBM coupon for $15.00 good for 30 days of free repairs on the typewriters, honored at any IBM service shop. He also sells calculators by Sharp, Canon, Casio, and Underwood, dictating machines, and checkwriters. Prices are *low*.

Mail Order Tip: For help with problems write Mail Order Action Line, DMMA, 6 East 43rd St., New York, NY 10017.

VENUS OFFICE SUPPLY CORP.
396 Broadway
New York, NY 10013
(212) 966-6900
Catalog: $9.50, refundable with $100.00 in orders
Minimum Order: $25.00
Accepts: check, MO

New Yorkers won't pay list price for anything if they can help it, and that includes rubber bands. That's why there's Venus Office Supply, where everything is discounted 20% to 33%, even rubber bands. They do all their business through the 370-plus page catalog, which gives only list prices—call or write for the lower Venus price on whatever you want. In addition to rubber bands, they sell paper clips, pens, pencils, paper, envelopes, office books and binders, calendars, scissors, sharpeners, waste-baskets, and reference books, plus a complete line of supplies for copying and word-processing machines and office furniture. They also do printing and make rubber stamps.

The brands available include Swingline, X-Acto, Dixon, Liquid Paper, National, Oxford, Eaton, BiC, Sheaffer, Pentel, Duotang, Rolodex, and Rhodia, to name a few. Venus is known for its wide selection and the hard-to-find items they carry, many of which aren't in the catalog (inquire if you don't see what you're looking for). It takes more than a bundle of rubber bands to meet the $25.00 minimum-order requirement, so plan on stocking up. After you buy $100.00 in goods, the catalog cost is refunded.

WALDNER'S
222 Old Country Road
Mineola, NY 11501
(516) 747-7300 (N.Y.S.)
(212) 895-1621 (N.Y.C. and inquiries)
(800) 645-6136 (rest of U.S.)
Information: price quote
Minimum Order: $15.00
Accepts: check, MO, MC, Visa, AE, DC

What's better than a discount? A closeout! Waldner's has tons of them in office products, which they showcase in ads in *The New York Times*. You can save up to 60% on things like canary and white legal pads, file folders, BiC pens, Steelmaster files and desks, chairs, Lexan chair mats, phone machines, and more. Call or write to see if they have what you're looking for. They ship by UPS and FOB Mineola on items that exceed UPS limits.

WOLFF OFFICE EQUIPMENT
1841 Broadway
New York, NY 10023
(212) 581-9080
Price List: free, SASE
Minimum Order: none
Accepts: certified check, MO, MC, Visa

Comparison shoppers know Wolff Office for their great prices on typewriters, calculators, dictating machines, telephone machines, and office furniture. They back up all they sell with manufacturers' warranties and their own repair department. The lines they carry include Olivetti, Olympia, Adler/Royal, SCM, Remington, IBM (rebuilt and reconditioned), Sharp, Sanyo, Hewlett-Packard, Texas Instruments, Victor, Phillips-Norelco, and Phone-Mate. Their free price list shows a sample of what's available, and they invite you to call or write for price quotes on other items.

SEE ALSO: Appliances, Audio, TV/Video
Books, Records, Tapes, Stationery, Films, Educational Supplies
Sports, Recreation, Toys, Games

17 | Sports
Recreation
Toys
Games

If you haven't been to a city lately, then you haven't seen the roller skaters who've joined the joggers and bicyclers on the streets to remind the rest of us how out of shape we are. Quiet as hawks, they glide by on tough plastic wheels, often dancing to headphone disco.

Most city sports are for indoors, though, which is why you'll find these sources best for activities like tennis, darts, and orgies. New Yorkers love to play, even though there's little room to roam—serious play helps relieve our many stresses. We like to go off to the country too, though, and the city's outfitters for hiking, skiing, backpacking, and horseback riding can't be outdone anywhere.

Young people and the young at heart will find many New York City suppliers dedicated to serving only them. Here is one of the largest concentrations of toys for adults. And, of course, we all know that F. A. O. Schwartz only pretends to be for kids.

BE A DOLL, INC.
99 Prince St.
New York, NY 10012
(212) 925-8487
Brochure: SASE
Minimum Order: none
Accepts: check, MO, MC, Visa

The marriage of two New York obsessions, novelty and narcissism, is seen in one of its more humorous manifestations at Be A Doll.

This is the firm that will take the photograph you send of any loved one, whether it's your mother, spouse, a friend or yourself, and transfer the image to the face of a rag doll with yarn hair and silk-screened overalls. The hopelessly spaced-out deserve a similarly personalized astronaut doll, a 27" creation in a silk-screened suit reminiscent of those seen on *Flash Gordon Visits Jupiter*. And now you can assure yourself of consistent program-ming quality without commercial interruption by installing Be On TV in your home. This stuffed moiré set, complete with antenna, dials, and plug, features the face of your choice on its screen. This may or may not give new meaning to the term "idiot box," depending on whose face is there.

The yarn-haired doll is under $25.00, the astronaut and TV are under $30.00, and all are unconditionally guaranteed. The gag possibilities for the dolls are endless, and if you've been meaning to "give yourself" to someone, there couldn't be a more painless way.

CAMP TOWN SPORTING GOODS, INC.
41 West 14th St.
New York, NY 10011
(212) 989-5056
Information: price quote by phone, or by letter with SASE
Minimum Order: $25.00
Accepts: check, MO, MC, Visa, AE

Camp Town sells camping equipment, sports goods, and sportswear at discount prices. Until they publish a catalog, they'll accept inquiries for price quotes by phone or mail (include a stamped, self-addressed envelope).

Camp Town carries canteens, stoves, coolers, jugs, tents, and other camping equipment by Coleman, Camptrails, and Eureka, hiking shoes by Timberline and Herman's, Adidas shoes and clothes, shoes by Puma, Nike, Converse, ProKeds, and Pony, AMF exercise bikes, Wilson softball bats, footballs, and tennis racquets, Marcroft paddle racquets, basketballs by Spalding, Seamco, and Wilson, National mitts, Everlast boxing bags and gloves, Billard weightlifting equipment and slant boards, and Bike braces and supportive aids. Camp Town also sells Brian Trottier sticks, Right-Gard pucks and balls, and roller skates for young Rangers or Islanders fans who have taken up the latest city sport, street hockey.

Write or call Camp Town with the stock, model, or style number and name of the product you're looking for, and they'll give you a price quote.

DARTS UNLIMITED, LTD.
30 East 20th St.
New York, NY 10003
(212) 533-8684
Catalog: $1.00
Minimum Order: $20.00
Accepts: check, MO, MC

We've heard of swimmer's ear, jogger's knee, and tennis elbow, but we've never heard of a single case of "dart wrist." The only hazard to this game, it appears, is being on the wrong side of the dart.

Darts Unlimited is devoted to darts and only darts. It seems that darts are as big in English pubs as pool is in bars here, and hence the best darts and equipment are made by British firms. One of these is Kwiz, which makes darts, feathers and shafts, cases, and scorekeepers. Kwiz makes brass-barrel darts, which, although the least expensive, are often preferred by professionals. These come with case and flights, and run from $2.80 for minidarts to $14.50 for the Ton-80 model. Then there are the Kwiz Tungsten Alloy series of darts in nickel/tungsten and copper/tungsten. They range from 16 to 36 grams each, feature feathers decorated with the Union Jack, a maple leaf, shamrocks, skull and crossbones, etc., and come complete with a leather case. They run from $48.00 to $72.00 each. Darts Unlimited also carries similar Winman tungsten alloy darts, which cost from $51.00 to $66.00 each.

Also sold here are replacement feathers of polyester, nylon, and turkey feathers, dart caddies, dart wallets, dart cabinets, scorebords, sharpeners, mats for marking off distance, dart nets, and the U.S Darting Association's *Rules and Game Book*. Unless you plan to use a photo of your least favorite person as a target, you'll need a dartboard. Darts Unlimited carries 4 bristle boards by Raven, Winman, Nodor, and Champion Choice, which run from $48.00 to $56.00.

Darts is a fad just waiting to happen, and if you've ever wanted to launch a trend, here's your chance. Darts may not give you a cardiovascular workout, but you *will* have the most flexible wrists around.

DESIGNPOINT

15 Christopher St.
New York, NY 10014
(212) 929-0550
Brochure: 50¢ and SASE
Minimum Order: $25.00 on credit cards
Accepts: check, MO, MC, Visa, AE

Mary Ellis has a son named Noah and a store that should be renamed The Ark. "Designpoint" recalls earlier days when Mary's original needlepoint designs and needleart materials inspired the store. When she became pregnant she lost interest in needlepoint and fell in love with toys. She named her son Noah and filled the tiny store with stuffed animals, animals on cards and clothing, animals at the bottom of mugs, and the like.

Most of Designpoint's customers are adults buying animals for themselves or other adults. You need no excuse to satisfy your yen for frogs or pigs here— they understand. Pigs do happen to be popular now, and there is an enormous stuffed one here in openwale corduroy with pink satin-lined ears and its own blue prize ribbon. The plush rhino will hurt no one, and the large white goose with a gold satin beak may never lay eggs but would be nice to have around anyway.

Alas and alack, these gems aren't available by mail now. What you *can* get are animal pillow kits and Designpoint's own animal silk-screened clothing. The pillow kits include the well-known Museum of the City of New York reproductions and Gorey animals. Among the old-fashioned animals are Jocko the monkey, Floss the puppy, Tabby, an owl, a rooster, a rabbit, and a mallard. Less traditional are the satin penguin, goblin, red macaw, and brightly colored toucan. Gorey brings his unique

touch to a pig, cat, bat, and rabbit. All the kits are silk-screened muslin.

Designpoint has come up with their own great animal silhouettes that they silk-screen on T-shirts and sweatshirts (sizes 12 months to XL), shorts, sweatpants, and tanktops. The motifs are so well done that they surpass cuteness, no mean feat when it comes to lambs and rabbits. They've got 25 of our favorite critters dancing in multiples across the clothing, with the basics like pigs, frogs, bears, cows, and cats in force, as well as less common creatures: turtles, giraffes, camels, unicorns, lions, and elephants.

Designpoint also sells the heavy nylon Passport bags that carry a 2-year guarantee, can be dry-cleaned, and don't have a logo. There are small and large duffles, a shoulder bag, backpack, briefcase, garment bag, and a suitcase in gray, black, red, and blue.

You'll have to ge to the store to see the other toys and novelties. If you're lucky, Noah will be there to demonstrate everything.

F. A. O. SCHWARZ

Fifth Ave. and 58th Street
New York, NY 10022
(212) 644-9400
Mail Order:
P.O. Box 218
Parsippany, NJ 07054
(201) 334-7715
Catalog: free
Minimum Order: none
Accepts: check, MO, MC, Visa, AE, CB, DC

F. A. O. Schwarz offers more possibilities for wish fulfullment per square inch than any other store in the city. It does help to be a child to enjoy the floors of toys, games, dolls, houses, books, and other juvenile pleasures at Schwarz, but adults usually find the store hard to resist. Even Bloomingdale's newest gadgets pale next to a miniature working model of a pickup truck that gets 65 miles per gallon and can hold a reasonably sized adult. Car models are also available, and prices are under $1,000.00.

F. A. O. Schwarz has gained its reputation among toy connoisseurs for its collections of stuffed animals by Steiff, Anima, and Trupa. Trupa is an Italian firm that creates stuffed rocking cats, St. Bernards, and *ducks*. Schwarz also has the freckled Monchhichi Monkeys and a plush Snoopy that stands over 5' tall and costs $295.00.

For little girls and serious collectors, there are Sindy and Sasha dolls, Sebino dolls (including "Moon," who comes in a hooded fur jumpsuit), Sekiguchi and Madame Alexander dolls, carriages, strollers, houses, furnishings, clothing, and more.

Budding thespians can explore their talents with the Marionette Theater ($75.00), puppets, makeup sets, and costumes. There are magic kits, plastic replicas of Centurian armor, kid-sized guitars, baby grands, rhythm bands, portable easels, sewing kits, vanities, fashion designing kits, Caran D'Ache colors, tool sets and workbenches, trains, telescopes, microscopes, walkie-talkies, sleds, bikes, log cabins, and on and on. Schwarz's games run from the latest in electronics to classic board games such as checkers and roulette. There are cars by Corgi, PlayArt, and Matchbox, and everything in construction sets from hardwood blocks to a 1,250-piece Loc Bloc set for $50.00.

F. A. O Schwarz has been bringing us the best and the newest in playthings since 1862. The Ultimate Toy Store isn't cheap, but neither is Tiffany's. Schwarz's free catalogs are published in late fall.

FAST FEET
118 East 59th St.
New York, NY 10022
(212) 838-2564
Information: price quote by phone or letter
Minimum Order: $15.00
Accepts: check, MO, MC, Visa, AE

Directly across the street from the snap, crackle, pop of Fiorucci is Fast Feet, a small shop with an extensive selection of sports footwear, tennis clothing, and running/jogging wear.

The store is a real family affair— everyone involved is related, and when we visited, David Breskin and his brother-in-law were manning the floor. David pointed out rows of shoes of every description, including black parachute boots that are made in France and worn by people who never leave the ground.

Fast Feet carries shoes by Adidas, Brooks, Converse, New Balance, Patrick,

Saucony, Topsiders, and Tretorn, and is especially big on Nikes now. Their store has Nike's video information system, which helps runners choose the proper Nike for their athletic purposes, anatomy, weaknesses, running styles, etc.

Fast Feet has a full line of running wear by Dolphin, GUTS, Frank Shorter, Nike, Bill Rodgers, Moving Comfort, and Pantera. They also carry tennis clothing by Fred Perry, Adidas, Ultra Sport, White Stag, and Tail. You can call or write with a style or model number, color, and size for any of the clothing or shoe firms listed, and Fast Feet will give you a price quote.

G & S SPORTING GOODS
43 Essex St.
New York, NY 10002
(212) 777-7590
Information: price quote
Minimum Order: none
Accepts: check, MO, MC, Visa

Children's toys by Fisher-Price, Mattel, Playskool, and other manufacturers are here at 15% to 25% off list price. G & S also sells sporting equipment, clothing and sneakers by Tretorn, Adidas, Pumas, Converse, Wilson, ProKeds, and Spalding at similar discounts. Write or call for a price quote.

GEM SPORTING GOODS, INC.
29 West 14th St.
New York, NY 10011
(212) 255-5830
Catalog: free
Minimum Order: none
Accepts: check, MO, MC, Visa

Gem has specialized in physical-fitness equipment since 1941, and sells more torturous-looking devices to that end than most sporting goods stores. There are pages of barbells by Simplex, York, and Hercules that run from $44.95 for the ladies' "Shape-Up" set to $439.95 for the York Olympic Standard 400-pound weights. Additional plates in all weights are available, as well as barbell bars and collars for securing the weights. Gem has a selection of dumbbells that run from a pound to 100 pounds a pair, including a beautiful chrome-plated set.

In the great art of body-building, weights are only the beginning. There are adjustable squat stands to support heavy barbells, curling stands, training belts to support the back, spring chest expenders, hand grips, and other muscle developers. Gem even carries a head harness from which weights are suspended to promote neck muscle development, and a "dipping" belt that is weighted and strapped around the waist and used while doing chinups or parallel-bar dips to increase muscle workout. There are ankle and wrist weights, weighted belts and vests by Everlast, exercise mats and benches, slant boards, exercise cycles by Tunturi, rowing machines, and Jogmaster treadmills for those rainy days.

Once you've built yourself up, you can let off steam with boxing and gymnastics. Gem has bag gloves and fight gloves ($10.95 to $32.95 a pair), headguards and mouthpieces, handwraps, jump ropes, training bags, gymnastic slippers, palm guards, and much more. The store itself carries other sports equipment, footwear, and clothing. Gem's sales-people are physical-fitness enthusiasts, offer advice on equipment and use, and will refer you to other sources if their goods don't meet your requirements.

GERRY COSBY & CO., INC.
Madison Square Garden
3 Penn. Plaza
New York, NY 10001
(212) 563-6464
Information: inquire with SASE
Minimum Order: $10.00
Accepts: check, MO, MC, Visa, AE

Gerry Cosby and Co. Inc. was established in 1939, and although their motto is "Hockey Is Happiness", they carry equipment and clothing for just about every other competitive sport except bowling, golfing, and skiing.

The firm outfits the New York Knickerbockers and the New York Rangers, and supplies to dozens of other pro teams, schools, and clubs. They were first with specialty merchandise like fiberglass goalie masks, hockey equipment and stick bags, ankle protectors, the popular V-neck jersey, and several other standard pieces of equipment. Cosby carries their own line, plus goods by Cooper, CCM, Koho, and skates by Bauer, CCM, Lange, and Micron. Everything is listed in their Ice Hockey Catalog.

Gerry Cosby also designed equipment for other sports. The type of shoulderpads currently worn by many college and pro football teams was his invention. Genuine pro football jerseys are available here—plain for $30.00, and with the number and name of your choice for up to $90.00. Their football lines include Cosby's, Wilson, Rawlings, Sand Knit, and Riddell.

Serious baseball fans know that Cosby's is the only place in the city they can find real professional shirts, gloves, and hats. Pro caps range from $11.00 to $12.00, and shirts run from $45.00 to $70.00, without numbers. Cosby's own line is featured here, but you'll also find equipment by Wilson, Rawlings, and Mizune in the store.

In addition to baseball, football, and ice hockey, Cosby sells national team soccer jerseys, boxing gear by Everlast and Tuf-Wear, racquetsports gear by Wilson, Head, and Ektelon, roller skates and wheels by Riedell, Hyde, and Sims, and footwear by Adidas, Puma, Nike, Converse, Spot-Bilt, and Brooks. They haven't put together a general sports catalog yet, but invite inquiries for goods made by the manufacturers listed. And when it comes to pro clothing, just pick your favorite team and player, and they'll probably have it.

HABER'S
33 Essex St.
New York, NY 10002
(212) 473-7007, 7008
Information: price quote by phone, or by letter with SASE
Minimum Order: $10.00
Accepts: check, MO, MC, Visa

What do sporting goods and office supplies have in common? They're both bought by institutions, which is why Haber's divides its store between the two types of merchandise. Although they sell to camps, settlement houses, schools, and the like, they're happy to give you the same kinds of savings—25% to 50% off list price—whether you buy by mail or purchase in the store.

Ben Waxman, the affable owner, rattled off a list of brands that will hit home with sports fans of every ilk: Davis, Converse, Nike, Adidas, Puma, Bancroft, Tretorn, Prince, Head, Wilson, Dunlop, Spalding, ProKeds, et al. He stocks all kinds of tennis gear, warmup suits, jogging clothing, equipment for baseball, football, basketball, racquetball, volleyball, badminton, and other sports, plus roller skates and ice skates. Haber's also carries the entire line of Coleman camping gear, including tents, coolers, heaters, and lamps. For those less athletically inclined, there are board games like Parcheesi and Monopoly, and toys by top manufacturers.

Those who would rather work than play are also provided for with all kinds of office supplies, from BiC pens to desks and filing cabinets. The pen department carries writing tools by Pentel, Flair, Lamy, Cross, Waterman of Paris, Dupont, Aurora, Sheaffer, and Pilot, all at considerable discounts. You can tally up your saving at Haber's in the records books by National, Wilson Jones, and Borman Pease, and stash the extra cash in your Buxton or Bill Blass wallet, which are also available at Haber's.

Ben Waxman welcomes inquiries by phone or letter (include a stamped, self-addressed envelope), and will give price quotes when you give him names and model or stock numbers of merchandise. Remember this place before the "back to school" supply rush and you'll save yourself a lot of time and money.

HUDSON'S

105 Third Ave.
New York, NY 10003
(212) 473-7320
Catalog: $3.00
Minimum Order: none
Accepts: check, MO, MC, Visa, AE

Hudson's roots are in Army/Navy surplus, but except for the occasional government-issue canteen, the fatigue pants, Army blankets, and combat boots you'd swear it was another mammoth camping-gear store.

Hudson's is known for its campwear, which ranges from very cheap surplus of indeterminable age to the newest down jackets, jeans, outerwear, shoes, and boots, by firms like Woolrich, Levi, Strauss, Schott, Lee, Timberland, Herman's, and Georgia, and Western boots by Nocona, Justin, Acme, and Dingo. They sell everything you need to survive in the wild, from sterno, dehydrated food, and electric socks, to canoes and tents. Hudson's has resident experts on outerwear, backpacks, and

climbing equipment who can give you the fine points on everything they carry. Some of the items are discounted.

H. KAUFFMAN & SONS SADDLERY CO.

139 East 24th St.
New York, NY 10010
(212) 684-6060
Catalog: free
Minimum Order: none
Accepts: check, MO, MC, Visa, AE, DC

Frozen in midprance, Kauffman's huge yellow wooden horse has been marking the presence of this famous saddlery for longer than anyone can remember.

H. Kauffman's was established in 1875 and is still run by the same family. A century ago, the store was in the center of the horse market, and the street was lined with stables. Today, the city's sole remaining stable is the Claremont Riding Academy on West 89th Street, which rents horses for use in its indoor rink and on the bridle paths in Central Park. It's not surprising to learn, then, that the majority of Kauffman's customers are not riders, but like the look of equestrian furnishings.

Kauffman may be best known for their handsome riding jackets, beautifully tailored in herringbone tweed, meltons, corduroy, and doubleknit, at $40.00 to $160.00 each. They make saddle suits, formal hunt suits, and even hunt buttons and club collars to order, for men, ladies, and children. There are ratcatcher shirts to wear under the coats, jerseys, riding gloves, socks, and raingear. They sell the necessary breeches and jodhpurs, ranch pants, and leather chaps, also made to order.

Riding boots inspired the fashion for low-heeled boots with straight uppers. People come to Kauffman for the real thing, in hand-shaped, black or brown box calfskin, with 19" uppers, butted fronts and side, $195.00 per pair in ladies' and men's sizes. There are field boots in leather with lacing at the insteps, Newmarket boots of canvas and rubber, also known as "mud boots," for $25.00, shiny black rubber boots for $20.00, jodhpur boots, and polo boots. Kauffman makes boots to order, and their boot-makers can alter boot legs and uppers.

No riding outfit is complete without a cap. They have all sorts of hunt caps, polo caps, hunt derbys, jockey caps, and even silk top hats for formal riding and hunts. In addition to the riding gear, they have a full line of Western clothing and accessories. You can get Frye, Justin, and Kauffman's own boots, as well as custom-made models that are Texas fantasies and start at $275.00. You can snaz up any boot with gold or silver boot tips and heel scallops, at $15.00 and $20.00 a pair, and add Stetsons, Western belts, bolo ties, bandanas, shirts, and fringed jackets to your wardrobe for that Urban Cowboy appeal.

The real stuff of riding occupies most of the catalog. There are English and Western saddles, stirrups, bridles, reins, browbands, gags, nosebands, martingales, hackamores, bits, horse blankets, covers, hoods, coolers, halters, horse boots, bandages and leg wraps, neck cradles, nuzzles, hobbles, grooming brushes, and supplies for tack room, stable, blacksmith, and vet.

Kauffman has much more—from leather-care products to hay, plus a line of gifts for the horse lover, and T-shirts, umbrellas, and tote bags printed with the famous Kauffman horses.

MILLER'S

123 East 24th St.
New York, NY 10010
Mail Order:
23 Murray Hill Parkway
East Rutherford, NJ 07073
(201) 460-1200
General Catalog: free
Christmas Catalog: free
Minimum Order: none
Accepts: check, MO, MC, Visa, AE

Miller's is the official saddler to the U.S. Equestrian Team, has supplied the Olympics Team, European and South American polo players, and serious riders from everywhere.

Miller's represents the finest in riding wear and accessories, saddles and horse hardware, tackroom accessories, books, and gifts. Their riding fashions include breeches, jodhpurs, chaps, hunt coats, riding coats, saddle suits, flycatcher shirts, riding gloves, ties, caps, helmets, and boots by Deauville, Caliente, Ecuyer, Elan, Equestrian, Equi-Stretch, Marlborough, Griffin, Prestige, Regency 4, Somerset, and Tress. There are also boot trees and racks, spurs, and leather-care preparations.

Miller's has superb saddles for hunts, dressage, polo, jumping, show, and cross-country riding. These include saddles from India, England, Argentina, Zaldi saddles from Spain, Passier saddles from Germany, and the Hermés jumping saddle from Paris, of beautiful Hermés leather, for $1,350.00. All the girths, stirrups, bridles, halters, saddle pads, reins, martingales, equipment for controlling, schooling, racing, showing, and breaking horses, hunt appointments, polo equipment, and crops and whips you need for handling the horse are here. Miller's also has a comprehensive collection of boots and wraps for treatment of the horse's foot and leg problems, horse blankets, sheets, and grooming needs, as well as odd items such as mane tamers, canteens, saddlebags, blanket pins, an electric grooming machine, blacksmith aprons, and stall screens. Miller's appeal to the "horsey set" is based on the fact that it carries the very best equipment and takes all matters equestrian seriously. The catalog goes so far as to include a guide to the "Correct Appointments for Hunting and Saddle Seat Riding," and a page explaining the origins and purposes of the U.S. Equestrian Team. The catalog lists virtually every item in the store except those in the Western Wear department, which features a fine selection of boots, shirts, jeans, and other goods and merits a visit to the store.

THE NEW YORK DOLL HOSPITAL

787 Lexington Ave.
New York, NY 10021
(212) 838-7527
Information: Inquire by letter with SASE
Minimum Order: none
Accepts: check, MO

The Chais family has been treating patients since 1900, and has been consulting in its second-floor room on Lexington Avenue for as long as anyone can remember. Their patients arrive in purses, shopping bags, and suitcases, and are laid on the counter for diagnosis by the Doll Doctor. His skills include repairs on porcelain, cloth, wood, papier-mâché, wax, pewter, tin, iron, wood, rubber, and plastic, and he specializes in restoring heirloom dolls. New eyes can be implanted and old ones made to work, limbs replaced and hair transplants done. While it *is* a doll

Genuine Major League
Baseball Hats from
Gerry Cosby & Co., Inc.

hospital, toy animals of the same materials are accepted for treatment.

The Doll Doctor, also known as Irving Chais, rarely encounters a hopeless case and always has something nice to say about the patients. He says that the most difficult repairs are rejuvenating soft rubber dolls that have hardened or disintegrated, and that often the body has to be replaced. "People are all basically the same—they all have livers, hearts, lungs—but dolls are all different," he states. When you write to him, give a complete description of the doll or toy and include a photo if possible, and he'll tell you whether he can help. You can also send the doll, insured, for an estimate. The hospital itself is peopled by hundreds of old dolls that stare silently from the walls. Some can be rented, some bought, and Mr. Chais does appraisals for governments, auctions, and individuals. Doll clothing, custom-made only, is available.

NEW YORK SCOUT SHOP

308 Fifth Ave.
New York, NY 10001
(212) 868-4744
Mail Order:
Boy Scouts of America
PO Box 175
Bellwood, IL 60104
Catalog: free
Minimum Order: none
Accepts: check, MO, MC, Visa, AE

Boy Scouts have been serving God, Country, and Little Old Ladies since 1908, when the organization was founded by a British Cavalry officer. Today, there are organizations in almost a hundred nations and merit badges for activities never dreamed of in 1908.

The Boy Scouts' version of just about "Scout approved" version of just about everything except the kitchen sink. Most of the items in the catalog are on display in their Fifth Avenue Scout Shop, which is manned by serious Scoutmasters and Eagle Scouts. There are uniforms for everyone from a size 4 Cub Scout to leaders with 50" waists, including a line of uniforms designed by Oscar de la Renta for women leaders, scarves, sweaters, jogging suits, rainwear, parkas, T-shirts, shorts, socks, ties, and more, all in the Scout colors of blue and gold, red and white, and olive drab and khaki and emblazoned with a fleur-de-lis or "BSA."

There are all kinds of books, badges, awards, desk accessories, jewelry, and leather goods that bear the logo and would be of little appeal to a non-Scout, as well as utilitarian camping and survival gear that is appropriated by civilians. We know of few young people who haven't at some time owned a green or khaki canvas Scout backpack, and their snakebite kit is so popular it's carried by other stores. The Scout handbook, an encyclopedic reference tool, is possibly the best survival text ever written, covering everything from fire-starting to snakebites and edible roots and berries. In the camping department, there are waterproof matchboxes, flint and steel fire-starters, first-aid and survival kits, tents, sleeping bags, backpacks, knives, axes, saws, camp cookware, and even a line of dehydrated food, all of which can be used by any outdoorsman (or outdoorswoman). In fact, we found everything at the shop we expected to find—except merit badges.

THE PLEASURE CHEST

20 W. 20th St.
New York, NY 10011
(212) 242-4185
Catalog: $5.00 bulk mail; $6.00 first class
Minimum Order: none
Accepts: check, MO, MC, Visa, DC

The Pleasure Chest is for those who take their unalienable rights very seriously. For them, the pursuit of happiness originates and terminates in the nerve endings. The Pleasure Chest sells all kinds of supplies and equipment to aid and abet this quest.

Their 224-page catalog begins with "novelties" and ends with "leather goods," which have nothing to do with French purses. In between is a full line of drug paraphernalia, lotions and creams, Fredericks of Hollywood-style lingerie, T-shirts, men's underwear and swimsuits, jewelry, enema equipment, and latex and rubber goods. Subtle it's not.

There are enough lubricants available here to grease every movable joint in Manhattan. They carry "Lube," which is even sold in gallon buckets, K-Y jelly, and good old Vaseline. There are creams to heat you up, creams to cool you down, and oils to keep everything running smoothly. They have Joy Jell, Mr. Prolong, Rush, Emotion Lotion, and Orgy Butter, to name a few.

Once you get revved up, there are all kinds of things to keep you going. Dildos take every possible form, as well as "vital French ticklers," vibrators, ben wa balls, and more. Those who need more acute sensations can choose from numerous items that clamp, bind, gag, choke, blind, spread, and harness different body parts. The full line of latex clothing and accessories should drive the susceptible into real rubber fever, and there are enough leather goods here to make a cow cry. Much of this merchandise is for the true sophisticate, but there are things here that even the most dilatory sexual dabbler can use.

One of the best things about the Pleasure Chest is the attitude of the salespeople. They are utterly open when it comes to preferences and dysfunctions and can help advise on solving all sorts of sexually related problems. It's always mildly enlightening or at least entertaining to stop in at one of the Pleasure Chest stores and listen to a discussion of the relative merits of quirts, cat-o'-nine-tails, and paddles, or see a straightjacket demonstrated. Whatever your addiction or affliction, there's help at the Pleasure Chest.

SPORT STRIPES

313 Columbus Ave.
New York, NY 10023
(212) 787-8000
Information: price quote by phone or letter
Minimum Order: $10.00
Accepts: check, MO, MC, Visa

The New York Road Runner's Marathon, which owes less to Greek culture than to New York fanaticism, must be seen to be appreciated. Thousands and thousands of scantily clad human beings inflict orthopedic torture on themselves, literally running around the city for twenty-six-plus miles, while thousands more cheer them on.

It goes without saying that these people wear shoes. Sport Stripes carries popular models of running shoes by Brooks, New Balance, Saucony, Puma, Tiger, Soma, Le Coq, Etonick, Autry, Batta, Tred II, and Pony. They also have metatarsal pads and other running accessories by Spenco, Gookinaid, and Time-Out Pads, when the bones and ligaments start to protest.

When you tire of running? Roller skate! Sport Stripes has the largest selection of roller skates in the state. They carry wheels and accessories by Kryptonics, Vanguard, Sims, Gyro, Rannelli, and Powell, and skating equipment by Riedell, Oberhammer, Chicago, Douglas Snyder, Suregrip, and Variflex.

Haven't skated since the age of ten? You can rent skates here and see whether you spend more time on your feet or your behind. Sport Stripes also services skates (we wondered where street skaters went to remedy the effects of running into/under a city bus). All the shoes, skates, and equipment are available by mail on a price-quote basis—call or write.

P.S.: Want to get an edge on the next fad? We're speculating on pogo sticks.

STUYVESANT BICYCLE

349 West 14th St.
New York, NY 10014
(212) 254-5200 (sales)
(212) 675-2160 (parts)
Catalog: $2.50
Minimum Order: $5.00
Accepts: check, MO, MC, Visa

Stuyvesant bicycle has 4 floors of bicycles, tricycles, tandems, mopeds, exercycles, and parts. The firm has been in business for thity-five years, and is run today by Sal Corso, who calls himself "owner, manager, and chief bottle washer." The bikes he sells include lines by Raleigh, Atala, Corso, Ross, Bianchi, Austro-Daimler, Puch, and others—from 1-speed kids' bikes to 18-speed models and racing bikes. There are parts by Suntour, Campagnola, Regina, and many other manufacturers, mopeds by Vespa, Piaggio, and Puch, and all sorts of things like horns, bells, lights, locks, touring equipment, tubes, biking clothing, pumps, toe clips, and much more.

Not only will Mr. Corso and his staff of bike fanatics answer all your questions, repair your bike, and store it (in winter, for a fee), but also they discount everything they sell, from 10% to 30%.

THE TOY BALLOON CORP.

204 East 38th St.
New York, NY 10016
(212) 682-3803
Price List: SASE
Minimum Order: $5.00
Accepts: check, MO

"Oh boy, balloons!" shrieks a 4-year-old

voice in the back of your head when you enter the Toy Balloon Corporation. Surrounding you is an inventory of, think of it, *millions* of balloons of every shape, size, color, and thickness. Doll balloons? They're here, as well as mouse head, dog, and other various novelty shapes, in addition to standard round and long balloons.

Those ordering by mail avail themselves of only a fraction of the stock, but even that is impressive. There are 2 kinds of long balloons, round balloons that run from 6" to 6' in diameter, special 10" clear, silver, gold, black, and purple balloons, marbelized and striped, and even polka-dotted balloons. Prices run from $4.00 for a gross of 6" round to $2.00 for 18" clear. Large dislay balloons are $2.00 for the 40" diameter balloon to $11.00 for a 6' round balloon, in white only. Inflation is no problem with the "blo pump" ($1.50), the metal hand pump ($7.50), or the vacuum-cleaner attachment ($1.50).

The main use for balloons? Advertising, it appears. The Toy Balloon Corp. will imprint just about anything on any balloon, for a nominal charge. Helium tanks can also be rented, if necessary. But as far as we're concerned, a balloon fulfills its destiny only when it is found, clustered with many others, at a child's birthday party.

SEE ALSO: Appliances, Audio, TV/Video
Art Supplies, Craft Supplies
Books, Records, Tapes, Stationery, Films, Educational Supplies
Clothing, Furs, Accessories

18 | Unusual
Rare

This category is comprised of things that don't really fit anywhere else in our catalog, but one could hardly call the purveyors "miscellaneous." Here you're sure to find the perfect gift for someone who has everything, or the ideal item that you don't need to have, but just have to have.

New York City is rare and unusual—it's one of a kind—and provides a market, with its incredible diversity of people, for nearly everything. The rarer and more unusual a thing is, the more likely it is to be found in New York and nowhere else. The city is like a rainbow, spanning the spectrum from the superb to the eccentric. And so we close our book with odd and unusual things, things that are, in a sense, more "New York" than anything, even the most luxe of goods. We can hardly imagine Hammacher-Schlemmer as a business that got its start in, say, Des Moines.

FIVE EGGS

436 Broadway
New York, NY 10012
(212) 226-1606
Catalog: free
Minimum Order: none
Accepts: check, MO, MC, Visa

The Japanese are masters of ingenious
methods of packaging that inspired the
book *How to Wrap Five Eggs*. When
Elaine McKay read the book years ago,
she was so taken with the elegance,
beauty, and propriety of the packaging
that she opened Five Eggs.

The Soho store observes Japanese
proportions in architecture and design,
uses stone, glass, and wood—not
plastic—in display, and is the "wrapper"
for an appealing array of goods Japanese.
As Elaine McKay observes, it "dispels
the notion that Japanese goods are all
tacky." Certainly not the cotton flannel
sleeping robes in traditional geometrics
(under $35.00), the cotton floral and
geometric bathrobes, or the colorful
scarves. For the home, there are traditional Shoji table lamps in black or
natural wood with non-flammable
screens, lovely small black iron teapots
in the traditional raised dot design (about
$45.00), and handpainted ceramic sake
sets (about $15.00). Elaine sells a sumi-e
painting set with ink, stones, seal, and
other items, packed in a charming wood
box ($20.00), a tiny basket filled with 12
minute handcarved wood charms
($10.00), and the traditional carp
windsock, a symbol of longevity and good
fortune, that is flown on Boy's Day, May 5.

The store sells many other decorative
and practical Japanese objects, all
beautifully displayed and unlike the sort
of things found at Azuma. Last but not
least, she sells the new version of the
classic that inspired the store, *How to
Wrap Five More Eggs,* which explains
the wrappings of all kinds of objects in
succinct, beautiful language, and is
under $20.00.

GREEK ISLAND, LTD.

215 E. 49th St.
New York, NY 10017
(212) 355-7547
Catalog: $1.00, refundable
Minimum Order: none
Accepts: check, MO, MC, Visa, AE, DC

Inspired by his own Greek heritage,
George Soter took a trip to Greece in the
1960s. Enthused by the crafts he found
being made there, he came back to the
United States and opened Greek Island.
Everything in the store is from Greece,
and this year the World Crafts Council,
which promotes, revives, re-establishes,
and extends handcraft skills, selected
Greek Island as the representative of the
Hellenic section.

The beautiful little store is hung with
brass plates, plants, and pictures. Greek
wine jugs sit in niches, and a table in the
middle of the store is covered with tin
and brass oil pourers and foods. On a
second level in the back of the store are
cubbyholes filled with distinctive all-
cotton sweatshirts ($22.50), striped T-
shirts ($13.50), and beautiful heavy
handknit wool sweaters from Crete and
Mykonos with cableknit patterns, Greek
key designs, and kangaroo packets.
Hanging in the back are some of the
designs Mr. Soter has made in Greece
expressly for the store. One of the
favorites is the vest and skirt of heavy
cotton, quilted, in striped blue or light
brown or a solid denim color. Another is
the Mykonos jacket, styled something
like a bomber jacket in handwoven
cream-colored wool with handknit cuffs,
collar and waist, and wood toggle
buttons ($85.00).

You can give the pierced ears of your
choice the lovely anti-evil-eye earrings,
blue stones set in silver ($6.00), or baby
hoop in sterling for $6.50. There are
silver bangles, bracelets with rams'
heads on them, and heavy silver chain
necklaces. Equally giftworthy are the
strings of fake amber worry beads, books
on all aspects of Greek life and history,
and the fisherman's flameless lighter, or
tsakmaki, a foot-long wick with a flint and
sparking wheel that is just $2.50.

Whether you're in the store or looking
through the catalog, don't miss the
edibles. Dolma, that mix of rice, herbs,
and onions stuffed in grape leaves, is
$1.85 for an 8½-ounce can. There are
grape leaves packed in brine for rolling
your own, good black and green Greek
olives, heady Hymattus honey perfumed
with wild thyme, olive oil by Nissa and
Minerva, and delectable quince and
rose-petal preserves ($3.50). Both the
Loumides Pappagalos coffee and the
small "briki" it's traditionally prepared in
are here, as well as delightful shish
kebab skewers in white metal with little
brass hens, fish, cows, sheep, rabbits, or

pigs on the ends. At just $1.25 each, they're bargains. Now, if the price of lamb would only fall . . .

HAMMACHER SCHLEMMER
145 East 57th St.
New York, NY 10022
(800) 228-5656 (orders only)
(212) 937-8181 (N.Y.C. orders, inquiries)
(914) 946-5353 (Westchester orders)
Catalog: free
Minimum Order: none
Accepts: check, MO, MC, Visa, AE, DC, Hammacher Schlemmer charge

Ambivalence aside, Hammacher Schlemmer has been fascinating New Yorkers since it opened as a hardware supply source in 1848 and kept them coming back with its winning combination of questionable taste and brilliant inventiveness. If you aren't up to the store, the seasonal catalogs convey that Schlemmer feeling beautifully.

The summer catalogs show different kinds of outdoor furniture, ranging from modern vinyl and aluminum chairs and chaises to a whole set done in Fiberglas made to look like wicker. There are mats for sunning, reflective Mylar tanning blankets, chaises and frames for volleyball games that float in the pool, electric outdoor grills, and reproductions of tire inner tubes for that swimming-hole feeling in your own pool.

While you're relaxing outside, you won't miss a single call if you have the Fone-A-Lert signal nearby. Better yet, get the FCC legal cordless portable telephone. With a minimum operating range of 3000' the sleek black-and-silver Checkmate ($595.00) is a boon to those whose extension lines aren't long enough to reach the tennis courts. There are other models with shorter reception ranges and smaller prices.

Keep the bugs away from your outdoor dinners with an electric insect lantern, or simply move the picnic table into the aluminum screen house, 12' across and topped by a vinyl roof ($269.50). You can bring out the ice in the handsome ice barrel on wheels, serve drinks in the gold-and-silver disposable cups, and broil the hot dogs with the solar cooker.

Hammacher Schlemmer's infamy comes not from summer incidentals, but from things like their famous electric carousel, a complete stereo system in an attaché

case, fine monogrammed bed and table linens, Cuisinart appliances, electric towel heaters, white-noise machines, kid-sized log cabins, and electric closets. The fantastically extravagant to the ultrapractical: New York City's absurdest department store has it all.

MATT MC GHEE
18 Christopher St.
New York, NY 10014
(212) 741-3138
Brochure: SASE
Minimum Order: none
Accepts: check, MO, AE

Somewhere in the past exists an imaginary era of wit and grace that transcends the commonplace and celebrates the rare and beautiful. Matt McGhee inhabits such a time.

Matt's store is established in a charming landmark building that dates from the 1820s. The very decor of his store expresses his talent for blending disparate elements that culminate in elegant, eclectic style. Walls covered in silk and ceilings covered in burlap meet Federal moldings and woodwork; comtemporary track lighting shares its task with silk-shaded lamps made from antique Chinese porcelains; modern glass *étagères* adjoin Oriental curio cabinets and English pine sideboards. Every object in the store is justified by rarity, beauty, or purity of design.

The front of the shop is dominated by the serene with marble Kuan-Yin, Chinese goddess of mercy, flanked by 2 comically fierce, antique marble temple guardian dogs. On shelves, in niches and display cases are a rich profusion of jars and vases of various shapes in glazes of oxblood, forest green, bright yellow, and mirror black ($25.00 to $200.00), nineteenth-century Japanese woodblock prints, antique baskets, and both antique and new teapots and tea sets. Matt occasionally comes upon troves of like objects—antique paper fans, primitive carved animals, Japanese Bungaku theater masks—which are added to the general display and replaced with new treasures as they are sold. Currently, Matt features a collection of mineral necklaces ranging from $30.00 to $350.00, with beads of lapis and malachite, rose quartz and rock crystal, turquoise, garnet and amethyst,

Foo Dog from Matt McGhee

jasper, jade, citron, and tourmaline, tigereye, moss agate, blue lace agate, and Apache tears. Augmenting this collection are unique old pieces: an Art Deco necklace of onyx and ivory beads, a mandarin's necklace of amber beads with seed inclusions, pearls, faceted jet, and strands of coral. Matt has an ensemble of delicate chokers strung with seed pearls, old and new emeralds, rubies, turquoise, and zircons, priced from $200.00 to $300.00. Recently he acquired a number of white, pink, and orange carnelians from old Parthia (third through the sixth century A.D.), which he is stringing into heavy necklaces.

Matt's fondness for what the Japanese call *okimono*, literally "place thing," has inspired his collection of Japanese netsuke. He has had one carving, a Kylin, cast in a limited edition of sterling silver—hollow for pendants, solid for collections. The Kylin, or *kirin* in Japanese, is a mythical beast of Chinese lore that "treads so lightly that it leaves no footprints; unequaled in virtue, profound in wisdom, its appearance on earth is a happy augury." Matt plans to introduce other exclusive limited editions, and is designing a line of porcelains that includes tableware as well as decorative pieces. The first vases have arrived; evocative of ancient Egyptian jars in shape, they are distinguished by coloring of celadon green, subtle mauve, thin ink blue, and light charcoal on the rim and throat that bleeds delicately into the crackled underglaze of pearl gray below— beautiful and quite special.

During the Christmas season, Matt offers handcarved, hand-decorated wood ornaments and handblown glass Christmas decorations, terra-cotta cherubs from Guatemala, wool teddy bears from mainland China, and brightly colored animals from Mexico. Of note at the time of this writing are the handcarved wooden Santa bent beneath his sack of toys, a miniature version of the "wooden soldier" nutcracker, a 2-dimensional Father Christmas of enameled pewter, iridescent glass balls, brilliant blue-and-green glass peacocks with brush tails, German music boxes with revolving platforms adorned with wooden Christmas angels, a painted wood Nativity set, and much more. Each year Matt designs new wreaths for the

holiday season. In 1980 it was pine cone wreaths from Italy garnished with brilliant red lacquered cranberries, crab apples, and other fruits, Della Robbia wreaths, and straw wreaths trimmed with ribbons, angels, and miniature fruits ($25.00 to $175.00).

The unbreakable Christmas ornaments, porcelain vases and jars, the Kylin and other items are available by mail—just send a stamped, self-addressed envelope for the brochure. New discoveries will be added as they occur.

Mat McGhee . . . "not just another place, another time."

THE MUSEUM OF MODERN ART BOOKSTORE AND GIFT SHOP
11 West 53rd St.
New York, NY 10019
(212) 956-7262
Catalog: $1.00
Minimum Order: $25.00 on charge cards
Accepts: check, MO, MC, Visa, AE

In the eyes of some, the Museum of Modern Art makes its greatest contribution to aesthetics not with the retrospectives of Picasso or Monet, but through the Design Collection. This is a permanent collection of functional and decorative objects, distinguished by their originality, timeless contemporary quality, and appeal. In addition to selling art books, prints, cards, and exhibition-related objects in its bookstore and gift shop, MOMA also sells copies of many of the originals in the Design Collection.

Some are well known: Fiskar scissors, Roll Dipper ice-cream scoops, the Braun coffee grinder, and the Sharp EL-8152 pocket calculator are almost common-place. Others aren't: A circular side table of steel and glass by designer Ellen Gray ($392.00), black neoprene rubber knobs and pulls by Masayuki Karokawa, the cranelike Tizio lamps, a glass and black enamel Le Corbusier table ($1,848.00), and the sleek Touch-Tone telephone from Denmark are a few of the more unusual pieces available.

MOMA chooses objects whose lines will never grow stale or clichéd—the Basaltware demitasse designed by Josiah Wedgwood in 1768 is as modern as the stainless-steel espresso maker from the Italian firm of Alessi. The Modern doesn't stop at home accessories. Since its addition to the Design Collection, the steel timepiece by Movado has become known as "The Museum Watch." A hatpin designed in 1908 by Percy Stamp is the model for an Art Nouveau sterling stickpin ($40.00), and an abstract floral fabric design created in 1900 and originally used on draperies is seen here on a light cotton scarf ($18.00).

MOMA's shop and catalog also offer a delightful array of "artful" puzzles, games, and toys for adults and children. Our favorites are the Bauhaus Blocks, used to "create houses, ships, landscapes, and animals in a spirit of happy invention." and "Capsela," by Play Jour. Capsela is a construction set of transparent plastic capsules that have mechanical or electronic functions, and can be connected to form motorized land or water toys. A set of Capsela is $26.00, and much more exciting than Tinkertoys.

The MOMA shop carries hundreds of art books, prints, calendars, stationery, Christmas cards, and posters, some of which appear in the catalog. Members of the Museum are entitled to discounts of 10% and 25% on items over $20.00, as well as free admission to the Museum, film screenings, a subscription to the Museum quarterly, invitations to previews, and more. Memberships begin at $35.00.

SCOTTISH PRODUCTS, INC.

24 East 60th St.
New York, NY 10022
(212) 755-9656
Catalog and Price List: $1.00
Minimum Order: none
Accepts: check, MO

There's a man on Long Island who wears the kilt he bought from Scottish Products to mow the lawn. Another man, who lives in the backwoods of Maine, has been honoring the traditions of the Scottish for at least thirty years. He, however, is Japanese.

Scottish Products has customers of all nationalities, owing not a little to the friendly, open-hearted manner of the people who run the store, and the fascinating things it sells. Nowhere else in New York City can you find such a selection of Balmorals (hats), sporrans (furred pouches), or Sgian Dbuhs (knives) that are part of formal Highland dress.

There are kilts made to order in your choice of hundreds of real tartans from $125.00, jackets of Harris tweed and doublets of barathea or superfine cloth, lace jabots and cuffs, kilt hose, Celtic dance pumps for men and women, and the Balmoral bonnets and Glengarry hats that finish the costume. The sporrans, purselike pouches of furred skins or leather that are worn in front of the kilt, could be used as shoulderbags by those who can carry off dramatic effects. The Sgian Dbuhs, black knives decorated with horn, sterling, pewter, and stone and worn in the stocking on the right leg of a Scotsman, would make fine additions to any collection of weaponry.

You can get all sorts of articles like ties, sashes, scarves, tam-o'shanters, and lap rugs made in genuine tartans, and the material itself is sold by the yard (2-yard minimum). There are 13 different kilt pins in shapes that include thistle and swords, sterling Celtic crosses, Luckenbooth brooches, bagpipe tietacks, and the huge round pins that are worn on the shoulder with the Highland costume.

For those with genealogical tendencies, Scottish Products has a list of almost 500 clans for which they have crests worked in metal thread embroidery on blazer badges, and coats of arms for over 100 families hand-screened on ceramic tiles ($4.50). Those who want clarification of their ancestry can consult the books sold here like *The Origin and Signification of Scottish Surnames, Scottish Clans and Tartans,* and a definitive 632-page tome called *Clans, Septs and Regiments of the Scottish Highlands.*

You don't have to be a Campbell or a MacKenzie to like thistles, Scottish Terriers, and bagpipes, which are used as motifs for designs worked into ashtrays, dishes, souvenir spoons, key chains, rugs, and stationery. There is a ceramic Loch Ness monster for $12.00, a miniature bagpipe player in a bottle, and beautiful carved wood molds for shortbread and butter.

Should you decide to take your Scottish heritage seriously, consider taking up bagpipes. Scottish Products sells 8 kinds of full pipes, practice chanters, and a full line of accessories and music books. Advice on bagpipes and all matters Scottish is given freely at the store, which lives up to the motto on its crest, "Better quality there canna be."

TALAS, DIVISION OF TECHNICAL LIBRARY SERVICES

130 Fifth Ave.
New York, NY 10011
(212) 675-0718
Catalog: $3.00
Minimum Order: $5.00
Accepts: check, MO

It's a little-known fact that most books that are made today will self-destruct in 20 years. This sad news comes from Elaine Haas, who is a chemist and the founder and president of Talas, which sells tools and materials for care and preservation of things made of paper, leather, and fabric.

Mrs. Haas attributes the slow suicide of modern books to the high acid content of paper made of wood fiber. Books of plant fiber (rag) have a much longer lifespan, but still need periodic care to offset the deleterious effects of central heating, air conditioning, sunlight, and bad handling procedures. Short of having a book completely rebound, there are many procedures you can perform that will reverse damages and extend the book life. You can deacidify the pages of a book by spraying it with Wei-To, and if the volume is a collector's edition you can put sheets of acid-free paper between each of the pages. You can use Talas Leather Protector to neutralize destructive acids on leather bindings. The Talas repertoire of goods for preservation extends well beyond books; for example, they carry Orvus WA paste by Procter & Gamble, highly recommended for use on washable, delicate textiles such as antique quilts and coverlets.

Under the direction of Mrs. Haas, Talas has developed a number of products to meet the needs of conservators, pioneered the sales of many items, including a special tape of archival quality, removable with water, which was described with such scientific accuracy in the old Talas catalog that the Library of Congress called to commend Mrs. Haas on the job she was doing. Which brings us to the only drawback to dealing with Talas:

Mrs. Haas has been working on cataloging her preservation supplies, bookbinding materials, marbled papers, dollhouse prints, and other esoterica for over a year. Because she'll settle for nothing less than an exhaustively detailed, accurate compendium of her services and wares, it's taking a while. Since the last one was so informative it was actually Xeroxed and given to students at art schools in Philadelphia and Chicago as a reference text on preservation materials and techniques, you know it's worth waiting for. If the catalog is still in the process of being put together when you write for it, inquire about the products you need for specific problems. They'll be glad to advise you and send you the supplies you need to save your books, repair the bindings, or wash your heirloom quilts.

WAX PAPER

172 Prince St.
New York, NY 10012
(212) 966-4590
Catalog: $2.50, refundable
Minimum Order: $10.00 on charge cards
Accepts: check, MO, MC, Visa, AE

Wax Paper is the novel name of a Baggie-size Soho shop that sells candles and stationery items. The store was formed in 1979 by Carolyn Faillace, who loves handmade papers, and Van deLune, who loves beautiful and precious things (see his listing under "Jewelry, Gems, and Watches"). Every item in the shop is handmade, and although the emphasis is on candles and paper, they now sell desk accessories, perfume bottles, glass paperweights, candlesticks, and other things suitable for gifting.

Carolyn's best sellers are her candles of variegated hues, displayed in 3 colorful rows that run from a "Festival" combination of multi-colored brights, to "Neutrals," which are dipped in beiges and grays. There are 10 color combinations in all, including a red, white, and green candle available at Christmas, and the pretty "Pastels," in shades of pink, baby blue, yellow, and mint green. The tapers are 9", 12", and 15" tall, and cost $2.75, $3.25, and $3.75 per pair. Wax Paper also sells birthday candles for $2.50 a dozen, and 2" ball candles for $1.00 each or $12.00 for a dozen packed in an egg carton, also in the same color range.

Their paper line is supplied by a woman in New England, who makes paper using beaten plant fibers—banana, iris, nasturtium, gladiolus—and colors them delicate shades of blue, lilac, peach, gray, buff, and other pastels. A packet of ten 6"-by-8" sheets and 5 envelopes is $7.25, and colors can be matched for special orders at no additional cost (there is a 2-month wait). The same woman has created abstract, decorative fans, using sprays of weeds embedded in a circle of handmade paper.

More practical are the handbound books covered with marbled paper. They range from $5.00 for the credit-card holder to $36.00 for the photo album. The medium-size book, with matching pencil and refillable notepad, is $9.50. Wax Paper also carries handbound, linen-covered books with abstract collage covers from $16.00 for the smallest to $42.00 for the 10" by 13" photo album.

Tucked away in a corner of the shop are beautifully made desk accessories of oak, cherry, walnut, mahogany, padouk, and zebra. Elegant storage is provided by the Shaker-type boxes of bird's-eye maple, sold in 5 sizes from $32.00 to $90.00 each. There are also lovely handblown perfume bottles, paper-weights, stoneware oil and kerosene lamps, candleholders, and cards. Wax Paper is planning a move to larger quarters, and will add different items to the store and catalog as they expand.

STEWART WILSON
221 Mott St.
New York, NY 10012
(212) 431-8835
Brochure: SASE
Minimum Order: none
Accepts: check, MO

Children play war games with little plastic men. Stewart Wilson takes the same little men, clothes them in pieces of fur, shiny fabrics, feathers, wire, curious scraps, and found objects, and creates Personas. He then adds a pin back and puts them in their own little plastic space cases. A signed, numbered Xerox copy of each is included for posterity's sake, as well as a magnifying glass for closer inspections. When not on your lapel, Personas travel via their own wild horses (also pins, $30.00), dear animals with fantastic manes of mink, little corrals carpeted in Astroturf, a Lucite sugar cube for coaxing, and their own Xerox-copy portraits.

Personas have the appeal of little toys and the curious attraction of kachinas and totem symbols. They are, we think, New Wave voodoo dolls. They cost, we know, $12.00 each. Each is, like a mantra, to be used/worn/worshiped by one person only, although Stewart ascribes no special powers to them. In fact, he ascribes no special powers to himself. His mini-malistic self-summary: "I have great weaknesses. I'll trudge through them."

Steward may trudge in the direction of fashion shortly. After dressing thousands of 2" plastic men, he is interested in working on the human form. His first creation is far from the maribou and satin confection one might expect. Imagine a plastic inflatable, ladies' rainhat that doesn't look like a flotation device. Clever! Chic! Cheap!

Stewart lives in Soho with a cat that is "cute but stupid" and many, many plants. He was born in North Carolina and brought up in Florida, and still thinks that New York City is magic. He is in the process of opening a gallery featuring "events," the first a show of calendars, inert and animate. Stewart's brochure of unimaginables is free (but send a stamped, self-addressed envelope for it).

SEE ALSO:
Art, Antiques, Restoration Services
Art Supplies, Craft Supplies
Books, Records, Tapes, Stationery, Films,
Educational Supplies
Cigars, Pipes, Tobacco
Clothing, Furs, Accesories
Food, Drink
Health, Beauty
Home
Jewelry, Gems, Watches
Music

FEEDBACK

*S*hop *New York By Mail* will be expanded and updated in future editions. We would appreciate suggestions from readers, feedback from readers regarding experiences with companies listed in this book, and information from businesses located in New York City that would like to be included in future editions. No charge is made for the listing; firms are included at the discretion of the editors of this book. Please write to:

SHOP NEW YORK BY MAIL
14 Gay Street, New York, New York 10014

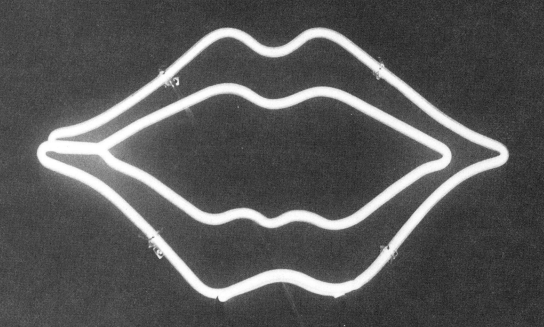

ACKNOWLEDGMENTS

The Print Project extends its thanks to the following people for allowing us to photograph their products:

Rudi Stern of Let There be Neon, for the photographs appearing on or facing the Introduction Page, the Feedback Page, and in Chapters 4, 11, and 17.

Pacifico Palumbo of Say It In Neon, for the photographs appearing in or facing the Title Page, Contents Page, and in Chapters 2, 9, 12, 13, 14, and 18.

David Davis of Fine Art Materials, Inc.

Ken Hansen for the use of his camera.

Bill Hyde of Balducci's.

Cindy Annchild and Michael McNulty of The Bath House.

Garry Bratman of Carroll Sound, Inc.

Paul Carmody of Gerry Cosby & Co., Inc.

Ronald Kopnicki of Matt McGhee.

INDEX